Basic
Gunsmithing

Other TAB books by the author:

Basic Gunsmithing

by John E. Traister

TAB BOOKS

BLUE RIDGE SUMMIT, PA. 17214

FIRST EDITION

FIRST PRINTING—SEPTEMBER 1979

Copyright © 1979 by TAB BOOKS

Printed in the United States of America

Library of Congress Cataloging in Publication Data

Traister, John E
    Basic gunsmithing.

    Includes index.
    1. Gunsmithing. I. Title.
TS535.T7   683.4'0028   79-17172
ISBN 0-8306-9756-X
ISBN 0-8306-1140-1 pbk.

Cover photos courtesy of Remington Arms Company, Inc., Smith and Wesson, and Trinidad State Junior College, Department of Gunsmithing, and Herold's Gun Shoppe, Waynesboro, PA

Preface

This book is aimed primarily at the growing numbers of people who want to keep their firearms in first-class condition at all times, and who want to have the added pleasure of doing the work themselves. In doing so, the gun enthusiast will also economize on all repairs and alterations as well as obtaining a better knowledge of firearms and shooting in general.

Upon thumbing through this book, almost every reader will immediately see a variety of small maintenance and gun-improvement jobs that can be performed at once. For example, procedures for properly cleaning rifles, shotguns, and handguns are completely covered in Chapter 5. Removing dents from stocks and touching up metal parts with gun blue are also covered. Perhaps your favorite shotgun has a dent in its barrel. Chapter 6 gives step-by-step procedures showing how to remove the dent. When you get to Chapter 8, you'll find out exactly how to reblue your favorite firearm for professional results.

Experienced shooters know that a smooth trigger pull is essential for good accuracy. Chapter 10 describes how to modify a stiff trigger pull into a smooth one. You'll also learn how to remodel firearms of all types.

Those who are thinking of opening a gun repair shop— either full- or part-time—will find this book invaluable for learning the techniques of gun repair jobs that are most frequently encountered. The seasoned gunsmith will also find a number of new hints of value that will warrant keeping a copy of this book on a shelf over the workbench.

This book is not meant to be a "crash" course on professional gunsmithing, as this can only be learned over a period of years under the guidance of professional gunsmiths. Even this is not a guarantee, but it is definitely compulsory if one wishes to become a pro.

Some of the jobs included in this book may be out of reach for a few readers—either due to lack of tools or mechanical ability; however, knowing the basic procedures will certainly not hurt anyone. It could still save you time and money by not attempting the job and being able to tell a professional what seems to be the problem.

In closing, I would like to emphasize the word *safety* and insist that you practice it when tinkering with any gun at home. Also, please be careful on the range or in the field, remembering that firearms only kill when in the hands of humans.

John E. Traister

Contents

Chapter 1

Tooling Up

High-quality work in any trade or profession can be accomplished only by the correct use of high-quality tools. Gun care and repairs are no exception—even for the beginner. The proper size and type of screwdriver, for example, must be selected to loosen and tighten screws so that the work will not be chamfered or the screw marked. Proper grades of sandpaper must be selected, then used in their proper order, when finishing a wood stock to obtain the best possible finish. Checkering tools must be kept sharp for high-quality fine-line checkering on stocks and forearms. These qualities can only be secured by the proper use of good-quality tools that are in first-class condition.

Those of you who have been doing a number of home repairs or who have other hobbies requiring the use of conventional tools will have probably acquired a substantial number of fine power and hand tools suitable for many gun repair jobs. If a few special tools are required for a particular project, most of them can be purchased without spending too much cash. Any jobs requiring expensive tools should be left to the professional gunsmith who is well equipped to handle almost any type of repair or alteration.

Tools commonly used by the amateur gunsmith are listed in the paragraph to follow. The first items are considered to be

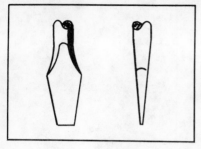

Fig. 1-1. Double-wedge screwdriver blade, front and side views, swaged on a punch press.

the minimum essential tools with which to do even the most minor gun repairs. Other tools are listed which may or may not be of interest to you, but still their use is explained. Tools should be of the best quality that the gunsmith can afford because many of them will surely find many other uses around the home.

SCREWDRIVERS

Since very few gun repairs can be made without removing a tight screw, the selection of a proper set of screwdrivers should be given careful consideration. The efficient holding power of the screwdriver depends upon the design of its blade, and the external force that may be applied. The blade should be fitted to the width of the slot for best results.

Bonanza Sports Manufacturing Company, 412 Western Avenue, Faribault, Minnesota 55021 has designed a number of precision screwdrivers especially for the mounting of scope sights and other requirements of gunsmiths. These screwdrivers are not of the double-wedge type swaged on a punch press as most other screwdrivers are. Rather, they are

Fig. 1-2. A double-wedge screwdriver being using in a deep screw slot, which usually results in the screw being scored.

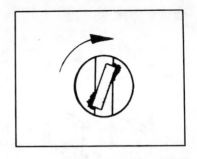

Fig. 1-3. Screw-head scoring resulting from using the wrong size of screwdriver.

ground to give complete metal-to-metal contact between the tip of the bit and the entire screw slot.

To illustrate the importance of a good screwdriver when working on firearms look at the drawings in Fig. 1-1. This is the double-wedge type swaged on a punch press. If such a screwdriver is used in a deep screw slot (Fig. 1-2) the blade transmits its torque to the top of the screw slot; with such a small area contacting the screwdriver the screw will be scored—or one section of the screw head will break off—if heavy pressure is applied (see Fig. 1-3). This wedge shape also tends to back the driver out of the screw slot.

A screwdriver like the one in Fig. 1-4, on the other hand, is ideal since the torque is applied at the bottom of the slot where the screw is the strongest, and the blade fills slot completely. Also note that the blade is the same width as the shank (Fig. 1-5) and has the same radius so it will not chamfer the work.

If you need to buy a supply of screwdrivers, a set like the one shown in Fig. 1-6 is ideal for the gunsmith or hobbyist.

Fig. 1-4. This type of screwdriver blade, manufactured by Bonanza Sports, fits down into the screwhead slot so that the torque is applied evenly.

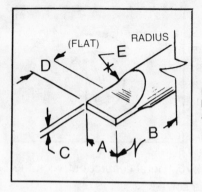

Fig. 1-5. Side view of the screwdriver blade in Fig. 1-4. Note that the blade and shank are the same width.

This set is manufactured by The Chapman Manufacturing Company, Route 7 at Saw Mill Road, Durham, Connecticut 06422 and sells for less than $20. It contains an extension, a midget ratchet, one screwdriver handle, twelve slotted head adapters, two Phillips-head adapter, and one Allen hex-type adapter.

Brownells, Inc., 200 South Front Street, Montezuma Iowa 50171 also has a good supply of screwdrivers specially designed for the gunsmith and hobbyist.

FILES

Files are probably the most important tools for the majority of gun repairs, but there are so many types and sizes that it is difficult for the amateur to even begin selecting a set that will handle most gun repair work; therefore, a brief description of several types is in order.

Pillar File. The pillar file is considered the standard gunsmithing file. Many jobs can be done with it which could not even be attempted with standard files. No. 0 is the coarsest and is used for fast removal of soft or untempered metal and for the final removal of wood. The No. 2 cut is fine for final fitting of precision parts and similar components. No. 4 is very smooth cut for finishing.

Round File. Common cuts for round files are No. 00 to No. 4. The coarser size (00) in used for fast removal of metal or as rasps to slightly enlarge or adjust accessory holes in wood stocks. Cuts 2 and 4 are for adjusting screw and pin holes, scope mount holes, fine cuts on tightly curved parts and all types of parallel round cuts.

Needle File. Needle files are very inexpensive and are used frequently on many gunsmithing jobs unsuited for any other type of file. They come in four popular types: equalling, square, three square, and half-round. An assorted set of twelve may be purchased from Brownells, Inc.

Lathe File. A lathe file is excellent for filing old rough military rifle barrels in a lathe. This type of file is rather heavy with about twice as much slant on the teeth as a standard file. This characteristic produces a sort of shearing cut when the barrel is turning in the lathe.

Hand File. A hand file will find many uses around a gun shop for dressing, striking off, shaping, cleaning up, metal removing of all types, etc. This type is recommended as one of the basic files for gun repair work.

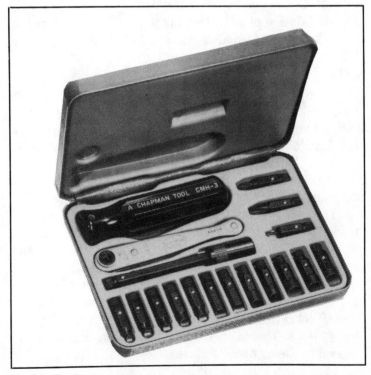

Fig. 1-6. The Chapman Manufacturing Company produces this tool kit for less than $20.

Mill File. The mill file is fine for draw-filing and finishing metals. The common cuts include No. 2 cut and smoother.

Knife File. The knife file with its narrow knife-blade type section is ideal for getting down into sharp angles and tight corners where no other file will reach.

Barrette File. The barrette file is another type of file designed for getting into tight places, coming right up to right angles, working over dovetails, slots, and other precision filing. Common cuts include No. 0 (coarse) and No. 1 (medium cut).

There are several other types of files for special jobs and for wood working. Cabinet rasp, half-round wood files, and cabinet files are standard tools for working on wood. Regardless of the type of file or rasp used, they will normally be used for one or more of the following purposes:

- Removal of surplus metal or wood.
- Correct errors on milled parts.
- Making of small metal parts.
- Fitting of wood or metal parts together more accurately.

VISES

A bench vise with 3½-inch jaws will find use around any home in addition to repairing guns. But don't buy a cheap one. It should be strong enough, in addition to being secured to a solid bench, that will allow you to remove rifle and pistol barrels. A plain swivel-base machinist's vise with a few modifications will suffice, but there are other types that have added advantages for gun repair work.

The utility workshop vise shown in Fig. 1-7 is recommended for the home craftsman who will perform occasional gun repairs. This is a rugged and moderately priced vise with serrated steel replaceable top jaws, steel replaceable pipe jaws, swivel base and large anvil enabling it to be used on many jobs around the home. One such vise is manufactured by Wilton Tool Division, 2400 East Devon Avenue, Des Plaines, Illinois 60018. The numbers in the illustration (Fig. 1-7) correspond to the following features:

1. Massive construction
2. Rugged box frame slide

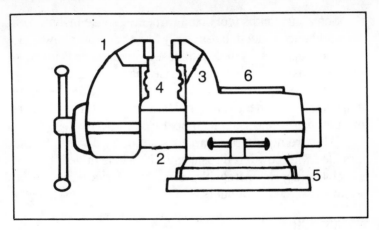

Fig. 1-7. Utility workshop vise manufactured by Wilton Tool.

3. Serrated steel, replaceable top jaws
4. Built-in pipe jaws
5. Swivel base
6. Large anvil

A ball joint vise enables one to hold the workpiece at the most favorable working position when filing, grinding, polishing, soldering, etc. Such vises, however, are not designed for rough treatment and should be used only as a second vise for gun repair work. This type of vise is equally suited for electronics and other fine work where speed and moderate strength count. The vise head and screw lock base has complete turn of 360 degrees, while the vise head also tilts to any angle within 90 degrees.

Accessory items for the ball joint base include bench clamp base, surface plates, end mount vise body and circuit board holder, etc. Other pieces are shown in Fig. 1-8. The part-time gunsmith won't have to worry about spending money on a tool that will not be used too much. There are dozens of other uses for this type of vise as the photos in Figs. 1-9 and 1-10 show.

In order to prevent marring of blued metal surfaces as well as wood finishes the bench vise should be equipped with removable copper, brass or lead jaws. You can even make a set of removable jaws out of leather or wood to serve the purpose.

Some gunsmiths feel that a carpenter's vise mounted on the workbench is needed especially for stock work; however, if a good machinist's vise is purchased, I feel there is no need for such a vise as the machinist's vise has taken care of nearly all jobs for the professional and will surely suffice for the home gunsmith. All you need is a pair of feltered wood jaws to insert into the vise when using it to hold wood.

When removing rifle barrels a set of hard maple blocks sprinkled with powdered rosin and with a hole drilled through the ·blocks approximately the diameter of the barrel to be removed will work wonders.

WORKBENCH

The varying sizes of work space and the people who use them are so diverse that it would be almost impossible to recommend a workbench to suit everyone; however, there are a few pointers that should be pointed out.

First of all, the work surface should be sturdy and firm. To help achieve this sturdiness, a shaky workbench can be braced and reinforced with bolted-on crosspiece supports. It is also recommended that the work surface have no cracks so that small parts will not be able to fall between them and become lost.

The workbench you now have in your basement, garage or other work area should be fine for the average gun repair—especially if a few modifications are made. For example, small drawers or compartments can be added. The legs can be made sturdier. Cracks can be sealed by securing a piece of plywood to the top of the bench, then cut or trimmed flush with the existing top. You can then face the edges with wooden strips (or perhaps metal) for a neat appearance.

Regardless of where your workbench is located or what type you may have, remember to provide good illumination. A 4-foot, two-tube fluorescent lamp fixture hung above the work surface will usually suffice.

GUN PARTS CONTAINERS

Like recommending a specific workbench design, containers for storing small gun parts and supplies will vary from individual to individual. Several factors enter into the proper

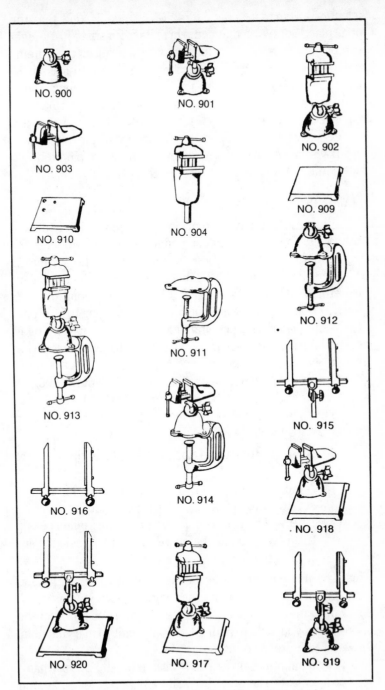

NO. 900
NO. 901
NO. 902
NO. 903
NO. 904
NO. 909
NO. 910
NO. 911
NO. 912
NO. 913
NO. 914
NO. 915
NO. 916
NO. 917
NO. 918
NO. 919
NO. 920

Fig. 1-8. Various accessory items for the PanaVise ball-joint base.

selection of suitable containers. Many people find that the small plastic drawers that come in units from six to forty-eight or more drawers are ideal for gun parts as well as other items needed around the house. Another person saved glass jars, nailed the tops to a wooden joist over the workbench, then screwed the jars into the lids. These made fine containers for gun parts such as springs, screws, etc. Tobacco tins are another source of containers for storing small parts, screws, etc. If you have a friend who smokes a brand of pipe tobacco that comes in tins ask him to save the cans for you.

HAMMERS

A hammer for use on firearms should be a striking tool, or better yet, an instrument designed for a particular operation. A good hammer for the home gunsmith would be a 4-ounce ball-peen hammer, about 12½ inches long, and a hammer face diameter of about ⅝ inch. Such a hammer is useful on such bench jobs as slight riveting, upsetting or swaging to hold pins or parts in place. The peening head can be set over a drilled hole and the hammer face given a sharp tap for quick deburring or light swaging of holes in nonferrous metals.

A no-mar hammer, available from Brownells, Inc., is another fine tool that will be greatly appreciated by the home gunsmith. Three types of nonsparking, non-marring tips in four sizes are available:

- **Amber Plastic**. A tough, fairly light tip for most general work
- **Nylon**. An extremely tough resilient tip that is very resistant to cracking, chipping or splitting
- **Phenolic**. A resin-impregnated cloth-reinforced tip that is very dense, highly resistant to abrasion, splitting or breaking

This hammer with its three heads is ideal for driving pins, installing or removing sights, searing inlays, pounding on all sorts of things or for the multitude of other jobs around the shop where you have to pound but don't want to mar the metal or wood you are working on.

A brass hammer tip is also available for the no-mar hammer to complete the set; this makes it a perfect all-around hammer for the hobbyist and professional alike.

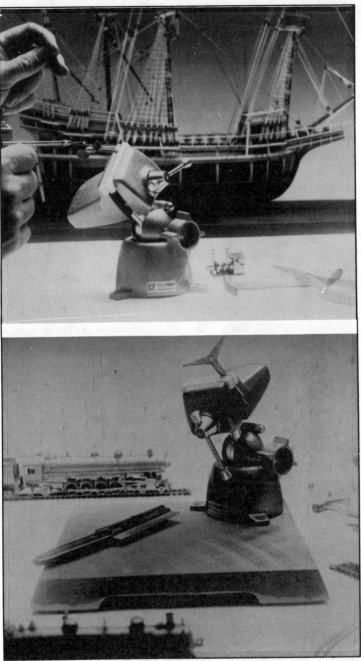

Fig. 1-9. The PanaVise ball-joint base can be used for model boat building (top) as well as model train construction(bottom).

Another hammer that might be of use to the home gunsmith is the rawhide mallet. You might even find a need for a hickory mallet.

PUNCHES

The home gunsmith will seldom tackle a gun repair job without needing a pin punch of some size. A set of seven punches—specially designed for gun repair work—is available from all gunsmithing supply houses for less than $15. This set will handle 90 percent of all the home gunsmith's needs. Each punch is made to fit a certain pin in a gun action, such as a cross pin, sear pin, etc. Besides five different pin punches, the set contains one starter punch and one center punch.

The increasing use of roll or spring pins in the newer guns may also require the use of a roll pin punch. Most sell for under $2 or they can be purchased in a set of seven punches for less than $10.

If you do much gun sight work a nylon front-sight drift punch is recommended. They're only about 50 cents each. This handy little punch is made to drive the front sight in or out without marring it or the rifle barrel.

CLAMPS

When installing recoil pads, forend tips, or making stock repairs, a web clamp will come in handy. Such a clamp is ideal for holding work of any shape and almost any size. Most are equipped with about 12 feet of heavy 600-pound break-strength nylon webbing which is designed to prevent marring of the work surfaces.

For close, precision holding of unusual shapes for welding, brazing, scribing, or drilling—such as in scope, sight or bolt work—machinist clamps will be of great help.

HAND GRINDER

While not an absolute necessity a hand grinder is a great convenience for many grinding, shaping and polishing jobs requiring a hand-held power tool that you can control with your finger tips. There are also numerous accessories available making the hand grinder useful on all work from the softest

Fig. 1-10. Even the smallest detail is no problem when using the PanaVise ball-joint base.

wood to the hardest steel. The kit shown in Fig. 1-11 is manufactured by Chicago Wheel & Manufacturing Company, 1101 West Monroe Street, Chicago, Illinois 60607; it is recommended as a good tool for the home gunsmith and can be purchased for around $50.

You may think that $50 is too much money to spend for a tool to fix an occasional gun. But the hand grinder has many other uses also. For example, with the many accessories, you can work on wood, metal, plastic, glass, and ceramics. It's a perfect tool for model makers, home repair buffs, ceramic hobbyists, sculptors, jewelry makers, wood-carvers, gunsmiths, mechanics, . . . you name it.

TORCH

The best all-around torch for the home gunsmith is the Pres-O-Lite kits available for around $20. This little torch produces a very hot, pointed flame (depending upon the nozzle) that actually encircles the work you are heating. It gives fast, safe, easy precisely controlled heating action for any job in the home gunsmith shop.

The torch will handle lead-tin soldering and silver soldering jobs on steel, copper, stainless steel, brass and others; however, it will not handle welding or brazing.

A gas welding torch is available from Brownells, Inc. that sells for less than $25. It is fine for many light-weight welding, brazing and soldering jobs around the home gunshop. It uses butane and a fuel oxidizer which produces a neutralizing flame and is more economical than former fuels. Each cylinder costs about $2 and will last from 15 to 30 minutes.

This small torch is only 5¼ inches long by 2 inches wide by 1¼ inches thick at the swivel joint. When adjusted for high heat, however, the temperature will exceed 5000°F. It will silver solder two copper pieces 1 inch by 2 inches by 1/16 inch and will handle welding and brazing rods up to 1/16-inch diameter.

While talking about torches, a word about heat is in order. Any type of heat applied to a firearm should be done with caution as heat can weaken any gun part to a dangerous level. You should never heat the receiver ring of a bolt-action rifle which has its locking system within this area. Heat that is low

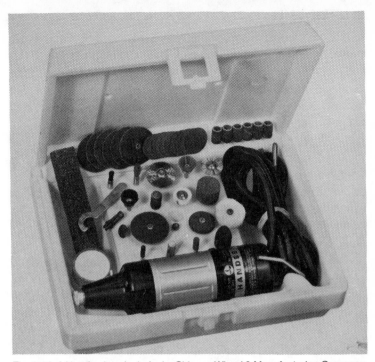

Fig. 1-11. A Handee hand grinder by Chicago Wheel & Manufacturing Company. It is great for those tiny jobs requiring a lot of control.

enough so that the bluing shows no discoloration is usually considered safe, but anything above this temperature can be dangerous. Only a professional should attempt to apply heat to any area around the locking system of a shotgun or rifle, a professional will know how to protect these areas with wet cloths wrapped around any part near these areas. This is so the heat will be confined to the part and not escape to the delicate area of the action.

Silver soldering on barrels can be safely done as the temperature needed for this operation is somewhat below that required for heat treating the barrel. Still, precautions must be taken, the main one being to apply the heat evenly over the barrel and not just to one spot. For example, if you're installing a front sight ramp to the muzzle end of the barrel the barrel should be heated all around the barrel and not just on top where the ramp is to be soldered. If heat is applied only to the top of the barrel, the barrel could become warped.

ELECTRIC DRILL

Every homeowner should have a ¼-inch or ⅜-inch drill motor with several attachments. They can be used to buff the car, drill pilot holes for inserting wood screws, and a multitude of other uses. The home gunsmith will also find such a tool indispensable for gun work. For example, when a small drill press attachment is purchased for the electric drill, it is useful for drilling holes to mount sights, scope mounts, and many other jobs. A buffing attachment consisting of a buffing pad is useful for polishing wood stocks. Wire brushes and similar attachments are good for polishing small parts. A sanding disk attachment is fine for fitting a recoil pad to a gun stock. A screwdriver attachment and many other accessories are available, too.

Electric drills are also provided with a small stand which can be bolted to the bench, converting the drill in a matter of minutes into a small electric grinder or buffer. A small table saw is another possibility.

It is recommended that the drill motor have a rheostat or similar control to vary the speed of the motor. Such a drill motor is available from Sears, Roebuck & Co., Black & Decker; and many other hand tool manufacturers. Just check at your local hardware or department store and look over the ones available.

A milling drill which can be used with any drilling machine and mills to any required shape is available from Frank Mittermeier, Inc., 3577 East Tremont Avenue, Bronx, New York 10465. This drill will mill in stainless sheet steel, sheet aluminum, sheet copper, sheet brass, sheet iron, wood, hard fiberboard, plastics, etc.

Frank Mittermeier, Inc. also sells a Forstner bit, which is a labor-saving auger bit that will bore any arc of a circle leaving a true polished surface. It can be guided in any direction—so necessary in inletting of gun stocks—without regard to grain of the wood or knots. The bit is guided by its circular rim instead of its center, which is the reason for its special adaptability in hard wood. This bit when used in a drill press will enable the home gunsmith to do most of the inletting of bolt-action stock blanks and save considerable time over the drill and chisel method.

The ¼-inch electric drill will also accept an engine-turning chuck. This tool consists of a steel holder with a ⅛-inch shank and an abrasive charged rubber tip. The specially made abrasive tip gives an even impression on steel. It further simplifies the work of engine turning and eliminates the danger of cutting deep rings.

When performing engine turning, it is recommended that a specially designed fixture is used to hold the bolt or other object to be decorated. The fixture containing the bolt is placed on a drill press table against a straightedge fence and clamped to the table so that the bolt body is centered under the engine-turning tool held in the drill chuck. The bolt is coated with abrasive compound; then the pattern may be started at either end of the bolt, but all rows of spots must start from the same end. The drill motor should be run at medium speed as it is brought down onto the bolt. Then the fixture is moved approximately one-half spot diameter and the brush is again brought down to overlap spots on the surface of the bolt. This continues for one row of spots. Then the bolt is rotated approximately one-half spot diameter and the process repeated. This continues until the bolt has been fully jeweled in the areas desired.

Another attachment for the ¼-inch drill motor is a shotgun barrel polishing head (Fig. 1-12) for polishing the bore of shotgun barrels. One such attachment is available from Frank Mittermeier, Inc. When four polishing strips are fastened centrally on the head the centrifugal force of the fast-revolving

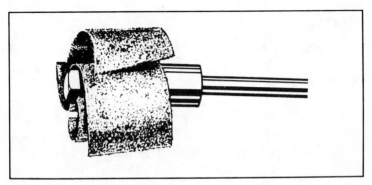

Fig. 1-12. A shotgun barrel polishing head available through Frank Mittermeier, Inc.

polishing head forces the strips to the wall of the bore with only the ends of the strips touching the wall and with air freely circulating to prevent overheating of the barrel. This allows the full length of the bore—from chamber through choke to muzzle—to be polished, smoothly, evenly and without interruption.

Polishing the choke to a mirror-like finish without changing its dimensions is now made easy with such an attachment for a ¼-inch electric drill. The polishing head comes attached to a 34-inch long steel rod, which is chucked in the hand drill. The speed can be up to 4800 RPM. In most cases the shotgun barrel will be clamped in a vise, the polishing head then inserted in the breech end of the barrel as shown in Fig. 1-13. Start the motor and push the revolving rod slowly forward and pull backward until the bore obtains a mirror-like polish.

Figure 1-14 shows many different shapes and sizes of mounted wheels and points to perform grinding, cutting, engraving and polishing of irregular and plain surfaces. An assortment of these wheels and points will take care of all grinding operations required on sight and telescope bases, reloading tools and dies, revolvers, pistols, rifles, shotguns, removing broken screws and taps, shaping butt plates, pistol grip caps and on many other jobs.

A minimum set of drill bits may be purchased for less than $5 and such a set should be all that is purchased initially; however, as new jobs arise, you may wish to obtain a complete set of wire-gauge drills and a set of fractional drills running from 1/16 inch to ¼ inch.

HACKSAW

Another tool which will find a great deal of work around the gunshop is a hacksaw. The best hacksaw frame is not expensive, so only the best should be purchased. Likewise, only the best tungsten high-speed hacksaw blades can be expected to hold up for all kinds of gun work. The hacksaw frame shown in Fig. 1-15 is one of the best designs and will eliminate all blade twist or wobble. The blade may be inserted in a conventional manner for cutting stock down to the surface and may also be inserted flat (Fig. 1-16) for cutting flush with the surface.

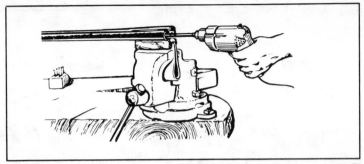

Fig. 1-13. Using the shotgun polishing head. Developed by German gunsmith R. Triebel, this handy device can be obtained through Frank Mittermeier, Inc.

The choice of teeth per inch on the blades will depend upon the type of work the saw is used on. In general, however, the thinner the material to be cut, the higher the number of teeth. Soft material requires fewer teeth per inch than hard material. Round hacksaw blades are also available for cutting wood, metal, plastics, tile, rubber, linoleum, leather, etc. The roundness of the blade also permits a cut along any line that can be drawn.

TAPS, SCREW REMOVERS, ETC.

There are many methods of breaking loose a frozen screw: soaking in water, using Liquid Wrench and heating the area around the screw with a torch until it breaks loose. All of these methods will work on certain jobs. But before doing anything, grind a screwdriver to exactly fit the slot to avoid any possibility of completely ruining the slot and making drilling necessary; however, at times, none of these methods will work and it becomes necessary to drill the screw to remove it. In this case, a high-speed center cutter should be used.

To use this device firmly fasten the gun to the drill press table and with the spindle at fairly high speed, bring the cutter down to the screw head several times, adjusting the position of the gun until you are certain that it is centered in the screw. Then apply pressure and cut the screw head until you have a deep center which will permit the proper undersized drill to start cutting without catching on the screw head slots and being thrown off center. The drill to use is one or two sizes under tap size.

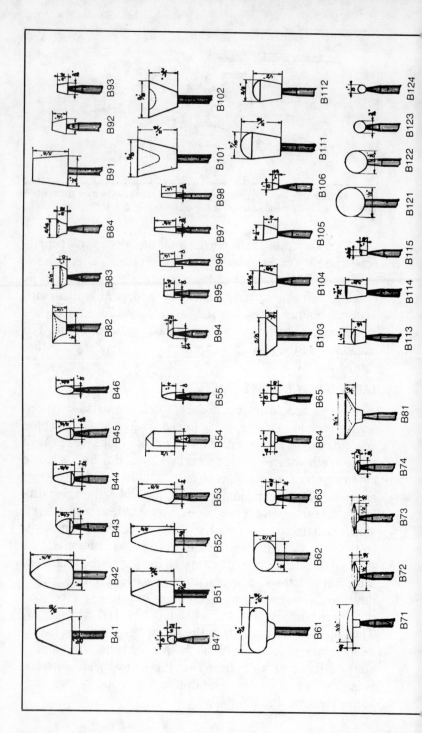

28

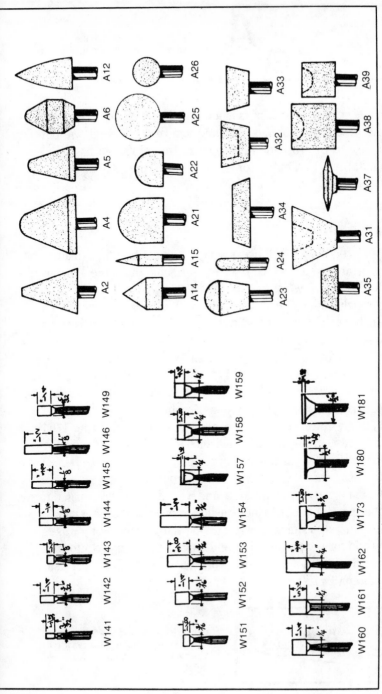

Fig. 1-14. Assortment of mounted wheels and points for grinding, polishing and cutting. These wheels can be ordered from Frank Mittermeier, Inc.

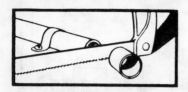

Fig. 1-15. A hacksaw with the blade mounted for normal operation.

A screw extractor is specially designed for removing broken screws, bolts, sights and similar items—all without damage to the threaded hole. Once the pilot hole has been drilled, the screw extractor is inserted and the left-hand spiral removes right-hand threaded screws.

PLANER-SHAPER

If you own a drill press you may have use for a planer-shaper attachment. One excellent attachment is the Wagner Safe-T-Planer, which is absolutely safe and will not grab or kick back under operation. They will fit drill presses with a ½-inch capacity chuck and will cut to a depth of ¼ inch and a diameter of 3⅛ inches at 3000 to 6000 RPM.

The illustrations in Fig. 1-17 show how the Safe-T-Planer works. The view in Fig. 1-17A shows how the cutters are tilted for bottom clearance and the conical grind insures a 90-degree cut for making tenons, rabbets, etc. Note in Fig. 1-17B how the cutting edges project beyond the shoulder 1/64 inch for fast, controlled cutting which eliminates any possibility of kickback. This cutting action remains the same (Fig. 1-17C) even after sharpening hundreds of times.

This planer is versatile and will do accurate planing, rabbeting, tenoning, panel raising, moulding and staving. It may be used to shape gun stocks and also for many other uses on wood for the homeowner and hobbyist. For more information, write Gilmore Pattern Works, P.O. Box 50231, Tulsa, Oklahoma 74150.

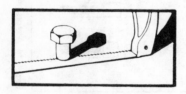

Fig. 1-16. The blade of a hacksaw can also be mounted sideways to cut flush with a large surface as shown here.

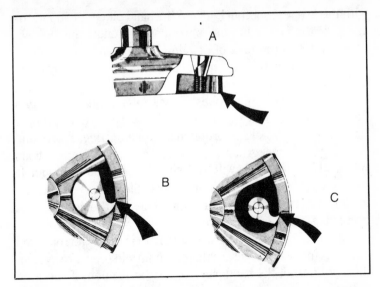

Fig. 1-17. The Wagner Safe-T-Planer. (A) A cutaway view showing how cutters are tilted for bottom clearance. Conical grind insures a 90-degree cut for making tenons, rabbets, etc. (B) Cutting edges project beyond the shoulder 1/64 inch for a fast controlled cut, eliminating any possibility of kickback. (C) Cutting action remains the same even after sharpening hundreds of times.

METAL & WOOD ENGRAVING TOOLS

Many artists and engravers are able to turn out high-quality work with only simple hand tools, but this skill is not learned overnight, not by a long shot; however, there is a machine capable of infinite control in supplying impact power to a hand piece which is suited for the beginner who hasn't a lifetime to learn or for the quality-oriented master who is production minded. The cost of the machine is around $500.

At first, a description of the tool might seem out of place in a book of this sort; however, the gunsmithing hobbyist whose interest lies in the direction of gun engraving can pay for the machine in a short period of time by taking engraving jobs from other shooters. In fact, a few hours a week spent on the machine might even bring in enough extra cash to equip an entire home workshop.

The power of the Gravermeister, manufactured by GRS Corporation, P.O. Box 1157, Boulder, Colorado 80302, is regulated through a foot pedal which serves the same function as the foot throttle in an automobile. Control is so precise that with the proper tool chucked into the hand piece, the operator can vary the power in ranges from stipple engraving on delicate crystal to the task of hogging metal from a steel die.

Delicate control of speed and power of this machine makes it ideal for performing almost any jewelry finishing tasks. With powerful strokes, it will raise a bead or form a bezel in seconds. With gentle strokes it will push over prongs, minimizing the breakage problem in stone-setting. Florentine finishing and background stippling, normally such tedious work, are amazingly swift and simple with this machine. It moves gravers, liners, beading tools, files, stones, etc. effortlessly in ranges from cutting steel dies to the delicate task of carving and finishing jewelry.

Bright smooth cuts are obtained in both ferrous and precious metals. The alternating vacuum and pressure system does not permit the hand piece to heat as happens if operated by air pressure alone.

Florentine and matt finishing will be the types most used on gun engraving. The florentine finish (checkered pattern) is used for two major purposes. An object such as a ring may be partially or completely florentined as a decorative finish or it may be used to complement another pattern.

It is applied with a tool called a liner, which is essentially a flat graver with equidistant V-shaped grooves cut into the bottom to produce parallel lines. Liners are categorized by width and number of lines per tool. The lower the width number, the narrower the tool; therefore, a #14-6 and a #18-6 would both cut six lines, but the #14 would be closer spaced because of its narrower width. Many different width and line combinations are available, but the liner generally favored by gun engravers for florentining is the #18-10.

Florentining consists of cutting crossed sets of lines. First, all of the lines in one direction are cut; then cross lines are applied at the preferred angle. A somewhat similar effect can be obtained by dragging the tip of the liner across the desired area. This action produces lines with no material removal. The stroke-speed setting and the speed with which the tool is pulled determine the spacing effect. If you drag the tool at a constant speed increasing the stroke speed results in closer spaced lines.

The liner is sharpened the same as a flat graver. The face of the tool is held at about a 45-degree angle and like most gravers would be polished after sharpening. In addition, the tip of the liner should be gently wiped a time or two on a sheet of crocus cloth to remove burrs thus permitting polished cuts.

Dental burrs offer a host of patterns for background matting as do bending tools. With up to 1200 strokes per minute and controlled power background matting is made extremely fast and simple with this machine.

When properly sharpened chisels are used, this machine is also useful for stock carving. Sharp, rapid blows of the machine render smooth, polished cuts in all kinds wood. For relief carving on wood, first layout the design. Next, with a scalpellike chisel gripped in the hand piece, follow the design outline backwards, not forward as one would in a normal cutting manner, at the same time applying power to the hand piece. Depth of the cut depends on the power supplied to the hand piece. Insert a scoop or gouge into the hand piece chuck and remove the background. As in metal work the background can be stamped with a variety of punches, which of course are held in the jaws of the hand piece. Rasps, files and cutters held in the hand piece speed up the work without compromising control.

For woodcarving this machine can be very useful for stock designs and the process may not be as difficult as one might imagine. Stan de Treville, Box 33021, San Diego, California 92103 offers decal carving patterns such as the running deer and the charging grizzly bear patterns. Each pattern sells for around $2.50 and is easily applied to the gun stock, where it provides outlines and guide lines for use in carving.

Just because you have a pattern, don't install it on an expensive gun stock and start carving away until you have gained some experience. Why not buy two patterns? Attach one to a flat piece of wood and practice on this first. Then, when you have gained confidence in your carving ability you can use the other pattern on a gun stock.

Carving of gun stocks can be an interesting and profitable hobby, even without the power machine described previously. It will greatly add to the pleasure you derive from owning your guns. With a little skill and patience you can transform an inexpensive, plain-looking gun into one that will be valuable and one that you will be proud to show your friends.

The pattern decal may be slid around on the stock and positioned more readily than a design drawn from a template or traced from a paper pattern. The decal will further adhere to a compound curved surface without forming wrinkles which distort the design. The thinness of the decal material—about 0.001 of an inch—permits carving right through the pattern without dulling the tools or tearing the pattern. However, all outlines of the design should be cut before removing any wood. The cuts should be kept shallow on the first cut, deepening them later where necessary to achieve the desired effect.

Those decals offered by Stan de Treville are printed in dark-brown on a contrasting background of yellow to show up clearly to avoid possible errors in cutting the design.

HAND BENDERS

A number of flat and coil springs may be made right in your own shop with a hand bender that is designed to multiform wire, flat metal and tubing fast. One such device is available from Karl A. Neise, Inc., 50-02 Roosevelt Avenue, Woodside, New York 11377. The unit consists of a compact, 6-pound fixed- or bench-mounted heavy-duty industrial bender light and portable enough for a tool kit. It makes precise sharp angle bends with ease in all wire and rod gauges up to 5/16 inch; and in 1-inch by ⅛-inch flat-metal forming curves, circles and coils to over 10 inches in diameter; and kink free small coils and radii in ⅛-inch, 3/16-inch and ¼-inch tubing. A special feature is the capability of forming closely adjacent wire bends in several planes, saving time and economically producing many parts.

MISCELLANEOUS TOOLS

There are several useful tools that can save the home gunsmith much time, but they should only be purchased when needed. For example, the T-handle wrench shown in Fig. 1-18 is designed specifically to fit the Weaver scope ring clamp nut. It will not mar or burr the nut slots and will fit over the screw

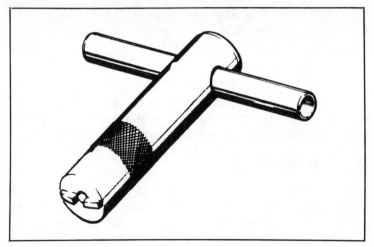

Fig. 1-18. T-handle wrench for removing Weaver scope ring clamp nuts and other makes.

end. This wrench also fits the imported scope rings similar to Weaver. They are available from Brownells, Inc.

The screw holder in Fig. 1-19 holds any #6 or #8 scope mount screw for grinding or filing. You can even rotate it to point a screw. You can chamfer a screw after shortening it for easier starting. Such a tool will prevent burning of fingers. If you have a lot of such work it is well worth the $5.

The swivel installation tool shown in Fig. 1-20 will allow you to install sling swivels without risk of damage to fine gun stocks. The V-jig has a hardened drill guide bushing and will automatically locate the 5/32-inch diameter drill furnished at the correct distance from the fore end or from the stock toe. It will guide the drill on the exact center of the stock edge or in the exact center of the barrel channel. The 7/32-inch diameter safety counterbore will counterbore the correct depth for the butt stock screw without risk of going too deep. The #10

Fig. 1-19. Screw holder for #6 or #8 scope mounting screws.

diameter drill and safety counterbore will drill and counter-bore, in one operation, the right diameter and depth for the fore-end screw and nut without risk of going too deep. All of the bits can be used in a ¼-inch electric drill or in a drill press.

Scope jigs—like the one in Fig. 1-21—are usually not warranted in the home gunshop. They are used mainly by the pro shops, but when drilling holes in the receiver to accept scope mounts, such jigs are indispensable.

SAFETY PRECAUTIONS

There are safety rules which apply to anyone handling firearms. In general, the basic rule is never to point a firearm at anyone or anything unless you intend to kill. This applies to either loaded or unloaded (you think) weapons. Secondly, make certain the firearm you intend to shoot is in good condition, the proper ammunition used, and that no obstructions, such as a cleaning brush, are in the chamber or bore.

Besides these basic rules, those who perform work on firearms should concern themselves with a few other basic principles.

■ Never apply heat to any part of a firearm unless you know what you are doing, then proceed with care

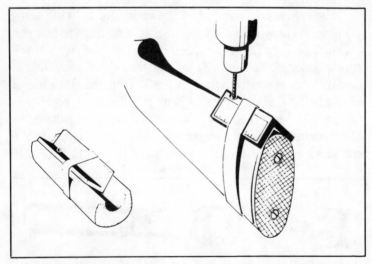

Fig. 1-20. Swivel installation tool for gun slings. The V-jig has a drill guide to locate the exact position of the fore and aft holes.

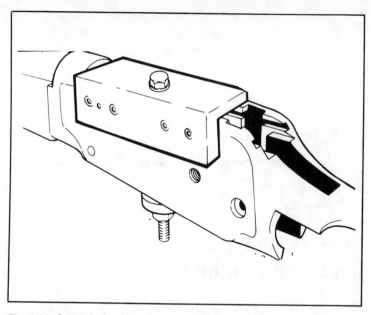

Fig. 1-21. Scope jig for drilling holes in the receiver for scope mounts.

■ Never remove excessive amounts of metal from a rifle action at points of stress, that is, receiver rings, etc.

■ When installing new parts make certain that these parts are functioning properly before firing the weapon

■ Watch trigger pulls

■ Always make certain that the gun is unloaded the moment you touch it, but always treat it as if it were loaded

Chapter 2

Understanding the Operation of Rifles

Everyone has heard the expression, "lock, stock and barrel," which means complete, everything, etc. The lock refers to the main mechanism on a muzzle-loading rifle, which consists of the hammer, trigger, side plate, cap in the case of cap-lock weapons or the flash pan in the case of flint-lock weapons, springs and other gadgets that help to control the ignition of the powder in the barrel. The stock, of course, is a wooden member in which the lock and barrel are imbedded. It offers the shooter a means of supporting the lock and barrel in a steady position against the shoulder. Upon firing the stock also acts to absorb the recoil against the shooter's shoulder. The barrel holds the powder charge, wading and the bullet or round ball before firing and acts as a guide for the projectile upon firing. Modern rifle barrels contain rifling and grooves which give the bullet a slight twist as it is pushed down the barrel. This twisting action helps the projectile to go straight upon being fired.

Modern rifles are very similar in design as the muzzle-loading rifle just described, except that the main mechanism on a modern rifle is the action instead of the lock. The stock and barrel are essentially the same.

Since the action is the main mechanism on modern rifles, this is also a means of identifying a rifle, that is, bolt action, slide action, lever action, etc. A brief explanation of each is order.

TYPES OF ACTIONS

Over the next few pages each type of action is explained. These are single-shot action, bolt action, lever action, pump action and semiatuomatic action. Although today many firearms manufacturers produce several types of actions, prototypes of each style were developed by individuals.

Single-shot Actions

There are several different types of single-shot actions, but probably the most common is the type referred to as a tip-up action. This type of action is employed by Savage on their Model 24 series of combination rifle/shotguns as well as other double-rifles and combination weapons.

Tip-up actions are usually unlocked by pivoting a lever located on the tang behind the hammer. Upon pivoting this lever the breech end of the barrel tips up, ejects the fired cartridge and leaves the chamber open for the insertion of a new cartridge. On tip-up actions with automatic ejectors the fired cartridge ejects upon opening. An unfired cartridge remains in the chamber and has to be removed by hand.

Another type of single-shot action is the falling-block action. The Ruger No. 1 Single-Shot, for example, uses an under-lever, falling-block action which follows the Farquharson design (Fig. 2-1). This type of action has been made in almost all sizes and designs to accept nearly every cartridge available.

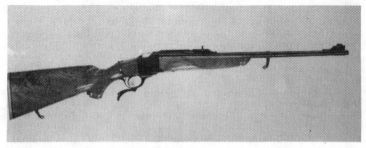

Fig. 2-1. Ruger No. 1 Single-Shot rifle with open sights. Comes in calibers .243, .270 and .30-06.

Fig. 2-2. The .30-40 Krag was the first bolt-action rifle used by U.S. Armed Forces.

The heart of the falling-block action is the massive receiver which forms a rigid connection between the barrel and the butt stock and the receiver together into a solid, rigid struction. A breech block is operated by a lever which holds the cartridge in place inside the barrel for firing. After firing the under-lever is pushed down and forward to release the breech block, providing ejection of the fired cartridge and leaving the chamber open for the insertion of a new cartridge.

Fig. 2-3. Lettering on the receiver of this .30-40 Krag shows that it was manufactured in 1894 at the Springfield Armory.

Fig. 2-4. Winchester Model 70. (A) Model 70 XTR. A new design of rear sight is one of the many features of the Model 70 XTR bolt-action rifle. (B) Model 70 African. (C) Model 70 cutaway.

The old Winchester high and low sidewall single-shot rifles also used the falling-block action.

The 1871 U.S. Springfield rifle utilized a trapdoor, single-shot action to house the .45-70-caliber cartridge. On this model the hinged breech block was lifted up like a trapdoor to eject the fired cartridge and for inserting a new one.

Another famous single-shot action is the rolling-block type, which was first produced around 1865. The breech block on this type of action was pivoted to roll back to eject the fired cartridge and to insert a new one.

There have also been a number of single-shot actions based on the bolt-action design. The bolt is lifted and pulled to the rear to eject a fired cartridge and to insert a new one. On most models the firing pin is cocked upon opening the bolt. On some models, however, the firing pin had to be cocked after the new cartridge was inserted by pulling back on a knurled knob at the rear of the bolt.

Bolt Actions

The bolt-action type is the one most used on center-fire rifles today. The action operates by a bolt which locks the cartridge in the chamber of the barrel and also ejects the cartridges—whether fired or not—when the bolt is opened. On bolt-action repeating rifles additional cartridges are housed in a clip or compartment in the action under the bolt and sometimes in a tubular magazine projecting under the barrel.

When the bolt handle is lifted and pulled to the rear the bolt ejects the fired cartridge, and when pushed forward the bolt cocks the firing pin (in most cases) and picks up a new cartridge from the magazine for insertion into the chamber. When the bolt handle is again locked the weapon is ready to fire. This procedure may be repeated for additional shots until the cartridges in the magazine are depleted.

Two of the earliest bolt-action rifles were the Mauser and the .30-40-caliber Krag—both being manufactured in the early 1890s (Figs. 2-2 and 2-3). The Mauser-type bolt-action is probably the most widely used action today and many center-fire rifles have been made up on this type of action.

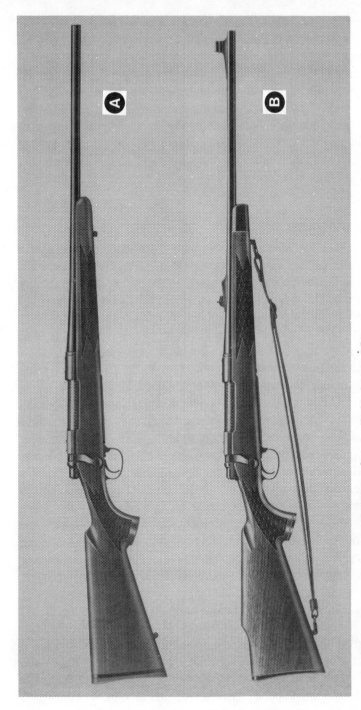

Fig. 2-5. Remington Model 700. (A) Model 700 Classic. (B) Model 700 BDL.

43

The strength of bolt-action rifles varies from weak to the strongest actions available and the better ones have bolts with an extra margin of safety for any cartridge that may be fired in them. The strength of the bolt depends upon the number and type of locking lugs and the method in which they enclose the cartridge head. Some of the better bolt-action rifles on the market today are the Winchester Model 70 (Fig. 2-4), Remington Model 700 (Fig. 2-5), Ruger M-77 (Fig. 2-6), Savage M110 and the Weatherby Mark V as well as the Mauser M98 as mentioned previously. This list is by no means complete—there are many others.

Lever Actions

Anyone who has ever watched a Western movie at the theater or on TV has certainly seen a lever-action rifle carried in the leather scabbord attached to the saddle and frequently used by the rider. The victory of the Sioux over the Seventh Cavalry in the valley of the Little Big Horn was accredited to the lever-action rifles used by the Sioux. The single-shot trapdoor Springfield rifles in the hands of the Seventh Cavalry were no match for the rapid-firing repeating lever-action rifles which the Sioux had somehow acquired.

The name that has become a byword for the repeating rifle is Winchester. The Winchester rifles were not the first successful repeating rifle though; both the Henry and Spencer came on the scene prior to Winchester. The Spencer lever-action repeater had a tubular magazine in the stock, this magazine fed ammunition at the rate of about ten shots a minute. When the finger lever was moved down, the breech would open extracting the empty cartridge and allowing the spring-powered magazine to feed a new cartridge into the chamber. The Henry repeater worked in a similar manner except when the breech opened as the lever was pulled down, the hammer would be cocked. The Spencer rifle hammer had to be manually cocked before the rifle could be fired.

The first Winchester Model 1866 was an improved design of the Henry. The magazine for this rifle was under the barrel as was the case with the Henry. The main difference was that the loading port was on the right side. The '66 was not to be the most popular Winchester rifle though. Models 1873,

Fig. 2-6. Ruger Model 77. (A) Basic Ruger M-77 bolt-action rifle, round top model. (B) Same as above but fitted with Lyman All-American scope and Buehler one-piece mount and rings.

1876, 1886 and 1894 were a progression of lever-action rifles that culminated in the 1894—becoming the popular deer rifle of today (Fig. 2-7).

The Winchester lever-action repeating rifle has a breech pin rod that serves to house the firing pin and to push new cartridges into the chamber. When the lever is pulled down the breech pin rod is pulled back, cocking the hammer. The lever simultaneously pushes the carrier block up, ejecting the empty casing and lifting a new cartridge up to the level of the breech rod pin. As the lever is closed the breech pin rod pushes the new cartridge into the chamber and locks in place. Since the hammer is cocked when the lever is pulled down the rifle is ready to fire.

In 1881 during the heyday of the Winchester lever-action rifles, the Marlin lever-action rifle was introduced. The Marlin rifle is very similar in looks to the Winchester model 94, at least on a superficial level. Actions on the two rifles are different in that the Marlin ejects fired cartridges to the side instead of through the receiver top. This gives the Marlin a distinct advantage when using a telescope sight. The top eject on the Winchester requires that a scope be mounted to the side (offset) so that it will not interfere with the ejecting cartridges. With the cartridges being ejected to the side on the Marlin, the scope can be mounted to the top of the receiver. The primary difference between the Marlin and Winchester actions is that on the Winchester an extractor holds the shell casing, pulling it out of the chamber as the bolt moves back.

The bolt on the Marlin rifle is pulled back by the movement of the lever in a forward swing. A spring-loaded ejector pushes the expended shell out of the breech. As the lever is moving forward the new shell is forced out of the magazine by spring tension and is then carried up to the chamber level by a carrier. When the lever is pulled back the bolt pushes the new cartridge into the chamber. The moving lever also hooks onto the locking bolt and pushes it into a slot in the bolt, locking it in place. When the bolt is opened, at the start of the cycle, the hammer is pushed back and cocked, so the rifle is ready to fire as soon as the lever is locked back in the closed position (see Fig. 2-8).

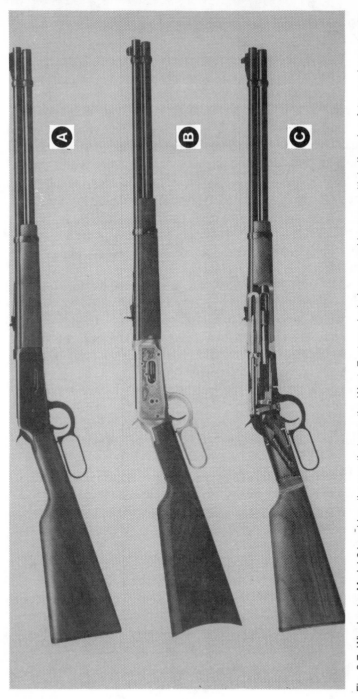

Fig. 2-7. Winchester Model 94 carbine, the gun that won the West. Features include exposed hammer with half-cock safety, receiver accepts several scope mounts, black serrated butt plate, hooded blade front sight, semibuckhorn rear sight, chromium molybdenum barrel and seven-shot capacity. (A) Standard Model 94. (B) Limited edition Model 94. (C) Cutaway of Model 94.

47

Pump Actions

Although the pump-action rifle is primarily an American rifle, it has never enjoyed the popularity that the bolt and lever-action repeaters have. This type of rifle is available in wide variety of calibers, from the .22-caliber rim-fire to some of the big-game cartridges. The pump-action rifle is the fastest manually operated rifle as far as rechambering and firing are concerned. Shooting from the shoulder the pump-action type is the easiest and smoothest action to operate when compared to the bolt- or lever-action types. The pump-action mechanism allows the shooter to cycle cartridges through the rifle without having to remove the trigger finger. The main drawback for the pump action rifle, as well as the lever-action style and automatic, is in its accuracy.

Since the pump-action rifle has a separate forestock which is subject to movement, the rifle's accuracy falls off. These rifles are also subject to creep in the trigger pull. Occasionally the pump-action rifle would not have enough power to eject a sticky cartridge. The most popular of the pump-action rifles are .22-caliber rim-fire types.

The pump-action rifle has been around since the late 1800s, having been introduced by Colt. These early pump-action rifles were adapted for use with relatively low-pressure cartridges. The Remington Model 14, which was introduced around 1912, was the first pump-action rifle that was capable of using high-powered cartridges. The Remington Model 141, a predecessor of the Model 14, is capable of handling many of the modern high-powered cartridges, such as the .30-06 and .270 calibers.

The basic pump-action type operates off of the movement of a forestock slide. As the slide moves rearward it pushes the bolt assembly back. When the bolt is back, the hammer is forced downward, causing the empty cartridge to eject. Shell ejection is governed by a circular spring in the forward end of the bolt. This spring holds the rim of the cartridge with a special clawlike protuberance inside the spring circle. When the bolt moves rearward the claw pulls the cartridge out of the chamber. Once the cartridge clear the

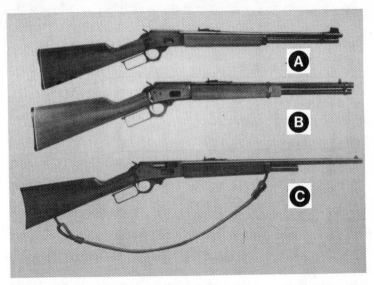

Fig. 2-8. Marlin lever-action rifle. (A) Model 1894 is produced as a .44-caliber Remington magnum with a 10-shot tubular magazine and barrel length of 20 inches. (B) Model 1894 carbine is produced as a .357-caliber magnum with a 9-shot tubular magazine and barrel length of 18½ inches. (C) Model 1895 is produced as a .45-70-caliber repeater. It has a 4-shot tubular magazine and a 22-inch barrel.

chamber a spring ejector in the bolt flips the casing out. When the casing is ejected, a spring-loaded magazine lifts a new cartridge up to the chamber level.

Moving the slide forward causes the bolt to move forward, chambering the new cartridge. The hammer, which was pushed back when the bolt was back, is held in the cocked position by a special sear that fits into a notch in the hammer. The bolt is locked in place by a turning action which allows special threads on the bolt to engage locking lugs. Threads on the bolt and the locking lugs act like the threads on a nut and bolt. When the slide is moved as far forward as it will travel the bolt turns in the locking lugs, locking the bolt in place. Once the locking lugs are engaged the rifle is ready to fire.

Semiautomatic Action

The fastest action that is available to the nonmilitary or law enforcement shooter is the semiautomatic. Although semiautomatic rifles are often referred to as *automatics*, this term is a misnomer. The semiautomatic rifle requires that the trigger be pulled each time that a shot is made. A truly automatic rifle requires only a single pull of the trigger to empty the rifle's magazine.

The primary advantage of the semiautomatic is firepower. The original purpose for this type of action was for military use since it gave a substantial advantage over the slower bolt-action weapons. Since World War II the tendency for military weapons has been toward the fully automatic rifle leaving the semiautomatic to the civilian.

For the hunter the semiautomatic action has more or less the same advantages as it does for military purposes, firepower. This type of action also has advantages when applied to the shotgun, but this will be taken up in the next chapter. The semiautomatic rifle finds its greatest use, as far as hunting is concerned, in brush and forest shooting. When shooting in heavy brush it is often necessary to be able to deliver several consecutive shots; the semiautomatic can do this quite effectively.

Semiautomatic actions can be powered by one of two different methods. The first method that we will discuss is the *recoil* method. The alternative is called the *force of expanding gases*.

Recoil-Powered Semiautomatic Action. The basic recoil-action semiautomatic is called the *blow-back* type (see Fig. 2-9). As the name implies the shell casing blows back against the breech block causing it to open. Since the breech block is heavier and also held by a spring, the bullet can go faster. While the breech is being thrown open by the force of the fired cartridge, it ejects the empty shell casing. When the spring stops the block, it starts to push the breech back to the closed position. As the breech block moves forward it picks up a new cartridge and pushes it into the firing chamber. When the breech was pushed back it also cocked the hammer; so once the breech is in the forward position the rifle is ready to fire.

Since the blow-back method depends on spring tension and the weight of the breech block, the cartridge power has to be limited. This type of system is usually employed on .22-

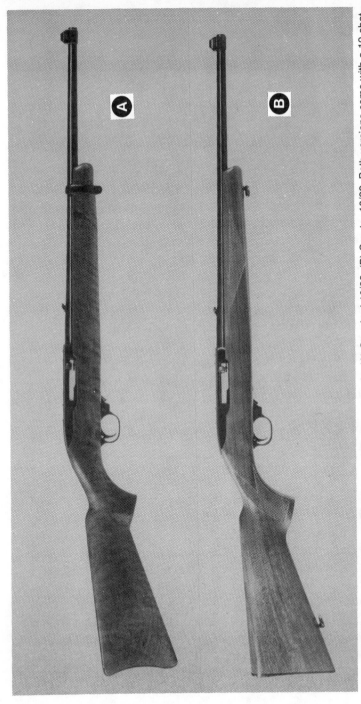

Fig. 2-9. Ruger 10/22 is an example of a blow-back semiautomatic. (A) Standard 10/22. (B) Sporter 10/22. Both versions come with a 10-shot magazine and a 18½-inch barrel.

51

caliber rifles and pistols. The blow-back type could theoretically be used with any cartridge but the breech block weight would be prohibitive. For a .30-06-caliber cartridge the breech block would have to weigh almost 30 pounds—definitely not a handy weight to be lugging through the forest.

Another recoil action is called the *short-recoil* type (see Fig. 2-10). With the short recoil, the breech block and the barrel are locked together. When the cartridge is fired the recoil from the bullet going forward pushes both the barrel and the breech back, compressing a spring. As soon as the bullet clears the barrel the breech and barrel separate, leaving the breech to carry onto the rear under the remaining momentum and the expansion of residual gas from the cartridge. At the extreme of the bolt movement a buffer stops the bolt and it is pushed back forward again by spring tension. The breech block picks up a new cartridge on the way forward and seats it in the chamber. The hammer is cocked when the breech is at the rearward position; so when the bolt has returned to the forward position and has locked the rifle is ready to fire. Since the breech and barrel only move a short distance, this system is called the short-recoil method.

The short-recoil type is somewhat stronger than the blow-back version since the weight of the barrel is added to the weight of the breech. This system is also stronger because the breech locks back into position rather than being held in position by spring tension.

The final recoil method that will be discussed here is called the *long-recoil* type. With the long-recoil system the barrel and the breech move together, as with the short-recoil method. The difference is that the barrel continues back all the way with the breech. When the barrel and breech reach the rear the breech is held by a special latch while the barrel returns to its forward position. The movement of the barrel forward causes the fired cartridge to be ejected. When the barrel reaches the forward position it causes a lever to release, which in turn releases the latch holding the breech open. Once the breech is released it travels forward picking up a new cartridge and pushes it into the chamber. The rearward movement of the breech and barrel cocks the hammer; so the

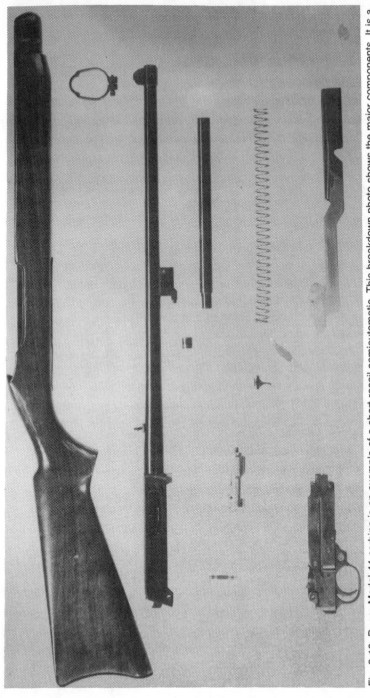

Fig. 2-10. Ruger Model 44 carbine is an example of a short-recoil semiautomatic. This breakdown photo shows the major components. It is a .44-caliber magnum with 12-groove rifling. Capacity is four rounds in the magazine and one in the chamber.

rifle is ready to fire as soon as both the breech and barrel are in the forward position.

The long-recoil method has been used successfully for the last 50 years or so. Remington manufactured two models, the 8 and the 81, which incorporated this system. These Remington rifles are chambered for the .25- , .30- and the .35-caliber Remington cartridges. With these rifles the barrel moves in a special sleeve, which has led to the common misconception that the rifle barrel could be removed changing it into a shotgun. The only real complaint aobut rifles using the long-recoil system is that they have a double-kick which may interfere with some hunters' shooting.

Gas-Operated Semiautomatic Action. Unlike the recoil method of operation for a semiautomatic rifle, the gas-operated automatic load rifle has only one basic configuration (see Fig. 2-11). Rifles that operate off of the gases that are generated by the expansion of gun powder have a hole in the barrel that leads to a piston chamber. When a cartridge is fired and the bullet passes the hole in the barrel some of the gases are forced out of the barrel. These gases go into a special chamber, usually below the barrel, and push a piston which is connected to the breech bolt. As the piston moves it unlocks the breech and pushes the bolt back. When the breech moves back, the expended cartridge is ejected and the firing pin is cocked. The breech encounters a recoil spring when it reaches the rearward position. This recoil spring pushes the breech, rod and piston back to their original position. When the breech is moving forward, it picks up a new cartridge leaving the rifle ready to fire.

The M1 carbine and Garand are probably the two most famous examples of the gas-operated semiautomatic rifles. These rifles were used very effectively during World War II and the Korean War, making the slower manually operated rifles obsolete as far as warfare was concerned. Gas-operated semiautomatic rifles are also very successful rifles when used for hunting. The Remington Model 740 *Woodmaster* is a good example. The Woodmaster comes in several high-powered rifle calibers, such as .30-06, .244 Remington and .308 Win-

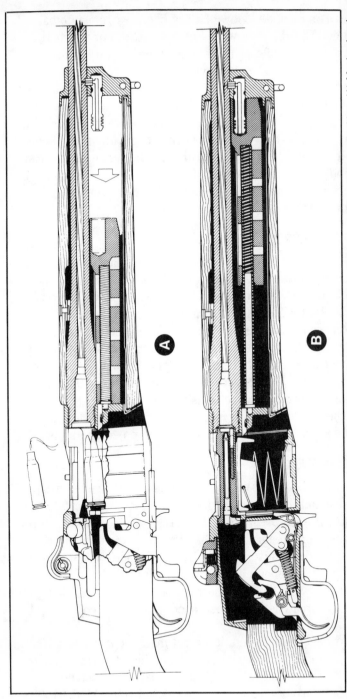

Fig. 2-11. Gas-operated semiautomatic action. Shown is a Ruger Mini-14 mechanism, which uses .223-caliber ammunition. (A) Mechanism is shown in full recoil. The bolt will be driven forward under pressure of the main spring to chamber the next cartridge. (B) Mechanism is shown with hammer cocked. Bolt is locked. Chamber and magazine are empty.

chester. An exploded view of a gas-operated semiautomatic, the Ruger Mini-14 is shown in Fig. 2-12. The semiautomatic is not as accurate a rifle as a bolt-action type but it does make up for any disadvantages by providing more firepower.

The semiautomatic rifle is not a good choice for anyone contemplating hand reloading. When the cartridges are fired and ejected by the semiautomatic rifle the casing is usually subjected to pretty severe treatment along with usually being difficult to find. The cases usually have to be resized if they can be found. For the action to function properly, a certain amount of breech pressure is required, and therefore reduced loads will not operate the mechanism.

THE RIFLE BARREL

The modern rifle barrel is the result of many generations of change. The first rifles had smoothbore barrels, resulting in very inaccurate instruments. When it was finally discovered that a bullet that had some spin to it was more accurate the smoothbore musket became a relic. The idea of putting spiral grooves in rifle barrels was brought to the United States by German immigrants that settled in the Pennsylvania Dutch country. These people were responsible for the development of the Kentucky rifle, which was well known for its accuracy. Since these rifles were so much more accurate the less accurate smoothbore rifles or muskets were no competition.

BARREL MATERIALS

Early rifle barrels only had to withstand pressures around 25,000 pounds per square inch or lower. Since these rifles had such low-breech pressures, the barrels could be made from relatively soft metals, such as iron and soft carbon steel. Bullets used in these rifles were only made of lead, again allowing for soft barrel materials. With the advent of high-temperature and high-pressure smokeless powder, though, barrel material had to be increased in strength correspondingly.

To begin the change in barrel material *ordinance* steel was introduced. Ordinance steel has a high tensile strength and is quite durable; it is also fairly easy to machine. The Springfield Armory used this type of steel in the Model 1903.

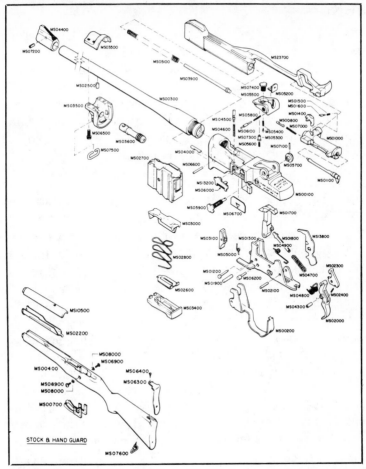

Fig. 2-12. Exploded view of the Ruger Mini-14. Part numbers are shown and replacements can be ordered from Sturm, Ruger & Company, Inc., Southport, Connecticut 06490.

Remington also produced high-powered rifles equipped with barrels manufactured from ordinance steel. Nickel steel was also used in rifle barrels made by Winchester. Although nickel steel is more difficult to machine it is more durable.

The modern rifle barrel is usually made from chrome-molybdenum steel. This type of steel was first used by Winchester after it was discovered that it could withstand the high pressures better than ordinance or nickel steel. *Chrom-moly*, as it is referred to, has a high tensile strength as well as being both durable and machinable.

TWIST

The amount of pitch that a rifle barrel's rifling has is called the twist. Twist is what determines the rate of spin that a bullet will have when it leaves the end of the rifle barrel. The amount of twist that is needed is dependent on the shape and sectional density of the bullet that is being fired. The smaller and more pointed a bullet, the more spin it needs to keep it on a straight path. Conversely the heavier bullets with blunt noses require less spin to keep them on target.

RIFLING

The rifling in a barrel is the spiral grooves that impart spin to a bullet as it traverses the length of the barrel. Several types of rifling have been used throughout the history of rifles but the most common modern rifling is called *Enfield*. Enfield rifling has a square shape which twists through the length of the rifle barrel. The number of grooves found in the barrel depends on the particular manufacturer and the rifle. Some rifles have as few as two grooves to as many as eight grooves. The most common barrels have either four or six rifling grooves.

Several methods exist for barrel rifling. The primary methods are referred to as the hammer or button methods. The hammer method of rifling consists of literally pounding the rifle barrel down over a special mandrel which imparts the proper rifling to the barrel. This method requires the use of a specially designed machine. Since the machines are fairly expensive, custom designed guns rarely have the riflings imprinted using the hammer method. The button method is a simple process of drawing a special button through a barrel blank. The buttons are similar in shape to a bullet, but are made from a very strong and hard metal alloy. As the button is pulled through the barrel, grooves on the button, that correspond to the proper twist and rifling, displace the metal of the barrel.

Chapter 3

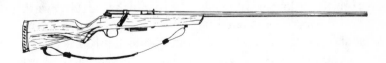

Understanding the Operation of Shotguns

In an historical perspective, the shotgun has been around longer than the rifle. The old muzzle-loading rifles were actually smoothbored and were therefore shotguns. Rifles didn't enter the scene until after the advent of rifling techniques. Modern shotguns differ considerably from their predecessors, especially in that they are loaded at the breech instead of through the muzzle.

Shotguns today come in several configurations. The single-barreled breakopen shotgun is the least expensive and simplest. Other types of actions commonly found in shotguns are semiautomatic, bolt and pump. The barrel configuration on a shotgun is not limited to only the single barrel. As in some of the big-game rifles, shotguns can have two barrels. Double-barreled shotguns have the barrels arranged either side by side or over and under (one barrel on top of the other).

With shotguns there is a different set of terms that need to be understood. Shotguns are sized into gauges and different barrels can have different chokes. With shotguns it is also important to understand the idea of pattern and to be able to distinguish between all of the different types of shot that can be used for each type of shooting.

Shotguns can be basically grouped under two categories, single and multiple barrels. Single-barreled shotguns are divided into several different action types. The double-barreled shotguns are limited, for the most part, to the breakopen configuration.

BREAKOPEN SHOTGUNS

Single-shot and double-barreled shotguns are usually of the breakopen configuration. Breakopen configuration refers to the fact that these guns open at the breech by allowing the barrels to fall downward, tipping the rear of the barrel upward. When the barrel is tipped up, the shells are placed in the chamber and the barrels are then lifted until they lock in place.

The breakopen single-shot shotgun is one of the least expensive shotguns on the market. Since it is relatively inexpensive it has been popular as a first shotgun for young people and also for the farmer. Single-barreled guns come in all of the major gauges from .410 to 12 gauge (.410 is actually a caliber). These guns have been used for shooting marauding pest animals as well as deer. Since the barrels break away at the breech these shotguns are probably the safest guns around.

Single-shot shotguns have also become quite popular at turkey shoots where they have proven themselves time and again. Some of the guns used at turkey shoots are fairly expensive when considering them as a single-barreled shotgun, but many of these guns have won their owners considerable sums of money. Trap shooting is another area in which the single-barreled shotgun is used. But again, these shotguns are usually pretty expensive and often times specially made.

As previously stated double-barreled shotguns come in two configurations, *side by side* and *over and under* (Fig. 3-1). The side-by-side type refers to the barrels being situated next to each other in a horizontal plane. This is the more familiar type of double-barreled shotgun and usually the type implied when simply referring to a piece as a double-barreled shotgun. The over-and-under type on the other hand is where one barrel is placed on top of the other.

Traditionally the side-by-side double-barreled shotgun has been used for small game and water fowl. The over-and-under double-barreled shotgun has been used for both hunting and trap shooting. The main advantage of the over-and-under version is that it has a single sighting plane. In other words

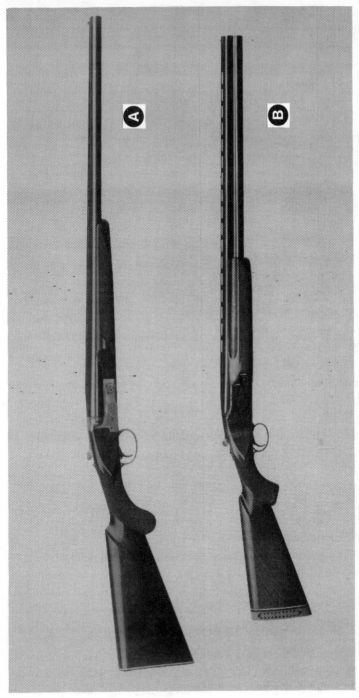

Fig. 3-1. Winchester double-barreled shotguns. (A) Model 23 side-by-side field gun. Available in gauges 12 through 20. (B) Model 101 over-and-under field magnum. Available in 12-gauge only.

only the top barrel can be seen while sighting. Many people disagree with this saying that the side-by-side double-barreled shotgun is just as accurate.

Barrels on double-barreled shotguns usually have two different chokes which give these guns an additional amount of versatility (choke will be discussed in greater detail later). With the choice in choke it becomes necessary to have a way of firing the barrels selectivity. On the less expensive shotguns two triggers are provided, one for each barrel. On more expensive double-barreled guns, the selection of barrels is accomplished through a lever, eliminating the need for two triggers. Another feature that is found on more expensive shotguns is a selective ejector. The selective ejector allows the shotgun to break open ejecting only the spent shell. This saves a lot of time when reloading in the field after discharging only one of the barrels.

The side-by-side double-barreled shotgun has lost some of its popularity in recent times because of the development of the over-and-under style. One of the possible reasons for this is that the average hunter is used to the single-barreled rifle and wants something that will sight in a similar manner. Some of the other advantages that might affect the decision on which to buy are the straight line recoil and the lack of crossfiring. The double-barreled side-by-side shotgun is subject to crossfiring since the barrels are usually designed so that the center of the shot pattern crosses at approximately 40 yards. When rifled slugs are being used, the right barrel shoots to the left, while the left barrel shoots to the right. The recoil follows the same basic idea; that is, the left barrel pushes to the right while the other barrel does the opposite. Once one gets used to this though, the side-by-side type is probably equal to the over-and-under method. The side-by-side double-barreled shotgun is still quite popular in Europe and seems to be coming back into the limelight (see Fig. 3-2).

PUMP OR SLIDE-ACTUATED REPEATING SHOTGUNS

In the late 1800s Winchester introduced the first successful repeating shotgun. The gun was designed by John Browning and was lever actuated. This particular gun was orginally

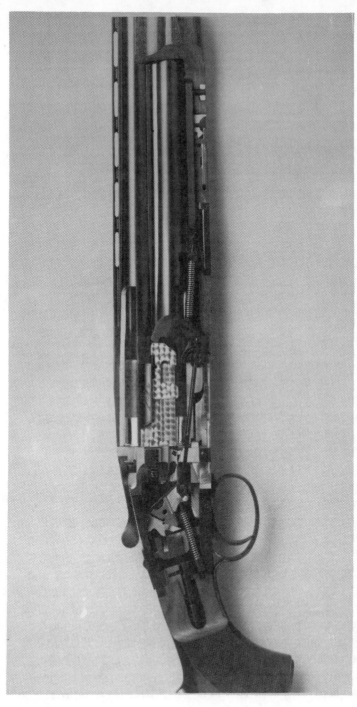

Fig. 3-2. Cutaway view of a Winchester Model 101, featuring ventilated rib barrel, combined barrel selector and safety, selective automatic ejectors, full length side rib, chromed bores and chambers, machined steel receiver and quick takedown.

63

equipped with a four-shot tubular magazine. When the chamber had a shell in it the shotgun had a total of five shells that could be fired as rapidly as the lever could be operated. This, however, was its downfall; the lever action was too slow.

Since the lever action was too slow for a shotgun, some other type of action needed to be developed. Winchester again was the company to popularize the new pump-action shotgun. The original Model 1893 was only produced for a short period of time, but the pump action was here to stay. The pump was faster than the lever action, plus the movements involved in using the pump did not affect the sighting capabilities as drastically.

By the early twentieth century Winchester had developed its Model 12 (Fig. 3-3), which is the oldest continuously produced, hammerless shotgun with a pump-type action. In a special presentation the one millionth Model 12 was presented to General Hap Arnold in 1953. Since its inception this shotgun has been produced in almost every shotgun configuration, from duck gun to trap gun.

Remington also produced pump shotguns starting around 1907. The original Remington ejected spent shells from the bottom of the receiver. This first Remington Model was designated the Model 10 and was produced for about 20 years. The Remington's action was quite a bit smoother in comparison to the Winchester, and it was definitely quieter. The present Model 870 is a very smooth action even though it was designed as a labor-saving action as far as manufacture is concerned.

The pump action in a shotgun like the Model 870 Remington is actuated by the movement of the forestock. When the forestock is pulled back a lever that attaches to the bolt moves rearward. The movement of this lever causes the spent shell to be ejected, and at the same time pushing the hammer back. The hammer engages a special sear that holds it in the cocked position. While the pump lever is being moved rearward it also moves a new shell into the carrier. The carrier is actuated by the bolt, which in turn is actuated by the lever attached to the pump. When the bolt is in the rearward position a special cam—the carrier dog—allows the carrier to drop

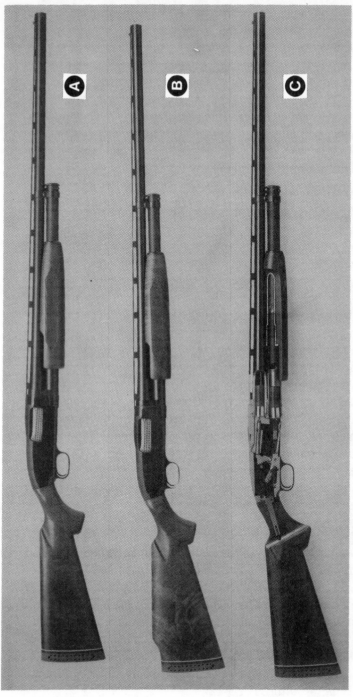

Fig. 3-3. Winchester Model 12 slide-action shotgun. (A) Model 12 trap gun with regular stock and ventilated rib. (B) Model 12 trap gun with Monte Carlo stock and ventilated rib. (C) Model 12 cutaway.

down to the level of the magazine. With the carrier in this position, the new shell that is moved into position by the pumping action can be picked up. As the bolt moves forward the carrier dog is forced down pushing the back end of the carrier down in a seesaw fashion, causing the front of the carrier to lift the new shell up to the breech. When the forestock is moved forward the rest of the way the bolt pushes the new shell into the chamber. When the bolt reaches its extreme forward position a special locking block closes into position making the action ready for firing.

BOLT-ACTION SHOTGUNS

For the most part the bolt-action shotgun has never been one of the top shotguns. The main reason for this is that this type of shotgun was made to compete in the low-price competition with the single-barreled shotgun. To make the bolt action as cheaply as possible most of the quality was left out.

The bolt-action type is designed, usually, after the Mauser-type action found in rifles. As a matter of fact the first bolt-action shotguns were modified World War I Mausers. Since the original bolt actions were put on the market a large number of these guns have been produced in several different gauges (see Fig. 3-5).

Although these guns are extremely inexpensive, as far as manufacture is concerned, they are reasonably strong and reliable (Fig. 3-6 through 3-9). Probably the best application that can be found for their use is with iron sights as a slug gun for deer hunting. The actions are extremely slow, and have to be rated as slower than the lever-action shotguns mentioned earlier.

AUTOLOADING SHOTGUNS

Around the turn of the century John Browning invented the first autoloading shotgun. Remington purchased the rights to market the gun in the United States, along with agreeing to pay Browning a royalty. The shotgun was designated the Remington Model 11 and was sold as such in America, while Browning retained the rights to sell it throughout the rest of the world as the Browning Automatic. For the most part all of the "automatic" shotguns operate off of the same principles (see Figs. 3-10 through 3-12).

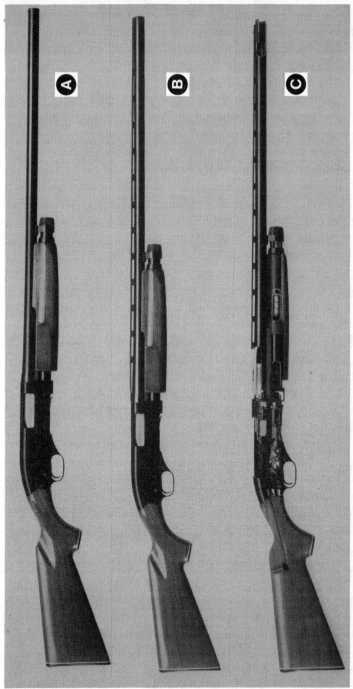

Fig. 3-4. Winchester Model 1300 slide-action shotgun, available in 12-gauge or 20-gauge versions. (A) Field gun with plain barrel. (B) Field gun with ventilated rib. (C) Cutaway of Model 1300.

The semiautomatic, as it is not actually automatic, shotgun operates off of the energy generated by the recoil. This method of actuating the action has proven itself, with time, as being the most dependable way for operating an autoloading shotgun. Basically, the recoil method can be separated into two separate groups, the long-recoil type and the short-recoil type. The original Model 11 Remington used a long-recoil system while the Browning Double Automatic and the Winchester Model 50 used the short-recoil method.

With the long-recoil type, as in the Model 11, barrel and breech are pushed back while still in contact with one another until they reach the rear of the shotgun. When the barrel and breech reach this rearward position they separate, with the barrel pulling itself forward. As the barrel moves forward it pulls away from the expended shell case. The shell casing is held in contact with the breech by a set of double extractors keeping the shell from moving forward with the barrel. As the barrel reaches its original position the shell is ejected by a special spring that is attached to the barrel. When the barrel is moving forward, it trips a mechanism allowing the breech to move forward. The forward momentum of the breech is caused by a spring in the stock which is compressed when the breech and barrel move rearward. When the breech is moving forward it picks up a new shell and pushes it into the chamber. This action leaves the gun ready to fire.

Since the long-recoil shotgun has a two-part recoil many people complain of the double-kick. When the shell is fired, the shooter feels the kick, but there is a second kick when the barrel and the breech slam home. Since all of the movements are controlled by the adjustments on the various springs that are involved, misadjustment can cause some rather jolting recoils.

To lessen the effects of the double-recoil, Browning and Winchester use a short-recoil system. With the Browning Double Automatic the barrel only recoils ⅝ inch, just enough to start the action moving. Winchester, on the other hand, has a fixed barrel and a floating chamber in its Model 50.

Winchester Model 50 has an inertia rod that runs into the shoulder stock. When a shell is fired, the chamber moves back approximately 1/10 inch, causing a special pin in the bolt to

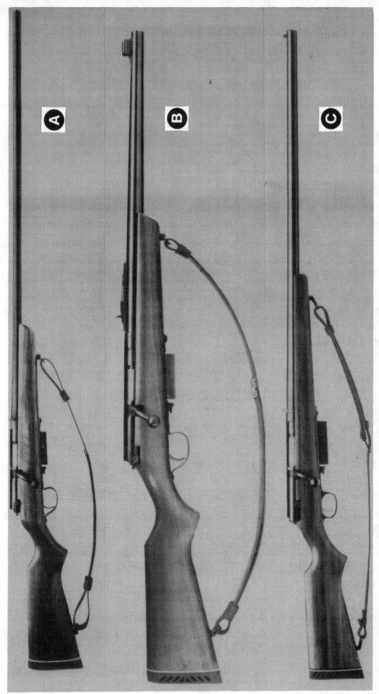

Fig. 3-5. Marlin bolt-action shotguns. (A) Model 55 Goose Gun. (B) Model 55S Slug Gun. (C) Model 5510 SuperGoose Gun.

kick the inertia rod back against a spring in the shoulder stock. The hammer is cocked as the inertia rod moves rearward. At the extreme rearward position of the inertia rod the bolt is opened and the shell is ejected. When the spent shell ejects a new shell is allowed to enter the carrier. While the spring pushes the inertia rod forward the bolt moves forward, picking up the shell on the carrier and pushing it into the chamber. This ends the cycle and the shotgun is ready to fire.

In recent years another method for powering autoloading shotguns has been developed—gas. The gas-operated semiatuomatic shotgun is a very smooth operating gun. This type of shotgun is modeled after the gas-operated high-powered rifle, deriving the gas power from the expended shell. The action uses expanding gas that pushes a piston actuating the movement of the bolt. The gas is taken from the barrel after the shot passes a speical port in the barrel. This type of action minimizes the amount of recoil the shooter has to withstand.

SHOTGUN GAUGES

When discussing a rifle the caliber refers to the size of the barrel bore. With shotguns the term is gauge. The original method for determining the gauge of a shotgun was to count the number of bore size lead balls that it took to make 1 pound. In other words, twelve balls having a diameter equal to the bore of a 12-gauge shotgun should weigh 1 pound. This method was to determine all of the shotgun gauges. Since modern shotguns usually are being used to shoot pellets rather than balls a different method was needed. The modern method of determining the gauge is based on the old numbering system—12 gauge, 16 gauge, etc.—but instead of checking the gauge using balls of lead, the new guns have been standardized. The standard size for the bore diameter on the 12-gauge shotgun is 0.775 inch, for the 16 gauge it is supposed to be 0.552 inch. There are slight differences between guns of the same gauge, as far as the bore is concerned, but these differences are not serious. As mentioned earlier the one exception to this is the .410 shotgun. This is really a misnomer; the .410 is a caliber, that is, 0.410 inch, and not a gauge size.

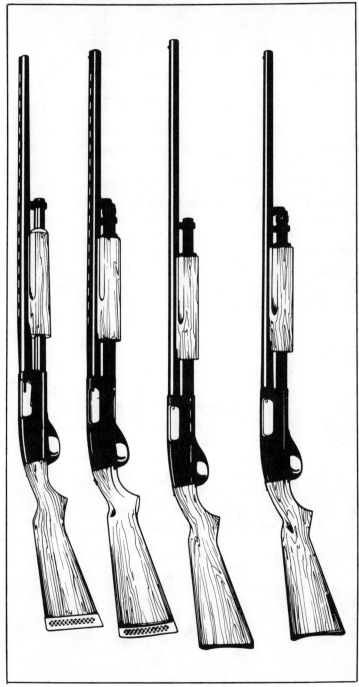

Fig. 3-6. Smith & Wesson slide-action shotguns. (A) Model 916 with 28-inch ventilated rib and recoil pad. (B) Model 916T with 28-inch ventilated rib and recoil pad. (C) Model 916 with 30-inch plain barrel. (D) Model 916T with 30-inch plain barrel.

Fig. 3-7. Marlin 120 Magnum slide-action shotgun.

Outside of actual size, each of the different shotgun gauges has its own set of characteristics. One of the main differences caused by different gauges is the amount of shot that the shell has. The larger the gauge for a particular size shell, the more shot that can be handled. The larger amount of shot that can be handled by a bigger gauged gun is an advantage since it means that the shot density will stay higher over a longer distance. When the shot density stays high with greater range the pattern thrown will be denser, meaning that the number of shot reaching the target will be greater. The idea of shot patterns will be discussed further in this chapter.

BARREL CHOKE

In order to concentrate the shot as it comes out of the barrel a taper is bored in the end of the barrel creating a constriction. When the shot passes through this constriction, it is pushed into a tighter group. Depending on the amount of constriction, the shotgun is classified as to a certain type of choke. When the constriction at the end of the barrel forces the shot into a group that will put 70 to 80 percent of the shot into a 30-inch diameter circle at 40 yards, the shotgun has a full choke. If 65 to 70 percent of the shot hits within the circle, the choke is referred to as an improved-modified type. Half-choke

Fig. 3-8. Remington 870 Wingmaster pump-action shotgun, field grade, with ventilated rib. Available in 12- , 16- and 20-gauge versions.

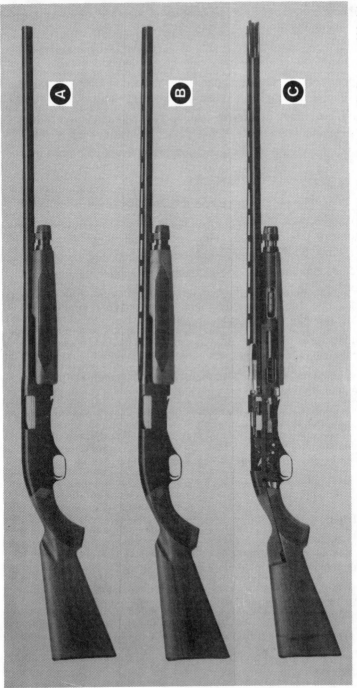

Fig. 3-9. Winchester Model 1200 slide-action shotgun. (A) Model 1200 with plain barrel. (B) Model 1200 with ventilated rib. (C) Cutaway of Model 1200.

or modified will put 55 to 65 percent of the shot in the target. The other choke names are: quarter-choke, improved-cylinder and straight-cylinder types. These last three chokes refer to 50 to 55 percent, 45 to 50 percent and 40 percent, respectively. Since the choke determination is dependent on the number of shot that actually hits the target in comparison with the number that leaves the end of the barrel, the determination is independent of gauge. In other words, the aforementioned percentages apply to an 8-gauge shotgun as well as to a .410.

The choke in a shotgun barrel is measured in terms of points. The point refers to one thousandths of an inch (0.001 inch) difference between the muzzle diameter and the bore diameter. This is usually used in manufacturing the guns to lend some type of standardization to a particular company's product. In actual practice guns from two different manufacturers may have the same gauge and the same number of points, but still throw substantially different patterns. This is due to the fact that even though barrels are supposed to be standardized, there are differences especially from one manufacturer to another.

If two barrels have two diameters that are different by as little as 0.020 inch, and the two barrels have the same number of points of choke, the patterns that they shoot will be quite different. Both guns will have the same choke and gauge designations. This leaves the gun owner only one true way of determining the amount of choke that his or her favorite shotgun has, namely, patterning.

SHOTGUN PATTERNING

As was just pointed out the choke on a shotgun determines what kind of pattern it will have; however, just because the manufacturer says that the gun has a certain choke, doesn't mean that it will shoot that particular pattern. Since the choke is susceptible to small variations in the manufacturer, two guns from two different manufacturers may have a different pattern. The only way to get around this is to pattern the gun yourself.

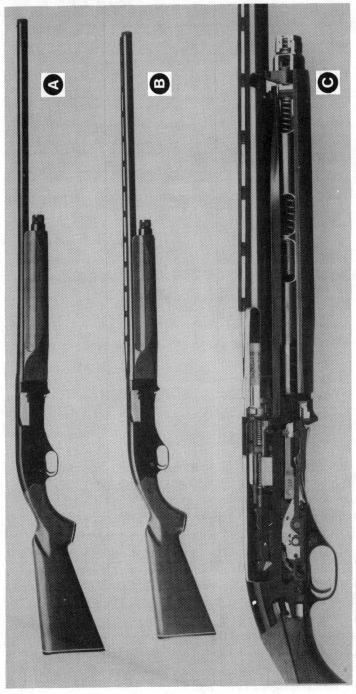

Fig. 3-10. Winchester Model 1500 XTR autoloading shotgun. (A) Model 1500 with plain barrel. (B) Model 1500 with ventilated rib. (C) Model 1500 cutaway.

Patterning a shotgun is a fairly simple procedure. Since the pattern is defined as the percentage of shot that hits within a circular target at a specified range, all that needs to be done is to set up a range that meets this criteria.

The target should be a piece of paper large enough to contain a thirty inch diameter circle. The circle can be drawn on the paper by tying a string around a pencil; then holding the string in the center, draw a circle with the pencil. Set the target up at a distance of 40 yards from the shooting line. Before firing determine the number of pellets in the particular shell that will be shot. The following list gives the shot, or pellet, size and the number of pellets that can be expected per ounce.

Shot Size	Pellets/Oz
BB	50
2	88
4	136
5	172
6	223
7	299
7½	350
8	409
9	585
10	868
11	1,380
12	2,385

Once the number of shot per ounce is known, the number of shot in a particular shell can be calculated by multiplying the number of ounces of shot in the shell that's to be fired times the number of shot per ounce for the particular type of shot. When the total number of shot has been determined, the shotgun should be fired at the target and the number of shot *inside* of the circle should be counted. The percentage pattern is calculated by dividing the number of shot counted inside of the circle by the number of shot in the shell before firing, then multiplying by one hundred. This will give a percentage that indicates the pattern for the shotgun when fired with the particular load that was tested. Once the pattern percentage has been determined, the choke for the shotgun can be determined from the following listing.

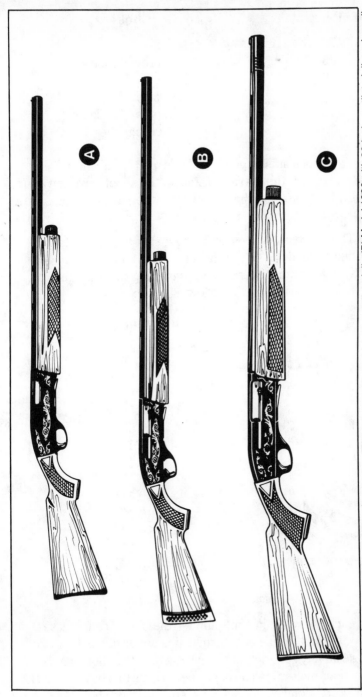

Fig. 3-11. Smith & Wesson autoloading shotguns. (A) Model 1000 with 28-inch ventilated rib. (B) Model 1000 with 30-inch ventilated rib and recoil pad. (C) Model 1000S skeet shotgun.

Percent	Choke
70–80	Full
65–70	Improved modified
55–65	Modified
50–55	Quarter
45–50	Improved cylinder
35–40	Skeet number 1

Once a particular shotgun has been patterned for several types of loads at the 40-yard distance, the shooter will have a better idea as to what he can expect when in the field.

SHOT SIZE

The process of choosing the best shot for a given type of shooting depends on several factors. First, though it is important to understand the terminology covering shot size, this can best be summarized in the following table:

Shot No.	Diameter (in.)
12	0.05
11	0.06
10	0.07
9	0.08
8	0.09
7½	0.095
6	0.11
5	0.12
4	0.13
2	0.15
BB	0.18
4 buck	0.24
3 buck	0.25
1 buck	0.30
0 buck	0.32
00 buck	0.33

With each decrease in shot number the shot size increases. The way that the size is determined is set at the factory. To get a relatively spherical pellet in large quantity shot manufacturers pour molten lead through special pans that have holes in them corresponding to the different sizes of shot. As the

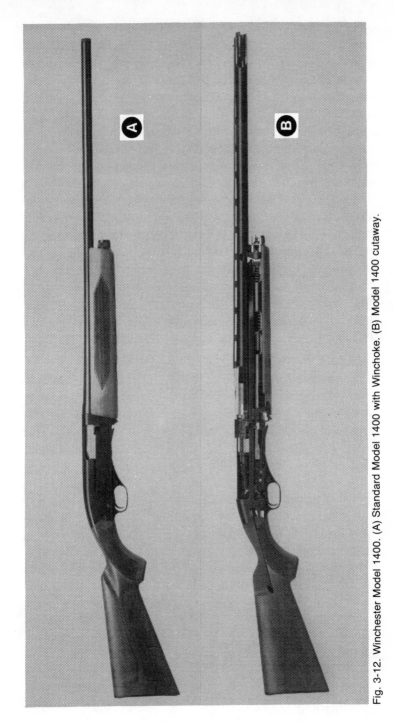

Fig. 3-12. Winchester Model 1400. (A) Standard Model 1400 with Winchoke. (B) Model 1400 cutaway.

molten lead drips through these pans, it forms more or less spherical pellets. The lead cools as the pellets fall through the air and into water, which is kept just below the pans. To aid in forming the spheroid shape, the lead is mixed with a small amount of arsenic. This process forms what are referred to as drop shot. Another type of shot is the chilled shot, which is made in the same manner with the difference being in the alloy of lead and antimony that is used. The shot can also be covered with copper by electrolytic processes, making the shot harder and more resistant to deformation.

Since chilled and copperized shot deform less, they produce tighter patterns than drop shot. In some marsh areas and wetlands it is being proposed that hunters not be allowed to use lead shot since it puts too much of the metal in the water, thereby affecting the aquatic life. In situations such as this, and where greater penetration with less deformation is wanted, steel shot has to be used. Steel shot is made similar to the lead shot, but it is much more expensive to produce, making the shot more costly to purchase.

CHOOSING THE RIGHT SHOT

The choice of shot size is, within certain limits, somewhat arbitrary. Each hunter usually has his own preferred shot size for a particular type of hunting. In general, though, the larger the target animal, the larger the shot size can be since the larger area afforded can be hit with a smaller number of shot. Another reason for using larger shot on larger game is that it will give deeper penetration due to the additional energy.

Although shot choice is relatively arbitrary, it's a good idea to have some place to start; there is no sense in using skeet load to go squirrel hunting (see Table 3-1). For hunting ducks several different shot types can be successfully used. Number 4 shot is a good choice for the duck hunter when anticipating long range or passing shots. Shot sizes of No. 5, 6 or 7½ are good for the closer shots. Hunting geese requires a greater punch; so large loads of the larger shot sizes should be used. For close range shooting at geese, a large number of hunters prefer the denser pattern that can be achieved by using No. 4 shot.

When hunting pheasant, it is a good idea to use No. 5 shot for long range and No. 6 shot for normal shooting. With

Table 3-1. Shot Size For Hunting.

Animal	Shot choice	Circumstance
ducks	No. 4 No. 5, 6, 7 ½	for long range or passing shots for closer shots
geese	No. 4	for close range shooting
pheasant	No. 5 No. 6	for long range shots for normal shooting
quail	No. 9 No. 7 ½, 8	for early in season for late season
doves, pigeons, white wings	No. 6 to No. 8	
woodcock	No. 8	for fast shooting

rabbits
  cottontail
  snowshoe, jackrabbit
	any of the lighter loads
	heavier load	

squirrels	No. 5, 6	
turkey	No. 2, 4, 5, and BB	
deer or black bear	12 or 16-gauge slugs or 0 and 00 buckshot	

pheasant hunting larger loads can be dangerous if you're hunting in large groups. Quail can usually be bagged with No. 9 shot early in the season, but as the bird's feathers get heavier, No. 7½ or No. 8 shot will do the job. Mourning doves, band-tailed pigeons and white wings can be hunted with shot ranging in size from No. 6 to No. 8. For fast shooting at wood cock, No. 8 shot is probably the best shot, but a lot of the choice will depend on the expected range.

Hunting rabbits like the cottontail can be accomplished with any of the lighter loads, but for snowshoe and jackrabbit the heavier loads will have to be used. Shot sizes of No. 5 and No. 6 are very effective on squirrels especially in high trees. The turkey hunter will probably get the best results from No. 2, 4, 5 and BB shots, depending on the range. For the larger game like deer and black bear, 12- and 16-gauge slugs are best, but many deer hunters prefer to use 0 and 00 buckshots where legal. These shot sizes are only recommendations giving a starting point from where the hunter can make his or her decision.

Chapter 4

Understanding the
Operation of Handguns

Handguns that are manufactured today can be separated into three groups—single shot, revolver, and semiautomatic. The single-shot pistol is usually used for target shooting. The revolver has several uses. Although it is not used extensively as a match-type shooting pistol, it is often found as a backup gun for the hunter and quite often as a personal defense weapon. The semiautomatic pistol is used in match shooting as well as for hunting and plinking around. This chapter covers each of these actions as well as discussing the advantages and disadvantages of each. Also in this chapter some of the causes and cures for common problems associated with handguns will be examined.

SINGLE-SHOT PISTOLS

Originally the first handguns were single-shot muzzle loaders that were only valuable as close-range weapons. Modern single-shot pistols are a vast improvement over this original idea. The new single-shot pistol is chambered in numerous cartridge sizes ranging from the .22-caliber rim-fire type on up to some of the heftier center-fire cartridges. These modern pistols are separated into two groups—tip-up action, and bolt actions.

The tip-up action was manufactured to the greatest extent by the Stevens Arms Company. This company relied heavily on the tip-up action for its pistols and made them in several calibers including the .410 shotgun shell. With the advent of the Federal Firearms Act, the .410, which is a shotgun shell, became illegal.

These single-shot pistols, manufactured by Stevens, had the appearance of the semiautomatic pistol. The primary problem that was encountered with them was that the front sight was mounted on the barrel while the rear sight was mounted on the receiver. This was a problem because, with age, the pivot between the barrel and the receiver would wear causing the barrel to become loose in relation to the receiver. When this happened, the pistol would loose its accuracy. Steven's final single-shot model incorporated sights that were both mounted on the barrel, alleviating the loose-barrel sighting problem.

One single-shot pistol that was produced for a relatively short period of time was the Model U.S.R.A. made by Harrington and Richardson Co. Considered by some to be one of the most accurate handguns ever produced in the United States, it is still actively sought after by both collectors and target shooters. This pistol was also of the tip-up version.

The bolt-action single-shot pistol is a later vintage single shot. These pistols are chambered in a large variety of calibers, ranging from the .22-caliber rim-fire type to some of the high-powered center-fire cartridges. These pistols are used for both varmint hunting and match-type shooting. Bolt actions for these pistols are strong enough to handle high-powered cartridges because the actions are modeled on high-powered rifle actions.

SEMIAUTOMATIC PISTOL

Semiautomatic pistol actions are divided into two systems based on the method controlling the action. The semiautomatics that use low-powered center-fire and rim-fire cartridges usually operate off of the blow-back system. This is the same method discussed in Chapter 2 on semiautomatic rifles. The way the system operates in a pistol is much the same. As with the rifles, the pistol doesn't employ a locking

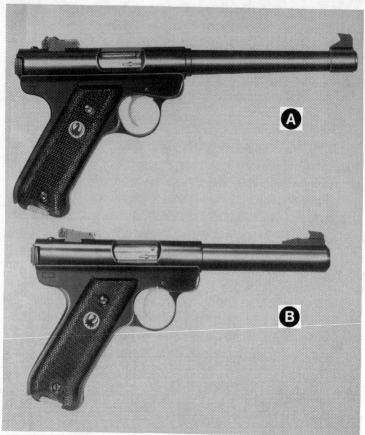

Fig. 4-1. Ruger .22-caliber autoloading pistols. (A) Mark I target model. (B) Mark I target model with bull barrel.

mechanism to hold the breech block (slide) in place. Instead, the weight of the breech and the power of the recoil spring keep the breech in place while the pistol is being fired.

The slide on an automatic pistol can extend over the barrel, as is the case with the .45- and .32-caliber Colt, or the slide can extend toward the rear of the receiver with the barrel being stationary. The latter case is usually more accurate and fairly trouble free.

The pistols that have a slide that extends towards the rear usually employ the blow-back system. These are the very successful .22-caliber rim-fire pistols. Some companies that have this type of pistol on the market are Ruger, High Stan-

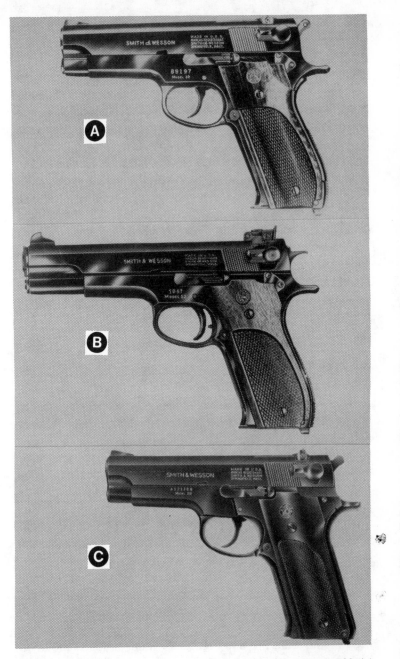

Fig. 4-2. Smith & Wesson semiautomatics. (A) 9-millimeter double-action Model 39. (B) .38-caliber S&M Special Model 52. (C) 9-millimeter double-action Model 59.

dard, Smith & Wesson and Colt along with many others. The reason that so many companies have used this basic design is that it is very accurate and reliable along with being able to handle the .22-caliber long-rifle cartridge.

Other semiautomatic pistols that incorporate a slide extending over the barrel operate off of a breech-block or delayed blow-back system. These pistols are the more powerful pistols, such as the .45, using centerfire ammunition. The delayed blow-back or breech-block system is similar to the system employed in the high-powered semiautomatic rifle. With this system the barrel and breech travel rearward for a short distance while they are still coupled. The barrel and breech only travel a short distance while they are attached; then they separate after the bullet has cleared the muzzle. The slide completes its trip to the rear of the gun, allowing the spent casing to be ejected and, as the slide returns, to pick up a new cartridge. When the breech contacts the barrel, they lock together and the pistol is ready to fire again (see Figs. 4-1 through 4-4).

REVOLVER

As with the semiautomatic pistol the revolver comes in two versions—the single action and the double action. In either case, the basic idea behind the revolver is that a cylinder rotates one chamber at a time allowing the pistol to be discharged from six to nine times, depending on the manufacture.

With the single-action revolver the hammer has to be pulled back after the trigger has been pulled before the pistol can be fired again. The double-action revolver cocks and fires the pistol with a single pull of the trigger (see Fig. 4-5). Double-action pistols can be fired as a single action, in that the hammer can be pulled back between each successive shot. The primary difference between the two pistols is in the speed with which they can be discharged. The double-action revolver is somewhat difficult to control since the tendency, when rapidly firing the pistol, is for each successive shot to be fired higher than the one before. Without practice the uninitiated will find the double-action type less accurate, not because of the gun, rather because of the inexperience of the shooter.

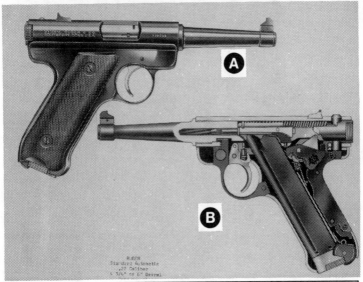

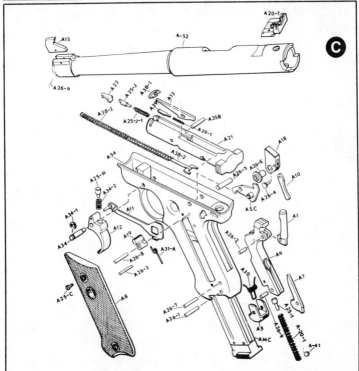

Fig. 4-3. Ruger standard .22-caliber semiautomatic Model RST4. (A) Full view.
(B) Cutaway view. (C) Exploded view.

Fig. 4-4. Smith & Wesson. Limited edition of Model 52 semiautomatic with highly engraved slide and frame.

For the sports-minded person the single-action pistol is probably a better choice since it affords a better trigger pull. The single-action pistol is also simpler in design, having a sear that engages the trigger and the hammer directly. Usually the parts in a single-action revolver are more reliable since they are rugged and the action is less complex.

Revolvers are available in a large variety of configurations as far as barrel length and chamber size are concerned. Cylinders can handle cartridges from the .22 to the .44 magnum. In the case of Ruger, some of their pistols have two cylinders, one for the lighter load cartridge and one for the magnum load. A good example of this is the Ruger Single-Six (Fig. 4-6) in .22 caliber, which is available with both the .22-caliber long-rifle cylinder and the .22-caliber magnum cylinder. See Figs. 4-9 through 4-25 for illustrations of various models of revolvers.

REVOLVER VERSUS SEMIAUTOMATIC

To try and get unbiased information on which gun is better, revolver or semiautomatic, is quite a trick. People that own revolvers usually swear by them as do the owners of semiautomatics. The best that can be done is to make some general comparisons; then decide from the information which gun best suits your particular needs.

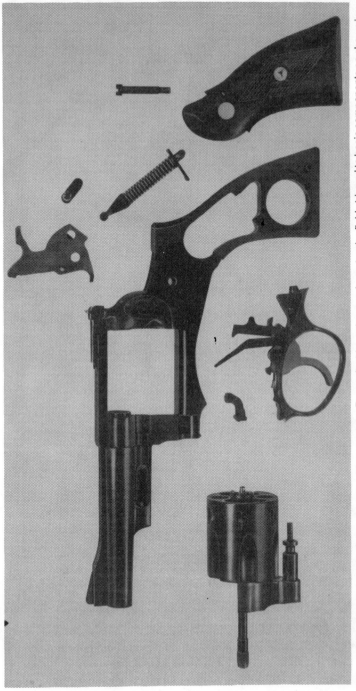

Fig. 4-5. Exploded view of a Ruger double-action revolver. Ruger double-action revolvers can be field stripped to basic components as shown in a matter of seconds using only a coin.

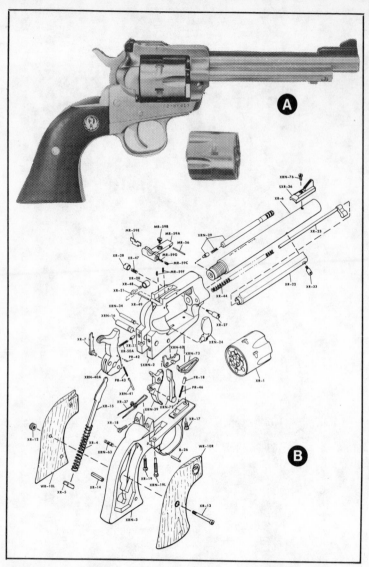

Fig. 4-6. Ruger Single-Six Convertible single-action revolver. (A) Side view showing both cylinders. (B) Exploded view with factory part numbers.

Since the revolver is manually operated, fewer accidents are likely to occur. This is not to say that the semiautomatic is unsafe, just that the semiautomatic has a greater potential for unintentional discharges. Automatics have a greater firepower, in that they can be fired very rapidly and in a lot of instances have a larger magazine. With proper respect, though, both firearms are safe.

With only a slight edge going to the revolver as far as safety is concerned, another facet that should be examined is maintenance. From the point of complexity, the revolver has to win again. The automatic is relatively complex, especially

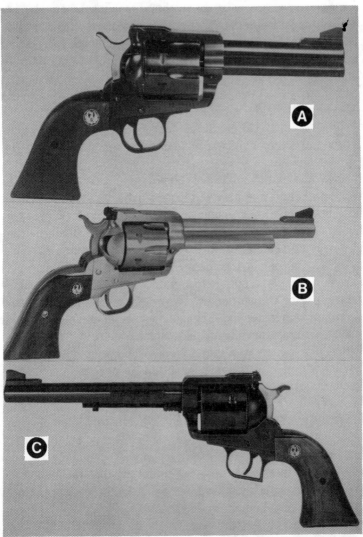

Fig. 4-7. Ruger revolvers. (A) Standard Blackhawk with 4⅝-inch barrel. Available in .357 magnum, .41 magnum and .45 calibers. (B) Stainless Blackhawk with 6½-inch barrel. (C) Super Blackhawk with 7½-inch barrel, .44 magnum.

when compared to the single-action revolver. Whenever a complex mechanism is compared to a manual or simple mechanism, the manual mechanism always ends up being easier to maintain. More parts are involved in the operation of a complex mechanism and tolerances are more critical.

Since most outdoor activities that involve the use of handguns require accuracy rather than firepower, the revolver again seems to be the pistol of choice. The semiautomatic, especially the ones equipped with barrels that are separate from the breech, may be slightly more accurate than the revolver. But in some cases, this advantage is outweighed by the fact that the revolver requires more from the shooter. Since the shooter is required to operate a harder trigger pull, the chances are that more concentration will be involved, especially when considering the novice shooter.

While on the subject of the novice shooter, the revolver has another advantage over the automatic. The novice will find the revolver a much simpler action to understand. The revolver will probably be cheaper in the long run to operate; there is no temptation to try to machine gun the target.

The automatic has many fans, though; many of the military organizations, both in the United States and foreign countries, prefer the automatic. Also, a large number of people competing in pistol shooting matches prefer the semiautomatic. As far as the military is concerned, the semiautomatic affords the firepower that a soldier needs for defense. The match shooter likes the semiautomatic because it affords a smoother action, especially in rapidfire competition. Another reason that the semiautomatic has a great popularity with match shooters is that the weight of the pistol is concentrated in the hand, while the weight of the revolver is just forward of the trigger guard.

The essence of these arguments is that the hunter or plinker will probably find all the pistol that he is looking for in the revolver. The person that is looking for a pistol to use in match shooting exclusively will probably do best with a semiautomatic. If the shooter is contemplating all three types of shooting, he will have to make the choice from a purely personal point of view, choosing the characteristics that appeal the greatest.

HANDGUNS & HUNTING

As in the case with the hunting rifle, the choice for a hunting pistol is governed to a large degree by the type of animal that is to be hunted. Even though this is true, there are a few considerations that should be taken into account in addition to the type of game that is to be pursued.

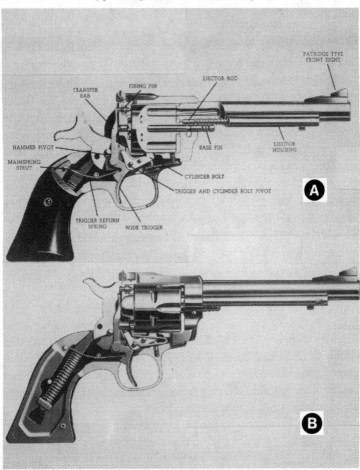

Fig. 4-8. Ruger Super Single-Six. (A) Mechanism shown with trigger pulled and hammer beginning to fall. Transfer bar is held in firing position between hammer and firing pin. Cylinder bolt is engaged in cylinder locking notch. (B) Mechanism shown at rest. Transfer bar is not in line between hammer and firing pin. This is the normal carrying position. All six chambers may be loaded.

One of these considerations is the weight of the pistol. Since the hunter will be carrying the pistol over long distances, the lightest possible gun will be an advantage. Weight will affect the steadiness of holding the gun on target. The heavier the gun the easier it is to hold in position. As a rule of thumb, though, guns of light caliber, such as the .22 or the .25, should weigh somewhere around 1.5 to 2 pounds. Pistols that are chambered in larger calibers, such as the .357 and .44 magnums, should weigh around 2.5 to 3 pounds.

Another consideration is the barrel length. The best barrel length for hunting is between 6 and 8 inches.

The reason that the barrel length is so important is twofold. First, the longer the barrel the longer the sighting length and the more accurately the gun can be aimed. Snub-nosed pistols are not the ideal gun for the hunter. The other reason that the barrel should be 6 to 8 inches long is that the long barrels give the bullet a longer time in the barrel. This means that the bullet has longer to use the energy from the expanding gases.

Sights that should be incorporated in a good hunting pistol should be adjustable. Many handguns have fixed rear sights which, when they get out of adjustment, stay that way. The micrometer-type sights found on good-quality target-type pistols are ideal for the hunting pistol. This type of sight affords both elevation and windage adjustments, which are critical for both hunting and target shooting.

Another option that the pistol hunter has, as far as sights are concerned, is the scope. Scopes have the distinct advantage of allowing the shooter to see both the target and the cross hairs in sharp focus. Pistol scopes are somewhat different from rifle scopes in that they have a much greater eye relief. The reason for the greater eye relief is that the pistol hunter sights at arm's length from the gun, usually. This means that the scope has to be in focus when the hunter's eye is as much as 17 inches from the end of the scope. The pistol scope usually has a magnification factor of 1.3 to 2.5, which is quite adequate since the pistol is not a long-range firearm.

Choosing the right caliber for a hunting pistol is dependent on the game animal that is going to be pursued. As with

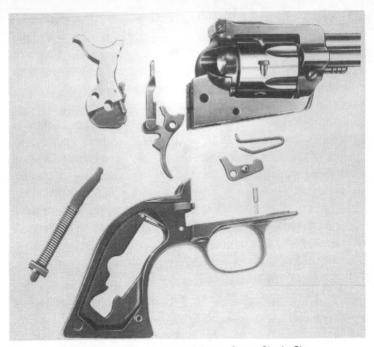

Fig. 4-9. View of internal components of Ruger Super Single-Six.

rifles, there is no handgun claiber that can be used on squirrel and deer. Instead the hunter will have to have a small caliber pistol for the small game and a larger caliber for big game.

The best caliber for small game is the .22. The .22 long rifle can handle rabbits, squirrels and small varmints. With practice the .22-caliber long rifle can be equally effective with larger varmints, such as the groundhog. The .22-caliber long rifle is inexpensive; so the hunter can practice with a pistol quite often without spending a great deal of money. Another advantage with some .22-caliber revolvers is that they can be purchased with the magnum cylinder. This means that the pistol can be changed from .22-caliber long rifle to .22 magnum just by changing the cylinder. The Ruger Single Six Convertible is available with this capability, increasing its versatility substantially. The .22-caliber magnum makes the pistol capable of bringing down animals the size of bobcats and even foxes.

When the hunter is going to be after deer or black bear, the pistol has to be chambered to handle a center-fire cartridge; the rimfire just doesn't have the muscle. Even with the centerfire cartridges the magnums are a better choice. The .44-, .38- and .45-caliber pistol loads will bring deer down but only at close range. These lighter loads have a greater tendency to wound resulting in lost game.

The best magnum loads for bigger game hunting are the .357 and the .44. Both of these cartridges are quite adequate for both deer and black bear, while the .44-caliber magnum is capable of bringing down even the mighty grizzly bear. These pistol loads pack quite a kick; in the case of the .44 magnum, the kick may be more than the shooter will want to bother with. In any case, the shooter contemplating big-game pistol hunting will have to get used to one of the magnums otherwise he will be going out unprepared.

TARGET SHOOTING

The first pistol that the target shooter should purchase is a good quality .22-caliber rimfire target pistol. With this pistol the shooter can concentrate on accuracy and not worry about the recoil that comes with high-powered target pistols. This is important since the novice will need to concentrate more on things like slow and even trigger squeeze and other shooting habits that he must develop.

As far as the choice between a revolver and semiautomatic is concerned, the target shooter is less limited. Since target matches are held at a regular range, the slight edge that the revolver has as far as safety is concerned becomes unimportant. This means that the target shooter can choose a gun concentrating on personal taste. As far as accuracy goes, there are revolvers that are just as accurate as the semiautomatics. The shooter may still be concerned with the complexity of the semiautomatic, though. Under target range conditions the semiautomatic is reliable.

Since target shooting requires the highest amount of accuracy, the target pistol should have a fairly long barrel. Reasons for this are similar to the reasons behind long barrel length in hunting pistols. The longer barrels give a longer sighting plane, making them more accurate. Usually the target pistol has a barrel that is from 6 to 9 inches in length. There is

Fig. 4-10. Smith & Wesson 1955 .45 Target revolver, Model 25, with 6½-inch barrel.

one distinctive exception, the .45-caliber Colt Gold Cup National Match pistol. This is a high-quality .45-caliber pistol that is expressly used for target shooting having only a 5-inch barrel.

The weight of a handgun used for target shooting is usually fairly heavy. This is because it is easier to steady a heavy gun. Since the target shooter doesn't have to lug the handgun over long distances the weight doesn't present a problem. The target pistol usually weighs around 2.5 to 3 pounds.

Without exception the target pistol has to have a good set of sights. The whole idea behind the target pistol is accuracy. It would not be to the shooter's advantage to have the proper barrel length, a good weight, but poor sights. The sights have to be adjustable for both windage and elevation. This way the shooter will be able to predict the shots according to the range that he is shooting.

HANDGUN PLINKING

The best pistol for plinking is the .22-caliber rimfire. With this pistol the shooter does not have to be concerned about the cost of ammunition. With the worries of cost eliminated the shooter can concentrate on the pleasures of plinking.

For those shooters to whom cost is not a particular concern, any pistol can be used for plinking. Many people buy some of the heavy-duty guns, such as the .357and the .44 magnums or the .38 and the .32, for house guns. These guns usually only get used for plinking which is somewhat of a waste but everyone has their idea of what is fun. Big guns usually make a lot of noise and give quite a kick, but this is part of the fun in plinking. It is rather amazing to see what a large caliber pistol can do to a tin can. Since the primary purpose, aside from fun, for plinking is to get a feel for guns, this is a good time to get used to the high-powered guns.

Chapter 5

Keep 'em Shootin'

A well-built firearm will last a lifetime, several lifetimes, if it is reasonably cared for. Besides longer life, increased accuracy and smoother operation will also result when the shooter spends a little time in keeping his or her firearms in first-class condition. The procedure only takes a few minutes for each weapon if the cleaning is done at regular intervals; however, once a firearm has been neglected, it becomes increasingly difficult to clean satisfactorily.

Necessary implements for keeping any sporting gun clean are few and inexpensive. All that is required is a powder solvent, such as the famous Hoppe's No. 9 (Fig. 5-1), a light gun oil for working parts and exterior surfaces, cleaning patches and a cleaning rod and perhaps an old toothbrush for getting in between those hard-to-reach places. There are other items, of course, which will make the job somewhat easier, but the items mentioned will suffice (see Figs. 5-2 and 5-3).

The bore of the rifle, shotgun or handgun should be first swabbed with a cotton flannel patch well saturated with the powder solvent. Cleaning should be done from the breech end of the barrel, if possible, with the muzzle resting on some clean, nonmarring surface. The patch should be run up and

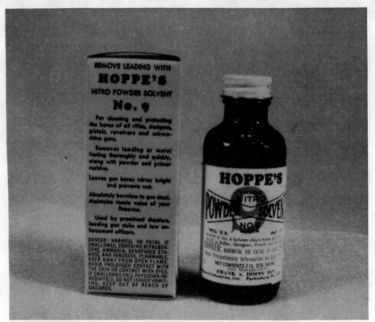
Fig. 5-1. Hoppe's No. 9 Nitro Powder solvent.

down the bore several times to saturate the powder residue thoroughly with the powder solvent.

Any one of the commercial solvents will work well in keeping the bore of your gun clean. I mentioned Hoppe's No. 9 previously. This is excellent for removing primer powder lead and metal fouling and also for preventing rust. Other good solvents include those manufactured by Birchwood Casey, Brite-Bore, and Marble.

Commercially made patches are best for cleaning rifles, shotguns and handguns because they are usually cut to fit the bore specified. They should be made from cotton flannel for best results. The patch is fitted in a small slot at the end of the cleaning rod so that it will be held in place during the cleaning operation.

If the firearm you are cleaning has been neglected for some time, you will need to use a wire brush (brass) to remove the sticky powder fouling partially loosened by the action of the solvent. Again, working from the breech end if possible, dip the brass brush into the powder solvent and run the brush up and down the bore with the cleaning rod. The brush should be pushed completely out of the barrel on each down stroke as reversing the direction of the brush inside the bore will ruin the brush.

After running the brass brush up and down the bore a half-dozen times or so, repeat the first operation; that is, install the patch-holding tip on your cleaning rod, insert a patch with powder solvent and swab the bore out again. Then use a clean patch with no solvent and wipe out the excess solvent. This may require as many as six clean patches. Run the first patch down, up, down and out at the muzzle end, but run the remaining patches through the bore only once—discarding each at the muzzle end. The final patch should show perfectly clean and dry. If not, the preceding operations must be repeated for a proper cleaning job.

The final step is oiling with a light gun oil. This will protect the gun for a period of approximately one month, depending on atmospheric conditions and how the gun is stored. If the gun is to be stored for a longer period than a month, use gun grease instead of the light oil.

Fig. 5-2. Hoppe's gun cleaning kit comes with everything you need to keep 'em clean.

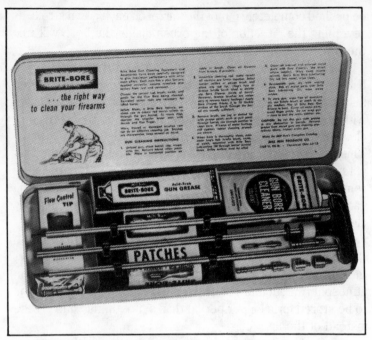

Fig. 5-3. Brite-Bore makes this universal kit to clean most any bore.

I mentioned previously that all guns should be cleaned from the breech end if at all possible. If not, be careful in running the rod into the muzzle, in that you don't create excess wear of the muzzle by rubbing against it with the rod. This can influence the accuracy of the weapon in the case of a rifle or pistol barrel.

Some shooters like to use a wooden or brass muzzle cap on pump, automatic, or level action rifles that cannot be cleaned from the breech end. This insures that undue wear will not be applied to the muzzle of the weapon. Also, if you use a plain jag tip for cleaning, the chamber of the rifle should be fitted with a cartridge case plugged with wood to prevent the patch from working loose as it sometimes does when pushed into the larger diameter of the chamber.

Frequency of the cleaning will vary with the use of the guns and the weather to which they are subjected. A good rule of thumb is to clean them after each firing. Also in humid areas or where used near salt water, guns should be cleaned or at least wiped off every few weeks.

When cared for as described previously, guns will rarely be injured from rust, fouling or corrosion from being handled by human hands.

GUN CLEANING TOOLS & ACCESSORIES

Now that you know the basic procedures for properly cleaning your firearms, let's take a look at some of the extra goodies that can make the job a little easier and perhaps better.

The types of cleaning tips commonly used for cleaning firearms are shown in Fig. 5-4. Of these types, the single slotted tip is the most popular. It has the advantage of holding onto the patch under all conditions, but has two disadvantages in that the patch sometimes jams when reversed inside the bore and the cleaning action is often one-sided, permitting the bare sides of the tip to rub against the rifling and perhaps causing damage.

The roll jag tip permits rolled or wrapped patches, and is preferred by many shooters for cleaning rifles that have to be wiped out from the muzzle end; this method is far safer than the plug and disk system because the flannel patch does not have to be dragged in. Accordingly, the rifling is preserved instead of being worn away at a most vital spot.

Drooped wire brushes are heavy brushes used on barrels that have been neglected for a long time. This type of brush will remove hard fouling and rust with ease. Most are made of bronze.

A flexible brass jag tip is preferred by many shooters for cleaning their weapons with a flannel patch. The patch is slipped into the slot of the jag and wrapped around it; the slot

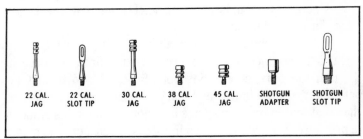

Fig. 5-4. Brite-Bore cleaning tips included in universal kit.

imparts a measure of flexibility, which causes the patch to press evenly on the bore, thereby squeezing the oil into the pores of the steel. The slot also permits the cleaner to be compressed by the choke, in the case of shotguns, which insures a thorough cleaning of the bore throughout its entire length.

Leather shotgun bore polisher tips contain several buff leather disks that absorb polishing materials, thereby aiding in repolishing the bores of shotguns which have been neglected. Such a bore polisher will also aid in keeping shotguns in perfect condition no matter in what weather they are used. Since no metal can possibly touch the shotgun bore, these polishers are recommended for use in most expensive shotguns.

Wool mop tips are fine for oiling the bores of rifles and shotguns, but they must be kept clean as much harm can be done by the fouling on the wool neutralizing the preserving powers of the oil (Fig. 5-5).

The plain jag tip gives a uniform cleaning action, and reverses perfectly inside the barrel. The patch sticks to the tip as long as it is inside the barrel, but any movement beyond the muzzle or chamber will cause the patch to come loose. To use this type of tip, merely center the patch on the tip and push it down the bore.

Rifle cleaning rods should be of either brass or steel. There are some aluminum rods on the market, but this soft metal has a habit of picking up bits of dirt which have an abrasive effect on the bore.

The rifle cleaning rod should also have a swivel joint so that the patch will rotate inside the bore as the patch is being pushed back and forth; that is, the patch will follow the twist of the rifling. Without this rotation, the patch will drag at right angles across the lands and will quickly destroy the sharp edges of the rifling, impairing accuracy.

The patch should be reasonably tight. If you want to get technical, the recommended pressure required to force it through the bore should be about 5 pounds. With factory patches it is sometimes necessary to purchase a size larger than that stated on the package in order to obtain this amount of pressure. For example, if your bore is .30 caliber, you might have to try .33- or .35-caliber patches.

Fig. 5-5. Wool and cotton swabs are available through Brite-Bore. They come in 12 per box.

A shotgun cleaning rod does not require a swivel joint because there is no rifling in a shotgun. Many experienced shooters prefer a high-quality all-wood cleaning rod for use on shotguns. In most cases these are made from prime, well-seasoned hickory wood. All woods will not make up into a suitable shotgun cleaning rod, nor is kiln dry wood satisfactory as it tends to make the wood brittle. For this reason, all hickory used for the better rods is air dried to prevent warpage, insuring the finish quality.

Besides powder fouling, the shooter must sometimes give consideration to metal fouling. It is not too common today except in the small-bore high-velocity rifles. This is due to a deposit of metal left by the bullet in the bore. When metal fouling is caused by lead bullets (with no jackets), the fouling is usually termed *leading*. A perfectly smooth bore will pick up very little metal fouling, whereas a badly neglected bore will always foul to some extent.

Regardless of the cause, metal fouling can cause poor accuracy until the metal fouling is corrected. Examine the bore with a bore sight. Any fouling will be visible by showing long streaks, flaky deposits or perhaps lumps of metal particles sticking to the lands and the grooves of the barrel. Metal fouling can be corrected if attended to promptly. To get rid of the fouling make a solution by mixing the following in a glass bottle:

Ammonium persulfate ....1 ounce
Ammonium carbonate ....200 grams
Water..4 ounces
Strong Ammonia...6 ounces

Powder the first two ingredients together and dissolve in water. Add the ammonia and store in a glass bottle.

For light fouling merely dip a patched tip into the solution and swab the bore as discussed earlier for powder solvent. Then clean and dry in a conventional manner. For the more serious conditions, first plug the chamber end of the barrel with a cork. Then use a plastic funnel inserted in the muzzle end of the barrel and pour the solution into the barrel. The barrel should be braced during this operation so that the chamber end is at the lower end, and the barrel in a vertical position. The funnel is to prevent any of the solution from touching the outside of the barrel which might injure the bluing or stock finish.

At first the solution will appear colorless, but will soon take on a blue appearance as it begins to dissolve the metallic deposits. Allow it to set for about 20 minutes before pouring out the solution. Then perform a normal cleaning of the firearm immediately. Also repeat the normal cleaning procedure frequently for the next few weeks—such as twice a week.

Leading can be removed with a wire brush, the metal-fouling solution mentioned previously, or mercuric ointment on a flannel patch. Some shooters pour a few ounces of mercury into the barrel after plugging one end. Then while holding a finger over the opposite end, the barrel is tilted up and down a few times. Common vinegar will sometimes do the job also.

As mentioned previously, leading is caused by a rough or pitted barrel and will sometimes cure itself after firing the weapon a few times. If the problem persists, the barrel should be lapped by a gunsmith. A brief description of the process follows:

A steel rod, slightly smaller than the bore diameter, is used in the barrel. One end is notched both length-wise and crosswise. The other end is set in a cross-handle with a ball bearing so that the rod can turn freely and follow the twist of the rifling when it is pushed through the barrel. First the barrel is cleaned of all foreign matter. Then a film of light gun oil is applied.

Cotton string wrapped tightly around the front of the rod, the tip of which is fluxed, is pushed through the barrel from the breech end until the tip is within an inch of the muzzle. The first few inches of the muzzle is then heated to a medium temperature. Then molten lead is poured into the barrel, which should fill about the first 3 inches of the barrel, the distance from the cotton string to the rod tip. When cool, the lead is pushed a short distance out of the muzzle in order to be trimmed.

The lap is then coated with oil and carefully pushed a couple of inches out of the muzzle. This portion is also oiled before applying the cutting compound, such as rottenstone. This lap is then worked back and forth through the bore from ten to perhaps thirty times—recoated after ten cycles. The lap is pushed through the bore with steady tension until the barrel has the same feel the entire length. The lap is then removed and cleaned with solvent, after which the barrel is slugged (measured).

Lapping a rifle barrel is not an easy job, and the brief description just given does not do the operation justice. It should only be attempted by a competent gunsmith.

Shotgun barrels, on the other hand, may be easily lapped or polished by the home gunsmith since they are smooth bored. Procedures for polishing a gun barrel were given in Chapter 1. Metal fouling in shotgun barrels can usually be corrected by polishing with some abrasive paper inserted in a polishing head powered by an electric drill or lathe.

One last point to remember about cleaning of firearms. Always run a clean patch through the bore of a rifle barrel prior to firing after it has been stored for some time. Excess oil in the barrel will cause the first few shots to go a bit wild. This final cleaning prior to firing also insures that no obstacle is in the barrel which may cause the barrel to rupture and injure the shooter.

TOUCHUP BLUING

The object of bluing metal parts on firearms is to dull the bright steel color of exposed metal parts which will also help to prevent rust. A well-blued firearm is also more pleasing to the eye, the same as a well-painted house is compared to one left unpainted.

Methods of completely bluing firearms will be discussed in later chapters, but for the present, we will be concerned with the use of cold bluing chemical for touchup work. Any firearm that is in use for any reasonable length of time will develop worn spots on various portions of the action, barrel, trigger guard, etc. Scratches are also common on hunting firearms. In most cases, it is not practical to reblue the entire weapon every time a scratch occurs, but the shooter wants this scratch remedied. Here is where cold blue comes in handy.

There are several brands of cold blue chemicals on the market. Some are better than others, and I will describe a few of the better ones on the market.

Oxpho-Blue

This gun blue, Oxpho-Blue, is designed for the gun owner who is not equipped to completely repolish his or her gun prior to bluing. It is ideal for touchup work. With this blue, all you need to do, in most cases, is dampen a piece of cotton flannel with the cold blue and apply it to the worn areas—just like you'd polish your shoes. The chemical goes through the oil on the gun, removes thin rust and blues the steel underneath. Some of the features of this bluing compound include:

- Absolutely no after rust
- Rust-preventing phosphatized surface formed under the blue
- Rust-removing qualities of the solution, making it unnecessary to remove mild rust in the usual manner
- Wetting characteristics of the solution, giving it the ability to penetrate oil and dirt on the surface of the gun, blue the metal underneath, remove rust and dirt and leave the gun blued
- High durability of the finish. Gives a finish as durable as the standard military finish
- Beauty of finish. Vigorous rubbing with No. 0 steel wool is part of the application—the more rubbing the more brilliant it becomes

Oxpho-Blue is available from Brownells, Inc. as are all the other cold blues described herein.

Cold Blues by Birchwood Casey

Another cold blue that works without degreasing the firearm is Super Blue manufactured by Birchwood Casey. The type of blue produces a deep blue-black finish and is fine for quick touchup of scratches or darkening gun sights. The same firm also manufactures Perma Blue—a cold blue that penetrates and blues steel instantly with a rich black finish that is claimed to outwear the original bluing. Casey's Paste Blue comes in tube form and is concentrated for deeper color and longer wear. This blue blends perfectly for touchups on firearms of all kinds.

Read and follow the manufacturer's instructions on the bottle or packed with the cold blue. In general, the area to be treated should be cleaned so that it is free of dirt, oil and grease. A safe cleaner-degreaser is made by Birchwood Casey and is an excellent degreaser and preblue conditioner. It removes all grease, oil, dirt, wax and silicone completely.

If a cotton-tipped applicator does not come with the bottle or tube of bluing solution, use any clean cotton swabs that are free of grease. Dip the swab in the bluing solution and apply to the area needing to be treated. You will see the bluing action take place immediately. Then repeat the procedure, applying the solution until the worn spot blends perfectly with the original blue. You may want to brighten up the spot with No. 0 steel wool, but do not rub too hard or you might rub off the touchup blue. Should this happen on your first try, merely use the degreaser solution, and apply more coats of cold blue until you have the shade you desire.

Treating Aluminum

The gun owner will also come across pieces of metal on firearms (especially modern ones) that will not accept conventional bluing methods. Aluminum and other nonsteel parts, for example, are sometimes used for trigger guards and similar parts on modern firearms. Anodizing is the only way aluminum can be blued and this is an expensive process—too expensive for the average do-it-yourself gunsmither; however, there is a way to get off the hook by painting.

Brownells, Inc. sells a special nitrocellulose lacquer developed for covering metal, and designed to combine all coats into one tough integrated finish. It dries dust free in 10 minutes and can be handled in 30 minutes. It dries, ready for use, overnight.

To apply this to an aluminum or other alloy that will not accept conventional bluing methods, first clean the part thoroughly and apply one coat of Gunsmith's Zinc Chromate Primer, which may be sprayed on the surface. Then spray on two light coats of the Aluma-Hyde (spray paint) and allow to dry in a dust-free area overnight. The finish wears almost as well as the original anodizing, and the color match is close.

Brass and solder may also be treated in a similar manner. Birchwood Casey makes a solution called Brass Black which may be used for touchup or complete refinishing of brass sights, screws, etc. Solder Black is an easy way to blacken tin-lead solders or the exposed silver solder on guns, machined parts and other metal items. This solution reacts with solder for a long-lasting finish.

Bluing With Heat

Another method of bluing small parts, such as pins, screws, etc., is to heat the part over an open flame until the part reaches blue in the color scale of heating, then quenching the part in oil. The color may be varied by repeated dipping in oil and burning off the oil. The oil can be regular household/shop oil such as the famous 3-in-1 oil, motor oil mixed with linseed oil, linseed oil mixed with Hoppe's No. 9 solvent, etc. Some shooters even use these different types of oil in combination, that is, dipping the hot part from one to another until the desired finish is obtained.

To perform this operation, set your torch (see Chapter 1) in a convenient location and adjust the flame to a point. The part must be heated until it turns a pale blue to a faint red. Then the part is dipped in a quenching oil as described previously. The part is usually held with a long-handled set of tongs. If the desired color is not reached on the first try, repeat the procedure until it is. You may also try a different temperature, such as heating the part until it turns blood red, about 1000 degrees Fahrenheit.

CLEANING BLACK-POWDER WEAPONS

Black powder is a mixture of charcoal, sulphur and saltpeter. The ingredients are ground together, pressed into hard cakes and subsequently broken into small pieces in order to pass through sieves of the proper mesh to obtain the desired granulation. The grains are then coated with graphite to retard the absorption of moisture, which gives the powder the black shiny appearance from which it gets its name.

Black powder will create powder fouling in rifle and pistol barrels much faster than smokeless powder. Those shooting these types of weapons must take extra care in cleaning their weapons (Fig. 5-6). Cleaning should commence after each shot; that is, after each shot, run a water-dampened patch to the bottom of the bore (in the powder chamber), letting it remain for perhaps 10 seconds to dissolve the powder residue. Then use a dry patch to absorb any moisture in the bore.

The finest accuracy can only be obtained by cleaning a rifle or pistol after each shot. This practice also serves another purpose. It eliminates any sparks that may be present immediately after the shot. If there was a spark in the bore and you poured the next charge of black powder into the barrel, you can imagine the results. . .kaboom!

Even with this cleaning after each shot, muzzle-loading rifles, using black powder, will eventually build up an accumulation of hard fouling in the cylinder passage. This causes misfires and will eventually close the passage so that the percussion cap cannot ignite the powder. To prevent this from

Fig. 5-6. Closeup view of a Ruger Old Army Percussion revolver.

happening, the cylinder should be removed after a hundred or so shots (Fig. 5-7). Clean out the fouling by immersing the cylinder in cold water. Water is the most effective solvent for black-powder residue. The cylinder must be dried before screwing it back in the barrel.

Some shooters of black-powder weapons like to disassemble their weapons after a couple of hundred shots and clean all metal parts with soapy water. They are then rinsed in clean water and dipped into a tank of boiling water for about 15 minutes. The water will dry immediately on the metal parts as soon as the pieces are taken from the tank due to the heat absorbed by the metal. Dry those parts in question; then liberally coat the bore with a good gun grease. Also give the same attention to other metal parts such as the hammer, lock plate and nipple.

Iron and steel barrels of muzzle-loading weapons will rust very quickly in warm, humid temperatures unless adequately protected. Those that have seen neglect will surely be a mess and may even be unsafe to fire.

SPRUCE UP YOUR GUN STOCK

If the finish on your gun stock is slightly scratched or marred, a few mintues a day can put the stock back into almost new condition. Of course, the old finish can be completely removed and a new finish applied, but much improvement can be had by just fixing up the existing finish.

Narrow cuts and scratches should be first filled with a wood filler that exactly matches the finish of your stock. Different shades of fillers may be purchased from most gun-smithing supply houses. Once the proper color has been selected, apply the filler according to the manufacturer's directions.

The tool used to repair dents should be a small spatula ground to a width of about ¾ inch and the blade shortened to about 4 inches. Then about an inch ahead of the handle start narrowing the blade until it is ½ inch wide or less at the point. Remove any burrs. Polish the blade until it is smooth and flexible.

On most light-colored walnut gun stocks the scratch or gouge should be first colored to match the surrounding wood.

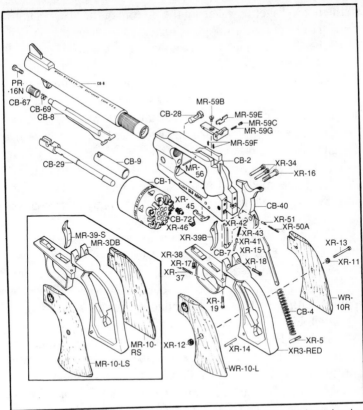

Fig. 5-7. Exploded view of a Ruger Old Army Percussion revolver showing factory part numbers.

Water-soluble stains are best for this step as they are more permanent than oil stains. An assortment of these dyes can be purchased from Brownells, Inc. This assortment can be used individually in water or blended to give a variety of colors for water staining gun stocks or any other types of wood. Once the stain has been applied, a transparent shellac stick should be used. On darker wood, various colors are available to get a perfect match.

Hold your knife in the flame of an alcohol lamp until it is hot enough to melt the shellac when pressed against the end of a shellac stick. These shellac sticks are designed specially for this type of work. When a small quantity of melted shellac has formed on the end of the spatula, immediately wipe it across the area to be repaired. This is best done by turning the blade

113

so the melted shellac will be on the bottom of the blade. Then, holding the knife at a 45-degree angle, draw it over the scratch or gouge. The motion should be quick but gentle. If the first pass does not completely fill the scratch, repeat the operation.

After the shellac has thoroughly hardened, lightly sand the repair down flush with the surrounding wood. Be careful not to damage any more of the existing finish while doing this. Repeat this entire procedure on all scratches that may be on the gun stock or forearm.

Mix two parts of raw linseed oil with one part turpentine and bring the mixture to a boil; then quickly remove the mixture from the burner. The mixture is highly inflammable; so be extremely careful while doing this.

Now warm the gun stock and apply successive coats of the hot mixture to it, letting each coat dry before putting on the next. Continue this operation until the stock and the scratches take on the depth of color you want. Plenty of rubbing with bare hands will produce a rich finish, and your stock will look like new.

Shallow dents in your stock may be removed by steaming them. Wet a cloth and place it over the dent, then apply a hot iron momentarily. The steam swells the wood fibers to the surface of the surrounding wood. For extremely small dents, you may want to use the tip of a soldering gun against the wet rag over the dent; however, be extremely careful not to burn the stock itself. It will only take a second or two for the damp rag to become dry; never leave the iron against the rag after the moisture has evaporated.

In the case of very large dents, scratches, etc., it is usually best to completely refinish the entire stock. This procedure will be fully explained later in the book.

Chapter 6

Simple Repairs

Most problems that occur with the majority of firearms are of a nature that even the rank beginner can handle them with little difficulty; however, before any repair work is undertaken, you should establish the exact cause of the trouble by carefully inspecting the firearm. Then, unless you feel that the problem is beyond your capabilities, you can use the information found in this chapter to remedy the situation.

REMOVING DENTS FROM SHOTGUN BARRELS

Due to the relatively thin barrels on most shotguns, dents are quite common. A weapon is accidently dropped, a piece of camping equipment falls on the gun in a case or any number of similar occurrences can cause a dented shotgun barrel.

An expanding dent plug is available from Frank Mittermeier, Inc., 3577 East Tremont Ave., Bronx, New York 10465. This is an excellent tool for removing dents in shotgun barrels. This plug is shown in Fig. 6-1. It has a center diameter of about 0.020 inches less than the standard diameter of the same bore that is, 12, 16 or 20 gauge. By turning the tapered screw it can be expanded to fit any oversized bore, and also it will not mar the bore because it is made of brass.

To remove a dent in a shotgun barrel, insert the plug in the chamber end of the dented barrel. Then use a wooden

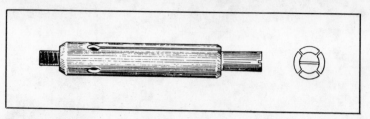

Fig. 6-1. Expandable dent removing plug for removing dents from shotgun barrels. Available through Frank Mittermeier, Inc.

dowel to push the plug directly under the dent. Expand the dent plug until it fits tight under the dent as shown in Fig. 6-2. Then use a brass hammer and tap around the edge of the dent with light blows. The light blows will force the dented metal up. Keep hammering until the dent is up or the plug comes loose. If the plug comes loose before the dent is completely out, repeat the process of expanding the dent plug, pushing it under the dent and hammering around the edge till the dent is completely up.

A dent in a shotgun barrel should never be forced up by the use of sheer force. The strain will sometimes cause minute cracks in the metal which may not be visible to the eye but will weaken the barrel at that particular spot. The hammering process, where the dented metal is slowly hammered back into its original position, is the only safe way of removing dents.

Some gunsmiths make or purchase a set of solid plugs which are used in the same way as the expanding dent plug except that instead of one expandable unit, several solid plugs are needed for each gauge, making the cost too high for most gunsmiths.

POLISHING SHOTGUN BARRELS

Polishing shotgun bores from chamber to muzzle is not an easy task as the barrel choke often may be damaged in the process. With a shotgun barrel polishing head (Fig. 1-12) the job is relatively simple, giving a mirrorlike finish throughout the entire bore. The polishing head consists of slots to fasten four polishing strips centrally. When the head is revolved at a rapid speed, centrifugal force forces the strips of polishing cloth to the wall of the bore. Only the ends of the strips touch the bore; this allows air to freely circulate inside of the bore which in turn prevents overheating of the barrel.

The polishing head comes attached to a 34-inch-long steel rod which is chucked in a conventional ¼-inch drill motor, lathe or grinder. The speed can be up to 4800 RPM.

Normally, the barrels are clamped in a vise as shown in Fig. 1-13. Then the chuck rod is inserted in the breech end of the barrel. Then the drill motor is started. The polishing head, (attached to the steel chuck rod), is slowly pushed forward and back through the bore.

Coarse polishing strips should be used for lead and scratch removal, while fine strips should be used for polishing. The strips may be changed by unscrewing the slotted bolt, removing the old strips and inserting new ones before tightening the bolt.

REMOVING BARREL OBSTRUCTIONS

The most common obstruction in rifle barrels is cleaning patches. This is caused by the cleaning patch being too tight on the cleaning rod tip. Usually such a patch can be removed by pouring about a half-teaspoon of gun oil down the bore and allowing the patch to soak a few minutes. This will soften the patch and allow it to be pushed out with a conventional cleaning rod. If this does not work, other, more complicated methods will have to be employed.

Screw shoulder type mandrels are available on the market which will fit on the end of a cleaning rod. Or you can make your own by soldering a common wood screw (one that will

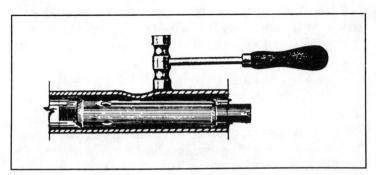

Fig. 6-2. Application of dent plug; that is, removing dent from shotgun barrel by tapping around the dent with a brass hammer (see Fig. 6-1).

freely slip down the bore withhout scratching it) to the end of a rod. The rod and screw may then be inserted into the barrel. When the screw tip touches the lodged patch, the rod and screw assembly is turned clockwise so as to engage the stuck patch. Once the screw is wound completely into the patch, both the screw and patch can be pulled out together.

In rare cases the two previously described methods will just not work on stubborn stuck patches. In this case make certain that it is indeed a stuck patch inside of the bore. Then heat the barrel around the area of the stuck patch until it will melt soft solder. If the heat is allowed to get no higher than this, it will not harm the barrel, bluing or bore, but will provide enough heat to char the patch to a point where it will become brittle and begin disintegrating. Then it can easily be pushed out with a cleaning rod.

RESTORING BARREL LIFE

Metal fouling can be reduced extensively by frequent cleanings of the bore. Nevertheless, most shooters will eventually run across a poor shooting rifle. One of the simplest ways of restoring barrel life is to use a special bore cleaner like J-B Bore Cleaner, available from most gun supply houses. It will remove lead, metal and powder fouling from rifles, pistols and also shotguns. In addition it will normally improve the accuracy of any weapon.

To use, first saturate a regular rifle cleaning patch with light oil or bore solvent and pass it through the bore. Then work J-B cleaner into a snug fitting patch and pass the patch back and forth through the bore five or ten times. Additional passes may be necessary within the first one-third of the bore directly ahead of the chamber as fouling is usually mass-produced in this area.

Again moisten a patch with light oil or bore solvent and pass the patch through the bore, followed with a clean dry patch.

If the weapon in question has been neglected for some time, it should be fired several times to heat up the barrel. Or else it can be warmed with a blow torch. This softens the fouling and is thereby easier to remove. While the barrel is still warm, apply the J-B cleaner as previously described.

Once the weapon has been cleaned and is free of fouling, a cleaning with J-B cleaner every 100 rounds of ammunition or so will usually keep the barrel in good shape. In between times, use methods described in Chapter 5.

REMOVING DENTS FROM GUNSTOCKS

During the normal use of any hunting weapon, minor dents and scratches are inevitable. Many of these dents can be raised without necessitating the complete refinishing of the gun stock. One method is to wet a cloth, place it over the dent. Then apply a hot soldering iron momentarily on the wet rag at the exact location of the dent. Don't leave the soldering iron tip on long enough to burn or cause the stock finish to bubble. Leave it there just long enough to cause the steam generated from the heat to swell the wood fibers to the surface.

When refinishing a gun stock, the same method may be used. Also, very minor scratches may be leveled at the time of refinishing with a sharp piece of glass, but care must be used as not to mar the wood.

Larger dents and cracks may be filled with a commercial wood filler. One method of repairing dents, scratches, deep tool marks, etc., is to use shellac sticks available from Brownells, Inc., Montezuma, Iowa. Such shellac sticks come in an assortment of various colors including white, ivory, transparent, medium and dark walnut, Circassian walnut and black.

To use shellac sticks on gun stocks, a small spatula no wider than ¾ inch and no longer than 4 inches should be used. This spatula should be no wider than ½ inch at the point. Heat the spatula in the flame of a torch or alcohol lamp until it is hot enough to melt the shellac when pressed against the end of the shellac stick. When a small quantity of melted shellac has formed on the end of the spatula, quickly wipe it across the area of the stock to be repaired. This is best done by turning the spatula blade so the melted shellac will be on the bottom of the blade. Hold the knife at a 45 degree angle as it is drawn over the scratch. If the first pass does not completely fill the crack, repeat until it does. After the melted shellac has thoroughly hardened in the scratch or crack, the area should be sanded down to the level of the surrounding stock. Finish the entire stock as discussed in Chapter 9.

When light colored stock woods are encountered, best results can be obtained by first coloring the gouge or scratch to match the surrounding wood. Birchwood Casey manufactures water stains that produce clear, true light proof colors without covering the natural beauty of the wood. If the first try is too dark, the color may be lightened by wiping the area with plain water. These water stains are available in walnut, cherry, mahogany and brown mahogany.

Once the defective area has been matched with the surrounding wood, use a transparent shellac stick to raise the dent or scratch to the same level as the surrounding areas. On darker wood use the various colors of shellac sticks available.

Another stock repair technique is to use a stock maker's fill stick, also available from Brownells, Inc. This is an economical and quick method of making stock repairs. Merely rub it in and wipe it off. Once applied the area may be finished with regular stock finishes, lacquer, varnishes, vinyls or any other type of finish. This method is especially useful for repairing finished stocks of the new synthetic-finish types which cannot be repaired by the hot shellac method previously described. Colors available include light, medium or dark brown or blonde.

BLUING SMALL GUN PARTS

Complete instructions for bluing firearms of all kinds are given in Chapter 8. Nevertheless, there are times when a few screws, pins or whatever may require bluing and the gunsmith does not want to go to the trouble of setting up the conventional bluing apparatus. One way to solve this problem is to use oil for bluing the small parts. To use this method, polish the parts as you would for conventional bluing methods. Then heat the polished parts slowly and evenly in the flame of a propane torch until they just begin to glow slightly when in a shadow. Then quench the part in raw linseed oil. The result will be a rich, deep blue that will probably match the rest of the firearm parts.

SOFT SOLDERING

Sight ramps, sight bases and other firearm accessories can be satisfactorily attached by soft soldering. As with any type of welding or soldering, the first step is to thoroughly clean the two parts to be joined. This includes all rust, bluing, oil, grease and the dirt. The part to be attached is then placed in the correct position on the barrel or action and outlined with a felt tip pen or with an ordinary lead pencil.

Once the areas on both pieces have been thoroughly cleaned, a coat of solder should be applied to the surfaces of each, that is, the side that will be bound together. The best solder to use is conventional half-and-half (50-50 or 50 percent in and 50 percent lead) solder without an acid core.

To coat the areas with solder, which is called tinning, heat the areas with a propane torch to a temperature high enough to melt the solder. Swab on soldering flux on the areas. Then spread a thin coat of melted solder completely over the areas to be joined. The correct technique here is to heat the metal, not the solder, with the torch. In this manner the metal will melt the solder when it reaches the proper temperature. If you heat the solder and drop it on the metal surface, it will not make a good bond. Wipe off any excess solder and allow the parts to cool to a temperature where they can be easily handled.

At this stage, the parts should be located exactly, then tightly planted in place with the two soldered surfaces together. Again heat the *parts* with a propane torch to a point where the solder is easily melted. Additional wire solder should be fed to the two joining areas either around the edges or possibly through screw holes in the pieces. Any excess solder should be wiped off immediately with a dry cloth just before they solidify.

Parts that have been properly cleaned and tinned and the joint thoroughly *sweated* together will be permanently attached and will take about any treatment that one would normally give a gun. If any blemishes occur from the heat, the spots may be touched up with one of the many instant blues on the market.

SILVER SOLDERING

Silver soldering normally requires more heat than soft soldering, but the joint is often stronger with silver solder than with soft solder.

If accessories are to be silver soldered to the barrel, the additional heat required sometimes induces oxidation inside the barrel which causes scale. Therefore, the bore should be protected. There are several commercial applicants on the market, but P.O. Ackley, the famous gunsmith from Colorado, recommends using two parts lamp black, three parts kitchen flour and four parts fine table salt. These ingredients are mixed into a thick liquid for coating the inside of the barrel near the area to be used. Once the bore has been coated with this mixture, the areas to be silver soldered are prepared as described previously for soft soldering.

To join two parts coat the joining surfaces of each with silver solder flux. Then lay a piece of silver solder wire on top of the flux. Clamp the two parts together and apply heat as evenly as possible until the silver solder melts. The heat must be applied as evenly as possible to avoid warping the metal parts.

When the proper temperature is reached, the flux will melt and probably come out from between the two parts. At this point, it is necessary only to keep the even heat going for another minute or so, then allow the area to cool.

BEAD SIGHT BASICS

It may seem like a simple matter indeed to unscrew an old shotgun sight bead from the muzzle of the barrel; then, just as easy, screw in a bright new silver or gold one in its place. Not so. When you start banging away, chances are the barrel is going to split or even be blown completely off if the threaded shank of the sight is allowed to protrude down into the bore. The results are almost as bad as though the barrel was tightly stuffed with cleaning patches.

The installation of a shotgun sight bead is certainly within the reach of almost any shotgun owner, provided he has access to a few simple tools and, more importantly follows certain procedures.

REMOVING THE OLD SIGHT

I've never run across a shotgun bead that gave any problems when it was being removed; most unscrew easily.

Nevertheless, if you should run across a stubborn thread, don't hesitate to use a good penetrating oil, such as WD-40, SS-P Super Penetrant and similar products. Apply the lubricant per the instructions on the container, wait about 15 minutes and try removing the sight with conventional pliers.

Should you accidentally wrench off the bead from the threaded shank, or if the bead is already off when you start the project, eliminating any gripping surface, the old threaded shank will have to be drilled out and a new thread tapped.

Most shotgun sight beads come in two thread sizes, that is, 3-56 and 6-48 use #45 and #31 drills respectively. Tap sizes will, of course, be the same as the screw threads. Bead sizes will be 0.067, 0.130 and 0.175 inch.

When drilling, use screw machine drills, which have short lengths, as the long ones tend to wander. Also use a drill jig if one is available. To use, merely align the barrel under the drill bit. Place the jig on the barrel, and line up the jig hole and bushing with the sight hole in the barrel or the spot where the hole is to be drilled if no hole exists. Tighten the jig clamp and you're ready to start drilling without using a center punch and with no further measuring.

Tap the hole with hand taps of 3 or 4 flute—preferably with the use of a tap guide. Use a special tapping compound such as Tap Magic. Do not use conventional cutting oil.

With the sight hole drilled, tapped and cleaned, be sure to select the proper size thread. This may seem like a silly statement to make, but many persons have gotten the threads

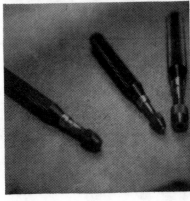

Fig. 6-3. Three sizes of shotgun sight installers.

Fig. 6-4. Scribing a line on the shank threads.

mixed up and tried to install one with the wrong size thread. In doing so, you'll end up with a jammed sight. Select one too small, and you have a sight that wobbles and will eventually work out or else protrude down into the bore to cause the problems as discussed previously.

INSTALLING THE SIGHT BEAD

Once the proper sight has been selected, with the proper thread, finish, size, and so forth, start the sight by hand or with a special shotgun sight installer as shown in Fig. 6-3. Run the

Fig. 6-5. Using a hand grinder with emery wheel to cut shank off the shotgun sight.

Fig. 6-6. Smooth up the sight shank with a small file or polishing bob until it is exactly flush with the contour of the bore.

threads to full depth. Then with a light as shown in Fig. 6-4, scribe a line on the shank threads where they are flush with the inside of the barrel bore.

Remove the sight and cut the shank off at the scribed line. This is best accomplished with a hand grinder and narrow emery wheel (Fig. 6-5) rather than with a hacksaw. The sight may be held in the sight installer, then the holder clamped in a small vise. The emery wheel will make a fast, smooth cut.

Fig. 6-7. Finished installation.

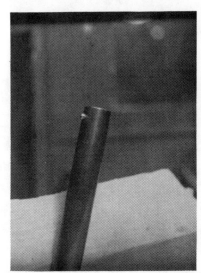

Continue by reinstalling the sight into the threaded hole. Then smooth the remaining shank with a small file or polishing bob until the shank is *exactly* flush with the contour of the bore (Fig. 6-6).

If the old screw comes out easily and a new hole does not have to be drilled and tapped, the entire operation should not take longer than 15 minutes. Drilling and tapping a new hole may take another 15 minutes. If the procedures just given are followed, the job is easy and perfectly safe (Fig. 6-7).

Chapter 7

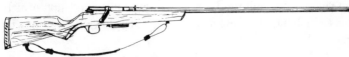

Installing Firearm
Gadgets Of Value

There are many useful accessories available for guns of all types which can improve the accuracy of the weapons, make them more convenient to carry, help to make shooting more pleasant by absorbing some of the recoil, and so forth. Most of these accessories are easy to install, making them a natural project for the home gunsmith. The items in this chapter are but few of the many available, but any gun owner will find at least one project that would be of help to his or her shooting enjoyment.

GUN SLINGS

The gun sling not only provides a means of comfortably carrying a firearm, but also is of tremendous assistance in steadying a weapon while firing, regardless if you are in the prone position, the sitting position, the kneeling position or the standing position. Every match shooter uses the sling in all positions, and few would attempt to shoot a match without a good rifle sling.

In adjusting the gun sling, the upper portion of the sling, called the loop, should be adjusted to such a length that it will come to within approximately 2 inches of the butt swivel. If the loop is too short, the butt cannot be fitted to the shoulder; if too loose the sling will not be tight around the arm. The rear portion of the sling, called the tail, should always be loose enough so that it will never be stretched tight when the shooter is in the firing position.

To place the sling on the shooter's arm, the arm should pass through the loop from its right to its left. This twists the upper portion of the sling so that its flat rests against the shooter's wrist. Then move the left hand in a circular motion, high and to the left, over the forward part of the sling. Grasp the forearm just in the rear of the front sling swivel. Then with the right hand, pull the loop as high up on the left-upper arm (for right-hand shooter) as it will go. Slip down the keeper to hold it there.

Once the sling is in place, the sling must never be held too tightly by brute strength alone. The muscles should be contracted only enough to hold the rifle up. Then the shooter should relax the other muscles and be calm. With experience, any person can learn to hold a rifle steady for accurate shooting.

The sporting sling differs slightly from the target rifle sling in that its main purpose is for carrying a rifle rather than using it to steady shots. While hunting with a rifle, in all but rare cases, the shooter does not have time to make sling adjustments and get into a steady position before firing. Most of the time, instant snap shots are required to hit a bouncing white-tailed deer as it darts through a thicket of timber. In a second or two the animal is out of sight.

One type of sling that is recommended for sporting rifles is Brownells Latigo sling. See Fig. 7-1. To install this sling, first take a yardstick or ruler and measure the distance between the two sling studs on the gun stock. Deduct 2 inches from this measure to allow for sling swivel bows. To illustrate, if the measure is 28½ inches, deduct 2 inches and use the figure 26½ inches.

Next remove the brass joining stud from the sling using either a screwdriver or a coin. Do not, however, disassemble the sling. On the terminal end of the strap you will find that the numbered holes are spaced more closely together. Locate hole 27 of these closely spaced holes and cut off the remaining end of the strap close to hole 28.

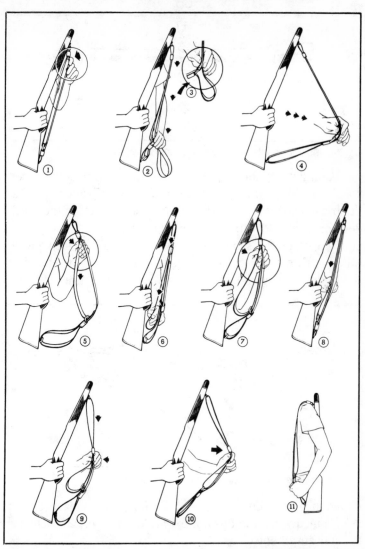

Fig. 7-1. Brownell's Latigo sling and how to use it. (1) Grasp the two outside straps of the Latigo immediately below the keeper. (2) Pull downward as far as you can for full extension of the sling. If this is too far for maximum sling comfort, pull downward only as far as needed to get your best length. A few tries will establish the correct length. (3) Change the position of your hold on the sling to include both main straps. (4) Quickly snap both straps outward. (5) To return the Latigo to the parade position grasp the inside of the sling just below the keeper at the top swivel. (6) Pull outward as far as you can. (7 & 8) If the sling is fully extended, pull down again as shown. (9) To use the Latigo as a carrying strap pull the sling approximately halfway down as shown in views 1 and 9. (10) Extend the sling to the desired length. (11) If the sling is not comfortable for carrying as shown it may be extended further to the desired length.

129

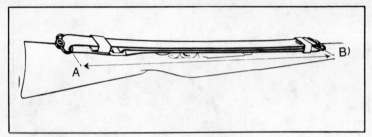

Fig. 7-2. Tips of swivels must be facing each other.

Continue by locating hole 27 again in the widely spaced hole. Match the two holes (both are number 27) and join using the brass joining stud. Position the sling and attach the quick detachable swivels to the mounting studs.

To attach the sling, the tip swivels should be facing each other as shown in Fig. 7-2. Measure distance AB as shown in the figure. Using the shortest whole inch to within ¾ inch,

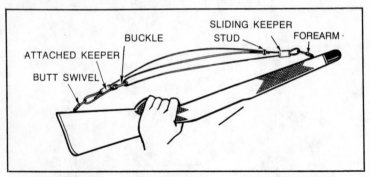

Fig. 7-3. Brownell's Latigo sling and its components.

obtain the correct measurement. That is, if the measurement is 27¾ inch when the tips are toward each other, 27 inches is the measurement to use.

Next to the holes punched on 2⅜-inch centers in the tongue end of the sling are numbers that match numbers

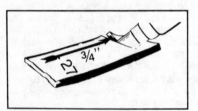

Fig. 7-4. Go beyond your measurement an extra ¾ inch.

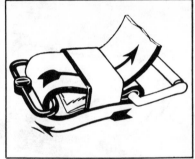

Fig. 7-5. After threading the sling through the swivel attach the keeper as shown.

beside holes on 1-inch centers punched in the buckle end. See Fig. 7-3. Beside one of the holes in the tongue end there will be a number corresponding to the measurement between the swivels. Cut off the sling at an extra ¾ inch beyond this hole as shown in Fig. 7-4.

Fig. 7-6. Feed the sling through the forearm swivel and back through the keeper.

Thread the sling through the swivel on the butt stock of the gun, and attach the keeper as shown in Fig. 7-5. Then thread the sling through the forearm swivel and back through the sliding keeper as shown in Fig. 7-6. Thread the sling through the loop of the buckle and bend back towards the outer strap of the sling, and pull it tight. The free end of the sling now becomes the center strap of the sling as shown in Fig. 7-7.

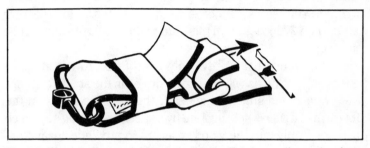

Fig. 7-7. Place the free end through the buckle. This is now the center strap.

Fig. 7-8. Tighten the screw with a coin.

Match the measurement number on the end of the sling with the same number on the buckle end. Put the female half of the stud through the holes and screw in the other half with a coin or screwdriver to tighten (Fig. 7-8). In case these holes cannot be matched due to tightness of the sling, attach the end to the nearest convenient hole and pull the sling into shooting position. Then refasten the stud to the proper hole. The sling will automatically correct the length when pulled to a tight position.

INSTALLING SLING STUDS

When installing a rifle sling on weapons without sling studs, it is necessary to measure and install these prior to following the instructions given previously in this chapter for installing the sling. Sling studs are normally placed at varying distances apart, usually between 26 and 28 inches, with the rear stud about 3 inches from the toe of the stock. For the average rifle stock, 3 inches from the butt toe for the rear stud, then 27 inches from this stud to the forearm stud, will be just about right for the average shooter.

If no studs have previously been fitted to the stock in question, two holes will have to be drilled in the stock to accept the swivels and studs. In general, the stud that goes on the forearm of a rifle is held in place by a special retaining nut which presses firmly into the wood so as not to protrude against the barrel. The rear stud screws directly into the wood.

To install the lower or rear stud to accept quick-detachable type swivels, the location must first be marked with scratch awl. Select a drill bit that exactly matches the size of the larger diameter of the screw; this will be the end nearest the swivels. With either a hand drill or an electric drill motor, drill this hole so that it will be approximately ¼ inch deep or the depth of the largest diameter of the screw stud. Use reasonable care so as to drill the hole straight and not at an angle.

Use a smaller drill to drill a pilot hole to about the same length of the screw stud. The swivel base can then be screwed into the wood, using a small metal pin or punch through the stud's eye for turning leverage if necessary. Be careful not to screw the stud in so deeply that it causes the wood to split.

The hole for the front stud is located in a similar manner. It is of great importance that this hole be centered exactly so that it is vertical to the forearm.

Although preferences differ, the recommended way of drilling this hole for the forearm stud is to drill from the outside to the inside. There is less chance of the wood splitting if the hole is drilled this way. This hole is drilled all the way through into the barrel channel of the stock. This hole must be slightly counterdrilled to a larger size in order to accept the retaining nut that will be pressed into the wood on the side nearest the barrel. In no circumstances should the retaining nut be allowed to come in contact with the rifle barrel; accuracy will be harmed greatly if it should.

RECOIL PADS

The primary purpose of a recoil pad is to cushion the gun's recoiling kick as the gun is fired. Sometimes, such a pad is used to extend the stock's length for a better fit. For example, one gun stock may have been fitted for a shooter with relatively short arms. Perhaps the gun was then purchased by a person with longer arms, making the stock entirely too short. Of course, the gun can be restocked, but in the case of a good walnut stock, the operation could be rather costly. It follows that a recoil pad of an inch or so thickness could lengthen the stock for a correct fit at a relatively low cost.

On the other hand, when a stock is of the correct length when fitted with a common thin butt plate, considerable wood may have to be removed when one of the thick recoil pads is attached.

Recoil pads for shotguns are normally manufactured in three different styles: skeet, field and trap design. The skeet style is designed for fast gun handling with a minimum degree of interference from the stock clinging to the fabric of the shooting coat. This type of pad will feature either a smooth surface or a rounded corrugated ribbing running lengthwise with the butt's outline. Furthermore, this type of pad is not concaved like many plates and pads, rather, it is nearly straight from heel to toe.

The standard field recoil pad, found on a great number of shotguns, is slightly concave in outline and features an extended toe. The corrugation that covers much of the pad's surface runs from side to side, or opposite to that on the skeet pad. This design is intended to discourage slippage of the stock after it has been placed to the shoulder.

The trap style recoil pad is very individualistic in design, giving improved accuracy and added comfort to a trapshooter. One characteristic is that the pad is deeply concaved about midway between the heel and toe. This pronounced concave design is intended to fit snugly over the shoulder muscles, to insure holding the stock in the identical position for each shot. If this type of pad is fitted correctly, surprising results can be obtained in the way of accuracy and comfort while firing.

To install a recoil pad, first measure in from the center of the butt a distance equal to the thickness of the new pad and strike a point. Then, with a flexible straightedge, run through the point just indicated and continue an equal distance or parallel with a line from heel to toe. Then scribe it for the cutoff line. This method is used when there will be no change in the gun's pitch. If, however, the down pitch is to be increased or decreased, the cutoff line must be altered accordingly.

Having scribed the cutoff line, use a fine-toothed saw to remove the surplus wood, being careful in doing so that the cut is square, even and clean. To insure a tight joint between the pad and stock, cut the stock slightly longer than necessary and work the new surface down with a disk sander or with a file.

Fig. 7-9. B-Square recoil pad jig from the Frank Mittermeier gun supply catalog. This jig enables the gunsmith to shape and install recoil pads on rifles and shotguns. Since the sanding and finishing are done on the jig there is no danger of damaging the stock.

During this operation test the stock often to insure that the face of the butt is flat and even.

When selecting the pad, be certain that it is long enough to permit the existing outline along both the comb and bottom of the stock to continue straight and unbroken. A handy device that can aid you in recoil pad installations is a recoil pad jig such as the one shown in Fig. 7-9, manufactured by B-Square and available through Frank Mittermeier, Inc. This jig enables the gunsmith to shape and install any shotgun or rifle recoil pad at the correct angle. Since all shaping and sanding of the pad is done off the stock, there is no danger of damaging the finish.

With the joint between the pad and stock even and tight, these two parts can be drawn together with the two pad screws provided for the purpose. It is best, however, to first apply a coat of linseed oil to the raw surface of the wood before attaching the pad permanently. Locate the holes for the screws so that the heel of the pad will be drawn up as near as possible in line with the top of the comb. To do so will reduce a considerable amount of work in dressing down the oversize pad to fit the stock's outline.

After securing the pad, wrap a piece of masking tape around the stock edge. This should be even with the base of the recoil pad to prevent marring the stock while sanding the pad down to the level of the existing stock.

Now, using a sanding disk or emery wheel, sand the newly installed recoil pad down to the correct size. If power tools are not available, dress the pad down as follows:

Hold the stock upright on a flat surface. With a fine-toothed hacksaw make a series of straight cuts, working around the stock and leaving a margin of about 1/16 inch. Be careful that the cuts around the toe are at outward angles similar to that of the stock. After this routing process with the saw, use a file to work the pad down to the stock size. Finally, with strips of emery cloth or sandpaper, finish the job.

Rifles seldom have recoil pads of the thickness that are normally installed on shotguns. They are normally thin metal butt plates. One unique design is called the trap butt plate. This plate is checkered chrome-moly steel with a trapdoor butt plate for custom installation on fine hunting rifles. A finger-nail notch is provided for easy opening and quick access to four spare cartridges, cleaning rod or other emergency equipment such as weatherproof matches, compasses, etc. Many other designs are available and can be seen in most gun and shooting supply catalogs.

INSTALLING IRON SIGHTS

Most factory firearms are manufactured with front and rear iron sights known as open sights. Many firearm experts will also tell you that such sights are not conducive to the best accuracy and that even the addition of a peep sight, mounted on the receiver of a rifle, will improve the accuracy tremendously. Open iron sights do, however, have their place in heavy brush or at close range where fast snap shots are necessary. In such cases, scopes and peep sights will only hinder the shooter.

Two peep sights manufactured by Williams can be adapted to practically any modern rifle without the need for any drilling or tapping (see Table 7-1). In other words, the installation of these two sights can easily be accomplished by anyone with a small screwdriver. One is known as the *Foolproof* receiver sight, which has internal micrometer adjustments that lock to prevent accidental movement of the sight setting selected. It is free from knobs and other obstructions that impair the shooter's field of view. The mounting holes are spaced to fit rifles which are factory drilled and tapped for receiver sights. This sight sells for around $20.

The other is the Williams 5D sight, which is similar in construction to the one mentioned previously, except that it does not have micrometer adjustments.

To install either of these sights to rifles that have been drilled and tapped at the factory, merely remove the set screws in the receiver of the rifle (the ones needed for this particular sight), place the sight on the receiver, and secure with the screws furnished with the sight. The chart in Table 7-2 shows several rifles in which these two sights will fit; however, all of them will not have factory-drilled holes. Holes will have to be drilled and tapped to accept the sight.

RECOIL REDUCERS

Heavy recoil from rifles and shotguns is probably one of the chief causes of flinching, causing the shooter to frequently miss the mark. There are several ways to reduce the recoil felt by the shooter. One of the most important aspects of eliminating felt recoil is the design of the rifle or shotgun stock. A gun stock that fits the shooter perfectly, with good straight line design, will do much to enable the shooter to absorb recoil even from the most powerful, hard-kicking weapons. Add to this a cushioned recoil pad and the recoil is hardly noticed.

In some cases, such as when lightweight shooters tackle a hard-kicking firearm, other steps must be taken to eliminate the recoil even more. One relatively inexpensive way is to install a Flinch-X recoil buffer. This pneumatic-action recoil buffer takes the hurt out of shotguns or rifle recoil of the firearm. This amazing little 7¾-ounce unit is shown in Fig. 7-10 and is easily installed in the buttstock. Some shooters are putting an extra one in the forearm too.

To install this unit, a 57/64-inch by 6-inch spur point drill is used. The unique ability of the spur point drill to cut straight,

Fig. 7-10. The Finch-X buffer for shotguns and the Rec-O-Chek buffer for rifles, both available through Brownells, Inc.

Table 7-1. Williams Foolproof and 5D Sight Chart.

MAKE	FP	5D
Benjamin 340, 342, 347 (need higher front sight)		5D-SH
British Pattern 14	FP-17	
Brno w/out d'tail receiver	FP-98	
Browning Centerfire Lever	FP-94	5D-94
Sq. Stern Shotgun*		
.22 Autos	FP-BR	5D-SSM
H.P. w/bolt	FP-98AP	5D-121
H.P. Auto	FP-BAR	
Crosman 160		
Daisy 99 & 299	FP-FN	5D-CR160
Dumoulin dril/tpt	FP-FN	5D-JEMS
Enfield 1917 & Br 14	FP-17	
FN drilled/tapped	FP-FN	5D-JEMS
Higgins (30-30 Lever)	FP-36	5D-94/36
Husqvarna w/out d'tail receiver	FP-98	
Crown Grade	FP-CGH	
Ithaca M-37*	FP-12/37	5D-12/37
M-49 .22 Saddle		5D-49
Jap 25 & 31	FP-JAP	5D-JEMS
Kodiak 260 series		5D-572
Krag, American	FP-Krag	5D-Krag
Norwegian	FP-N Krag	5D-N Krag
Lee Enfield British short magazine	FP-SMLE	5D-SMLE
Marlin		
A-1		5D-81
36 & 336	FP-36	5D-94/36
39A	FP-39	5D-39A
56, 57, 62		5D-56/989
80, 81	FP-88/100	5D-81
94		5D-94/36
93		

MAKE	FP	5D
740 AP stock	FP-740AP	5D-760N/
740 above #64,046		740/742
740 .30/06 & .280 above #207,200 & .308 above #22,000		
742	FP-740AP	5D-760N/
760 above 154,965	FP-740AP	740/742
760 w/ AP stock	FP-740AP	5D-12/37
788	FP-788	5D-12/37
788LH	FP-788LH	5D-SSM
870*	FP-12/37	5D-RU
1100*	FP-12/37	5D-56/989
Sq. Stern Shotgun*	FP-SSM	
Ruger 10/22&44 Mag	FP-RU	
Sako Finnwolf	FP-88/100	
Savage (see Stevens)		
Sq. Stern S gun*	FP-SSM	5D-SSM
.22 Auto		5D-550
99	FP-99	
99DL w/top tang safety	FP-99S	
110	I-P-110	5D-706N
170	FP-740AP	
Sears Centerfire Lever (30-30 Lever)	FP-94	5D-94/36
Sherdian Model C	FP-36	5D-SH
Shotguns Sq. Stern*		
Pump/Flat Rec's*	FP-SSM	5D-SSM
Smith & Wesson rifle	FP-12/37	5D-12/37
Springfield	FP-CGH	
'03	FP-A3	5D-JEMS
'03/A3	FP-A3	5D-03/A3
S & Larson 54J, 60, 65	FP-S & L.	

Stevens / Savage, Mossberg, Remington, Winchester, Weatherby firing-pin & aperture reference

Model		
99 Auto Load		5D-56/989
99 & 989		5D-56/989
.44 Mag & 444		5D-94/36
Mauser 98		5D-JEMS
Mossberg		
800	FP-36	
3000	FP-98	
BSA	FP-70, FP-70AP	5D-70
	FP-70AP	5D-70
Remington		
8*	FP-SSM	5D-SSM
11-48*	FP-12/37	5D-12/37
11 Nylon		5D-510
12	FP-121	5D-121
12 Nylon		5D-510
14	FP-14	
24	FP-BR	
30 Express	FP-17	
31*	FP-12/37	5D-12/37
48 Sptr	FP-12/37	5D-12/37
58*	FP-12/37	5D-12/37
66		5D-760N/740742
81*	FP-SSM	5D-SSM
121	FP-121	
141	FP-14	
241	FP-BR	
510- 11- 12- 13		5D-510
550 Auto	FP-740AP	5D-550
552 & 572	FP-600	5D-572
552 BDL & 572 BDL	FP-70AP	5D-572
600 & 660	FP-98AP	
700	FP-70	5D-70
700 Left Hand		5D-JEMS
721, 722, 725		5D-70

Model		
Stevens		
Stevens/Savage (will fit some not drill'd		5D-550
22/410 & 20 ga		5D-22/410
300 series	FP-340	
620*		5D-12/37
Swiss 1911 7.5	FP-SW	
.30 Carbine (G vt)	FP-30 Car	
Winchester		
9422	FP-94	5D-94/36
05, 07, & 10	FP-71	5D-12/37
12*, 1200, 1400	FP-12/37	5D-12/37
1500		5D-12/37
25*	FP-12/37	
52 Round Rec'r	FP-52	5D-70
54	FP-70	
55	FP-94	
64	FP-94	5D-94/36
65	FP-94	
70 Old Style	FP-70	5D-70
70 New Style	FP-70AP	
71	FP-71	
74		5D-74
77		5D-77
86	FP-71	5D-56/989
88	FP-88/100	5D-94/36
94	FP-94	5D-56/989
95	FP-95	5D-12/37
100 Auto	FP-88/100	5D-12/37
150 & 190	FP-12/37	5D-12/37
241	FP-94	5D-760N/740742
250-5, 270-5, 290 above w/ramp	FP-12/37	
670 & 770 New	FP-70AP	5D-70
Weatherby, Mk/5	FP-98	
Mk/10	FP-FN	

*4D01C97 Shotgun aperture optional—advise. Extra shotgun or interchangeable aperture available. (Courtesy Brownell s)

true holes in any grain structure makes it a real lifesaver when installing these popular recoil buffers.

Another means of reducing recoil is to use a muzzle brake on the barrel. While there are several different models available, most work on a gas trap propulsion principle with a prequick outlet for surplus gas to escape—usually from jet-type sharp-angle ports. Such recoil reducers claim to cut recoil from 20 to 60 percent. This means that the movement of the shooter's body backward and the muzzle jump upward are reduced to a minimum. The installation of these muzzle brakes requires about ⅜ inch of barrel extending forward of the gun sight which is threaded, using a thread of approximately 28 per inch; then the muzzle break is screwed on.

Some confident gunsmiths can also provide a muzzle brake on a rifle or shotgun by making it an integral part of the barrel; that is, small ports are drilled around the muzzle of the barrel to allow gas to escape. This action reduces the kick and muzzle movement of the firearm.

TELESCOPE SIGHTS

Many shooters have improved their marksmanship overnight with the installation of a telescope sight on their rifles (see Fig. 7-11). Most modern rifles are drilled and tapped at the factory to accept telescope sight bases. Nevertheless, there are numerous rifles in use that have not been previously drilled and tapped; therefore, this operation will have to be done prior to installing a telescope sight.

A sight jig is very helpful, but not essential, in drilling and tapping for scope bases. One of the best is manufactured by Forster Products of Lanark, Illinois. The use of this device makes the drilling and tapping operation almost foolproof; however, a certain amount of orientation with it is necessary. The manufacturer gives the following instructions for its use.

This fixture was especially designed for accurately drilling and tapping rifle actions and barrels for top mounts and target scope blocks, receiver sights, ramp sights and beads on single-barreled shotguns as well as side mounts whenever the mounting holes are in line with the centerline of the barrel. The V-blocks align the gun by the barrel. Even if the action is

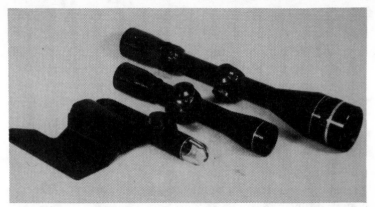

Fig. 7-11. Telescope sights. Here are three of the many telescope sights handled by Harold's Gun Shoppe in Waynesboro, Pennsylvania. The small one on the left is a Weaver Quick-Point, Model S-1100, intended for shotguns. The medium size one in the center is a Leupold M8-4X. The largest one, located on the right side, is a Leupold 3.5 × 10, Model Vari-X III.

not exactly in line with the barrel, the fixture automatically corrects this error and drills the holes true with the barrel.

The gun to be drilled and tapped should be removed from the stock. It is not usually necessary to remove the trigger mechanism on bolt actions. The Savage 99 requires only the removal of the forearm. The Remington 760 requires the removal of the slide bolt as well as the bolt mechanism. Tubular magazine rifles must have the magazine removed before the drilling operation. The barrel is then laid in the V-blocks, with the action over the end of the fixture having the clearance slot. Whenever possible, the barrel to be drilled should be so positioned that the action is close to the rear V-block, with the cylindrical or straight portion of the barrel supported by the V-block.

Slide the overarm in place over that portion of the action to be drilled and raise the rear V-block up to bring the action in contact with the correct size drill bushing. Next, measure the diameter of the barrel with a micrometer at the points of contact at the front and rear V-blocks. As most barrels are tapered it will be necessary to raise the front V-block.

To arrive at the exact difference in height, subtract the small diameter from the larger diameter, multiply this value by 0.707 and raise the front V-block that much higher than the rear V-block. This can be done very satisfactorily by measuring with a machinist's rule or, if extreme accuracy is desired, by means of a feeler gauge between the top of the machined boss and the bottom of the V-block. Next, clamp the barrel lightly, using the aluminum pads under the clamp screws to avoid marring the barrel.

On bolt actions, raise the flat top support pad into firm contact with the flat bottom of the action. This squares the action and acts as a support during the drilling operation. The clamp on top of the leveling block is used to hold the action when it is desirable to remove the clamp from the rear V-block so that the overarm may be moved over any part of the action. Now tighten the clamps.

Actions that have no flat bottom surface can be aligned by means of a square from either the top of the overarm or any other machined surface on the fixture. The gun also can be aligned by use of a level, but in this case be sure the fixture is level before lining up the gun.

One method used by many gunsmiths to locate mounts is to place the mount on the action or barrel in the desired position and mark the forward hole on the gun with a scriber or pencil. Next, with the locator pin, point down in the front hole of the overarm, slide it over the gun so the point lines up with the mark and lock in place. Drill and tap this hole. Now screw the mount to the gun with one screw. Loosen the overarm and with the tapered point of the locator pin, locate the overarm over the second hole in the mount and lock in place. Lock the spacer block against the overarm. The overarm then can be moved out of the way, the mount removed and the overarm set against the spacer block. The second hole is then drilled and tapped. Other holes in the mount can be located and drilled in the same way. Do not drill the holes with the mount in place as this may prevent drilling the holes on the true center of the action.

When drilling for receiver sights, line up the barrel in the V-blocks in the usual way, but turn the action sideways and square it by means of a small square laid on top of the overarm. Locate the first hole and proceed as previously outlined. The same procedure is followed when mounting side mounts, but holds true only if all holes are in line with the center line of the barrel.

If the desired holes are not on the center line of the barrel, the fixture can still be used to hold the gun squarely and steadily in the drill press. In this case the overarm is not used.

When drilling and tapping for a ramp sight, the gun is turned around, the muzzle end being at the notched end of the fixture. The V-blocks in this case are raised high enough so the drill bushings will contact the barrel. Allowance must be made for the taper in the barrel as previously explained. In this case, it will be necessary to square the gun with a level. Shotgun beads are mounted by following the same procedure.

Go easy at first and double-check your setups to be sure that you are drilling the holes exactly where you want them. Make sure also that the V-blocks align squarely, by tightening the screws gently at first so that the flat of the screw contacts the flat of the shaft squarely. A twisted V-block will throw you off due to the taper in the barrel, and especially so if the barrel is supported at a point where the taper is abrupt. Extreme care should be used to prevent chips from getting between the finished surfaces of the overarm and the body of the fixture when the overarm is moved. This is equally true of the spacer block. If chips are allowed to lodge between the two surfaces they will impair the inherent accuracy of the fixture. Brush away all chips with a small dry brush before loosening the overarm and spacer block. Do not use too much force when tightening the screws holding the overarm and spacer block.

Chapter 8

Simplified Bluing Methods

There is no better way to learn the mechanics of firearms than to blue a gun. To correctly blue, a gun must be completely dismantled piece by piece. Each type of gun has its own peculiarities. After bluing a few weapons, the theory of a gun's mechanical operation becomes ingrained in one's mind. Continued dismantling and handling of guns soon leads the person to know, almost automatically, which pieces are worn, which pieces should be replaced, etc.

A person who sets up a hot bluing operation in his home workshop will not only be able to take care of personal firearms that need bluing, but will also have a good source of extra income. One can easily charge from $30 to $75 for each gun, with materials only around $5 for each gun blued. Many gunsmith hobbyists who have learned the basic principles of gun bluing have earned upward from $300 a month bluing firearms for shooters in their neighborhoods.

In general, there are two common methods of bluing firearms: the cold method and the hot method. There are several different variations of these two methods regarding the type of bluing solution, the temperature of the solution, and other similar items. Nevertheless, the quality of a blue job, regardless of the method used depends almost entirely on the skill of the person doing the job.

If the gun being blued is expertly polished to a mirror finish, all surfaces are true and bright, corners sharp, no funnelled screwholes and ground-off screw heads, the gun is on the right track for getting an expert blue job. But there is more. The gun must be carefully cleaned and degreased just before applying the bluing solution. Then if the person follows the instructions with the type of bluing solution used, the finished weapon should have an excellent finish, regardless of the bluing method.

TOUCHUP BLUING

If firearms are given the care that they deserve, a good blue job will last the lifetime of the gun owner except for a few spots that will occasionally need to be touched up.

While there are dozens of cold blue solutions on the market, three types seem to be the most popular with gun owners, gunsmiths and hobbyists. A description of each follows:

- **Oxpho Blue.** This bluing solution, Oxpho Blue, is distributed by Brownells and is designed for the gun owner who is not equipped to completely repolish a gun prior to bluing. All you need to do, in most cases, is to dampen a piece of cotton flannel and go after the gun much like you would polish a pair of shoes. The chemical penetrates oil and rust and blues the steeel underneath, removing the rust at the same time. Tests have proven that this blue is the toughest cold blue on the market, or at least of those tested.

- **Dicropan T-4.** Dicropan T-4 is another tough bluing solution which is applied similarly to Oxpho Blue previously described. Although not quite as tough as the former, it is easier to apply and gives deep density of color. A 4-ounce bottle sells for around $4 and will blue several guns.

- **Casey's Perma Blue.** Perma Blue solution penetrates and blues steel instantly and produces a rich black finish that normally wears as long or better than the gun's original finish. Experience with this type of cold bluing solution has proved it to be one of the best for resisting rust.

For touchup work on any weapon, with any of the previously mentioned bluing solutions, merely following the directions on the labels of the containers.

FINISHING ALUMINUMS AND ALLOYS

Modern firearms are containing more and more aluminum and non steel parts, making conventional gun bluing methods useless. Parts normally consisting of aluminum or non steel materials are the trigger guard and floor plates of some rifles. Anodizing is the only way aluminum can be glued and the expense of setting up for this operation prohibits its use for the home gunsmith.

A product called Brownell's Aluma-Hyde is a spray black paint for aluminums and alloys and is one method of getting off the hook when running into an aluminum or non steel part during the bluing of an entire firearm. It is a special nitrocellulose lacquer developed for covering metal, and designed to combine all coats into one tough integrated finish.

To apply this finish, polish the metal and first apply a zinc chromate primer before applying two light coats directly from the spray can. It dries dust-free in 10 minutes, can be handled in 30 minutes, and dries to a hard, tough finish overnight. The result is a tough, scratch resistant, semi gloss finish, matching very closely the original finish. The part can be recoated anytime.

WIPE ON COLD BLUE METHOD

For those who are not set up for buffing and polishing operations, the gun parts to be blued should be cleaned with a cleaner-degreaser to remove all grease, oil and dirt. This is normally applied with a sponge and then wiped dry with a service cloth. One type of cleaner-degreaser sells for less than $2 a bottle and is manufactured by Birchwood Casey. This solution completely removes all grease, oil, dirt, wax, silicone, and so forth. It produces no harmful fumes and will not gum up.

Remove all the old bluing and any rust on the gun with emery cloth or use a liquid blue and rust remover. The latter replaces much hand work when preparing guns for rebluing.

Most brands provide a rust inhibiting film that protects the metal up to 72 hours should you not have time to complete the project in one operation. After applying the rust remover, use a small piece of steel wool to scrub all parts to be blued. Before using the steel wool, however, it should be cleaned; it comes from the factory soaked in oil to prevent rusting. To clean the wool, soak liberally in wood alcohol, then take it to a safe place *outdoors* to ignite, burning off all the oil and alcohol. Never burn it inside or allow the fumes to be inhaled.

The next step is to brighten all parts to be blued with a fine-grit abrasive cloth. Work around the barrel from the muzzle to the breech with a rapid shoe -shine motion, removing all rough spots and pits that you can. If the barrel is pitted very badly, a flat file may have to be used, but do so very carefully.

Rough barrels can also be worked down and smoothed better by using a special type of draw file as shown in Fig. 8-1. This type of file is available from Frank Mittermeier, Inc. and can be used on single and double-barreled guns, on straight and taper barrels and close to fixed sight bases, ribs and places otherwise inaccessible. Its concave shape eliminates flat spots on the barrel and eliminates the need for most cross-polishing. This draw file is 3½ inches long, which allows a firm

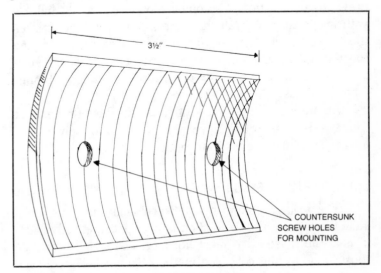

Fig. 8-1. Barrel draw file for working down barrels.

grip. It can be mounted on a wood handle by using wood screws through the two countersunk holes. The circular teeth cut fast and are spaced at the right intervals to prevent pinning and with it nasty deep scratches. For those who do not have a lathe, it is the best tool for working down and smoothing barrels of any type except those that are not round (e.g., ictagon, etc.).

Once all parts to be blued are polished, clean them again with a cleaner-degreaser using a sponge. Wear clean gloves to handle the parts after this final cleaning as skin oil will affect the final results of the bluing job. Finger marks, for example, will leave marks on the parts when blued.

Apply the cold blue solution with a cotton swab and allow the bluing solution to work for about 1 minute; wipe it off with a clean service cloth and polish the blued surface with fine steel wool that has been cleaned as described previously. Repeat the operation described in this paragraph at least three times to obtain a rich dark blue that thoroughly covers all the area. Four or five times may be necessary to obtain the desired shade.

When the desired shade is obtained, wipe the entire surface of the blued steel with a rust preventive such as Birchwood Casey's Sheath with FPR. This is a polarized rust preventive consisting of a combination of chemicals and oils with an extremely high affinity for iron and steel. It neutralizes the corrosive action of moisture, sweat and salt water, drying to a thin nongumming film which lasts through indefinite storage. It is also harmless to wood, leather and non-ferrous metals.

Another good rust preventive is Rig Rust Preventive. This type is in the form of a grease that is easy to apply to guns for absolute rust prevention from any cause.

DIP COLD BLUE METHOD

The main trouble with wipe on cold blues is that streaks sometimes result if the solution is not applied exactly right. This is the reason that most hot blue jobs look better than those done by the cold blue method. Nevertheless, a relatively new cold bluing method has been introduced by Bir-

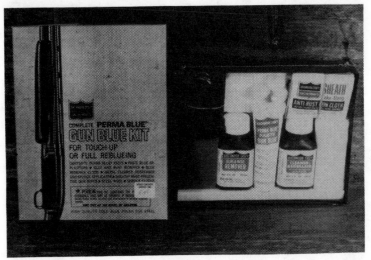
Fig. 8-2. Birchwood Casey Perma Blue kit.

chwood Casey called Perma Blue Immersion Bluing Kit. (Fig. 8-2) It is designed for bluing guns and steel parts of all kinds.

The manufacturer of this method recommends wearing rubber gloves to keep finger prints off the metal parts and to avoid any possible skin irritations.

Begin the operation by disassembling the gun or parts to be blued. If you run into any difficulty in this phase of the operation, write the manufacturer of the gun for disassembly instructions or check your local library for the book *The Encyclopedia of Modern Firearms Parts & Assembly Vol. 1* by Bob Brownell. This book has over 1,600 exploded views, photos, blueprints, sketches, schematic drawings, cutaway photos and drawings, explaining in detail how to disassemble most American firearms.

Take the cleaner-degreaser that comes with the kit and pour an amount into the plastic tank with equal parts of hot water to cover the gun parts to be blued. Let the parts soak for 2 to 3 minutes; then scrub them with a sponge. Remove the parts and rinse them under running water in a laundry sink or similar sink. Wipe all parts dry with a clean dry cloth.

The old finish must be removed by using blue and rust remover, then polishing the metal parts with an abrasive cloth. The barrel and round parts may be placed in a padded vise and polished with a rapid shoe-shine motion. For pitted areas, rub vigorously with blue and rust remover and let stand for 15 minutes before rinsing.

After removing all the old finish, repeat the cleaning step described previously, using the same solution in the tank. This solution may then be poured into a plastic container and saved for use again. Be careful not to let any of the parts to be blued come in contact with your fingers as in doing so, marks will be left on the finish. Keep the parts clean, away from any oily surfaces, etc.

Rinse the tank; then prepare the bluing solution by mixing one part of Perma Blue with three parts of water. Use only room temperature water as heating is not necessary. This should make 1 gallon of bluing solution if the entire bottle in the kit is used.

When the mixed bluing solution is in the tank, immerse all steel parts, barrel and so forth to be blued in the solution for about 1 minute. The use of wood dowels or plastic-coated wire to hold the gun barrel is a good method to keep it from resting on the bottom and to insure an even bluing of all sides. Agitate the solution gently during this 1 minute interval: then remove the parts and barrel to rinse with hot water. All of the blued parts should then be left to dry for about 30 minutes. Stand the barrel up and lay the smaller parts on a clean cotton rag.

After the parts have dried, polish all of the parts with fine steel wool, cleaned as described earlier in this chapter. Be sure to run a small pad of steel wool through the barrel with a cleaning rod to polish the inside also.

If a darker shade of blue is desired than obtained from the first immersion, repeat the steps from immersing the parts in the bluing solution two or three times until a darker more uniform blue is obtained. For hardened receivers or areas that appear streaky, rub with steel wool while immersed in the bluing solution. When the desired shade of blue is obtained, the bluing solution may be poured from the tank into a plastic container for reuse.

Use an antirust gun cloth and apply a generous coating to all metal parts. Let the parts stand for several hours before wiping off excess. The inside of the bore must be oiled also to prevent rusting.

HOT BLUING METHOD

Metal tanks, thermostat, a source of even heat, and other factors contribute to making hot bluing impractical for the average shooter with only one or two guns to blue every 5 years or so. It is usually best to take the gun to a qualified gunsmith who is set up for professional bluing jobs and get the job done there. Nevertheless, if the home gunsmith wants to make gun bluing a part-time profession, or a gun club with several members wants to set up a bluing operation for its members, then it's a whole new ball game.

Herter's, Inc. of Waseca, Minnesota supplies a hot bluing kit that is especially suited to the home gunsmith. It contains a steel bluing tank 36 inches long, approximately 8 pounds (enough for about five guns) of bluing compound, 2 ounces of blue remover, Vite cleaner, two sheets of crocus cloth and complete detailed instructions. The kit at this time sells for under $15. If the user follows instructions, a real professional gunsmith finish can be obtained with this kit.

In general, the hot bluing process involves much the same work as is required for cold bluing; that is, all metal parts to be blued are cleaned with a degreaser, rust and old blue are removed, the metal polished to a mirrorlike finish with all scratches and dents removed, then the parts are degreased again. Regular degreasing compound can be used for this process, but most professionals utilize a tank of boiling water to dip the steel parts in just prior to dipping the same parts in a tank of bluing solution, which is made from bluing salts disolved in hot water. The solution, for best results, must be brought to a temperature as specified by the manufacturer of the bluing salts. This is where a bluing thermometer comes in handy. When the salts are mixed with water, the solution is heated to a temperature of between 240 and 285 degrees Fahrenheit to produce the desired finish on the gun parts and barrel.

It is usually desirable not to blue the inside of the barrel or bore; therefore, some means of plugging up the muzzle and receiver end of the barrel becomes necessary. Tapered dowels are the favorite of gunsmiths for plugging the barrel. They also act as handles to lower the barrel into the tank. Different sizes will obviously be needed for different size bores, although since the dowels are tapered, they will normally fit more than one caliber.

BROWNING

Up to the time of the Spanish-American War, when smokeless powder was introduced for loading cartridges and shot shells, Damascus or twist barrels represented the finest in steel barrels. Many of these fine guns are still around and their owners may wish to finish them with the traditional brown finish.

Because of the method of manufacture of Damascus barrels, the grain of the metal is so arranged that it appears on the outside of the barrel in the form of irregular links or spirals. These variations account for the beautiful design which many Damascus barrels show. The intricate pattern is brought forth in its full beauty by browning, not bluing.

The cheapest Damascus barrels were the so called *band* Damascus while the better types were called, according to quality, *horseshoe, rose, Bernard, Crolle, moire* and *Laminette*. Other fine types of Damascus included those made in England, known as *Laminated Steel*. Nevertheless, even the better grades of Damascus steel barrels have been found to be unsafe with modern smokeless powder loads and should never be fired with same. Keep them on the wall where they belong.

Most of the muzzle loaders were also browned instead of blued. For restoring such weapons to their original condition, they should be browned. (Fig. 8-3 and 8-4)

A gun browner called Plum Brown is manufactured by Birchwood Casey and chemically browns steel instead of bluing. It's easy to use and gives deep color and metal penetration. Gun browner is applied very similarly to the cold blue methods as discussed earlier.

COLD BLUE FOR DOUBLE-BARRELED SHOTGUNS

It is generally not recommended to blue double-barreled shotguns by the hot blue methods as the high temperatures (as high as 285 degrees Fahrenheit) may cause the soldered

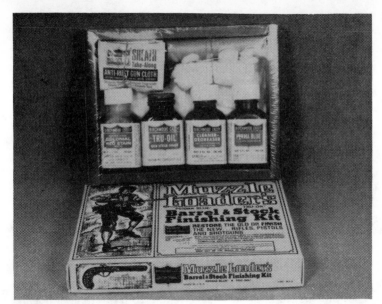

Fig. 8-3. Birchwood Casey Muzzle Loader's Barrel & Stock Finishing Kit. This kit is available in blue and brown.

barrels to come loose; therefore, a cold bluing method is desirable. Brownells Inc. distributes a professional cold blue for double-barreled shotguns shotguns called Dicropan IM.

To use the professional cold blue, polish and clean the gun as described earlier in this chapter. Then boil all barrels and

Fig. 8-4. Olde Time Finishing Kit, manufactured by Connecticut Valley Arms, Inc. The pistol shown is owned by Harold's Gun Shoppe, Waynesboro, Pennsylvania and is a replica of a Philadelphia derringer finished with the Olde Time kit.

parts in clean water. Continue by making a nitric acid solution on the barrels and parts after taking the parts from the boiling water. Swab all metal surfaces thoroughly until the parts become cool; then return them to the tank of boiling water for another 10 minutes.

Mix 5 ounces of water to 1 ounce of the bluing compound to make the blackening solution. Then again take the parts out of the boiling water and swab on the blackening solution with a cotton pad, rubbing rigorously until all parts are cool. Apply more solution until the surface is wet. Take some fine steel wool and rub hard all over the metal surfaces. Return all of the blued parts to the boiling water again until they are again hot. Remove loose rust and repeat the blackening solution application operation. Return to the tank and let boil a few minutes before repeating this operation; that is, remove all rust and return to the tank to reheat.

The last time the parts are taken from the tank of boiling water, and while the parts are still hot, apply a heavy coat of good upper-cylinder lubricant as used in automobiles. When cool, remove the oil and apply wax or light gun oil.

Chapter 9

Gun Stock Work

Gun stocks provide a foundation for the barrel and action of a firearm. The design of the stock and the precision with which the barrel and action are inletted in the stock have much to do with the accuracy of the weapon as well as the amount of recoil and other important factors.

Most gun stocks are made from wood although some are made from fiberglass or plastic. The main woods used for gun stocks are as follows:

■**American Black Walnut** This is the most popular of all gun stock woods. Better grades of gun stock walnut come from trees grown in forests rather than in open fields. Prices are largely governed by the beauty of the figure and grain. Walnut is a quality close grained and strong wood with good weight and is ideal for any type of rifle or shotgun.

■**French Walnut** This is a very dense grained wood, but also relatively light in weight with excellent warpage resistance. Many professional gunsmiths consider this to be the best of all gun stock woods. It is somewhat lighter in color than American black walnut and runs about twice as much in price.

■**Wild Cherry** This type of wood has a good dense grain, is light in weight and has excellent strength. It is the only North American wood suitable for mounting printers' engravings due to its ability not to shrink or swell.

- ■**Maple** Maple has the same weight as walnut in most cases, although some rifle blanks may be somewhat heavier. It has a good dense grain, is very strong and has good resistance against warpage. Maple is, however, one of the hardest woods to work, especially when used as a gun stock.

- ■**Myrtlewood** This wood is sometimes referred to as Oregon myrtle. It is a very good gun stock wood if it is dried properly and thoroughly. Myrtlewood has a very dense grain and is very light in color as compared to American walnut.

- ■**Claro Walnut** This wood is close to American walnut in quality, but is somewhat lighter. It is normally used on the cheaper weapons as it is less expensive and easier to work than American black walnut.

Practically all types of wood have been used for stocking rifles and shotguns, but some of the more common include Osage orange, apple, red gum, beech and birch.

All gun stocks are laid out with the grain of the wood; that is, the direction of the fibers upon the surface run lengthwise with the stock.

STOCK DESIGNS

The most common type of rifle stock manufactured today consists of what is known as the sporter stock. Such designs are available in the widest selection of woods and grades of wood available. Typical specifications for a sporter stock include:

- ■ Approximately 33 to 34 inches overall length
- ■ Trigger pull of 13¾ inches
- ■ Drop at heel about 1½ inches
- ■ Drop at toe about 6¾ inches
- ■ Height of comb must clear bolt on bolt action rifles when the bolt is in full open position
- ■ Forearm length from the front of the receiver varies considerably, but a good average is 12 inches

Target stocks are made to practically the same specifications as sporter stocks except that the area of the forearm and action is somewhat wider. Such a stock is necessary on a rifle with a large barrel diameter, so typical of rifles used for bench rest shooting and varmint hunting.

Mannlicher style stocks are made to practically the same dimensions as sporter stocks in the butt section, but the forearm extends to the muzzle of the barrel. Rarely are rifles with barrels longer than 22 inches stocked with Mannlicher type stocks. More common are barrel lengths of 18 and 20 inches.

REFINISHING GUN STOCKS

Before refinishing any type of stock, the barrel and action should be removed along with all metal parts, such as sling swivels, butt plates, etc. This will make the wood stock accessible and prevent the metal parts from becoming scratched or damaged.

The old finish may be removed in many different ways, but one of the easiest is to use a solution manufactured by Jet-Aer Corp. called Gun Stock Finish Stripper. It is safe to use on all types of wood and removes the old stock finish very quickly.

To use the stock finish stripper, first spread newspaper or other protective material beneath the stock to protect the work area. Spray one entire side of the stock. Immediately the old finish will begin to bubble and in 3 to 5 minutes the old finish will have been penetrated enough to remove. Then wipe the surface clean with an old rag, followed by steel wool. If the first coat of finish remover does not remove all of the finish, apply another coat as stated before until all of the old finish is removed.

If the stock being refinished has checkering, a stiff bristle brush may have to be used to remove the finish from the crevices. Many gunsmiths find that a stiff toothbrush works fine.

Before applying the new finish, the entire surface of the stock must be thoroughly cleaned with turpentine and allowed to dry.

Fig. 9-1. After the stock has dried rub the wood down with steel wool until smooth. It may be necessary to apply water and rub it down several times before the desired result is obtained. Continue until the grain of the wood will not rise any further.

Any type of varnish remover may also be used to soften the stock finish, but several applications will normally be necessary. For any stubborn spots, use a piece of glass for scraping, but don't scrape over any checkering or carvings for obvious reasons.

Number 0 sandpaper is then used to dull the stock surface before applying a hot lye solution consisting of 3 level tablespoons of lye to 1 gallon of boiling water. Rubber gloves must be used with this solution as well as protective goggles because any contact with the skin or eyes will cause injuries. Scrub the stock well with this solution using a stiff scrub brush, then rinse thoroughly in clear water. Once dry, the stock is ready for finishing.

FINISHING GUN STOCKS

Regardless of whether an old stock is being refinished or a new stock is to be finished for the first time, the procedure is the same. The first step is to smooth the bare wood until the surface is as smooth as glass. One way to accomplish this is to wet the stock with water and let it dry, either naturally or with heat lamps. This procedure raises the grain of the wood. Once dry, the stock is rubbed with steel wool across the grain (Fig. 9-1) until the surface is smooth. Apply water again and repeat the procedure just described. Continue this operation until the grain no longer rises after wetting.

After the stock surface is as smooth as possible, some type of wood filler, and possibly stain, should be applied to the stock (Fig. 9-2). One excellent brand is Birchwood Casey's Gun Stock Filler. This filler is used to prepare all types of gun stocks for final finishing. It has a warm walnut tone that helps bring out the beauty of the stock and dries to a clear noncloudy finish. This, or some other filler, should be applied to the

Fig. 9-2. Applying wood filler. Try Birchwood Casey's Gun Stock Filler to prepare the stock for final finishing.

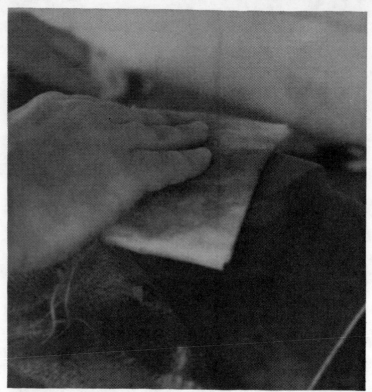

Fig. 9-3. Using a gunsmith's tack cloth to remove dust.

stock, wiped across the grain with a rag, and left to dry for at least 4 hours, preferably overnight.

When the filler has dried sufficiently on the stock, go over the entire surface with a very fine grade of steel wool before applying the stock finish.

To apply most types of stock finish, first wipe the surface with a gunsmith's tack cloth (Fig. 9-3) to remove all dust or other particles that will prevent the final finish from being completely smooth. Apply the stock finishing oil directly from the container to the stock, using your fingers (Fig. 9-4) or a cloth to evenly spread the oil with the grain of the wood. Allow this first coat to dry at least 2 hours, longer if possible. When the first coat is dry, sand the entire surface very lightly with No. 00 steel wool and apply another coat of stock finish. Repeat these steps until the desired luster is attained; this will usually take three or four coats.

When the final coat has dried completely, at least 24 hours, a good gun stock wax should be applied to the stock surface to protect the finish and to dress up the final finish. Another coating is Birchwood Casey's Stock Sheen, which is a good final polish for finished gun stocks. Just apply it directly from the bottle; it requires no hand rubbing, no rottenstone, no pumice. It also protects the finish against handling and weather.

Gun stock finish over checkered areas is usually applied with a soft bristle tooth brush and rubbed with the same until the finish takes hold. The same holds true for carvings and other indentations on the wood.

CHECKERING

Checkering pistol grips and forearms on gun stocks does require a certain degree of skill, but for the most part, patience

Fig. 9-4. Stock finishing oil can be best applied by hand as shown here.

and practice will take care of the job. The most difficult part of gun stock checkering is correctly laying out the pattern and making the first few cuts for the guide lines; the remainder of the work requires a great deal of patience and a reasonable amount of care.

Before starting a checkering job, look over the checkering jobs on some other guns to get a mental picture of what a checkering design should look like. Some designs are quite simple while others are extremely fancy. A checkering job does not have to be fancy in order to look professional. The important thing is to carefully layout and cut neat clean lines.

Once you have decided upon the pattern you want, practice checkering a portion of the pattern on an old discarded gunstock or on scrap pieces of wood, particularly on pieces which have some curved surfaces. To lay out a pattern on a curved surface, take a flexible rule and carefully draw in the shape of the pattern, using the rule as a straightedge. The first lines drawn will be the borderlines. Next draw in the two master guidelines. These lines will cross one another right in the middle of the pattern at an angle of approximately 36 to 38 degrees. This cross should run parallel to the longest length of the pattern.

Obtaining parallel lines on a curved pistol grip may seem difficult at first glance, but if you take a flexible steel rule and wrap it around the pistol grip tightly so that one edge is on the cross line as discussed in the previous paragraph, and trace this line right around the pistol grip, it will be straight. It may look a little like a cork screw, but it is straight to the surface of the wood.

When straight starting lines have been drawn, lightly cut down the center of these lines with a pocket knife to act as a starting groove for the checkering tool. But do not cut these lines very deep. The first cuts are made with a single-line cutter. Then use a two-line cutter and cut a line adjacent to each of the master lines. Care must be taken on each parallel cut because the grain of the wood, if running somewhat but not quite parallel to the line that is being cut, will have a tendency to lead the cutter off to one side or the other, making the spacing more or less than it should be (Fig. 9-5).

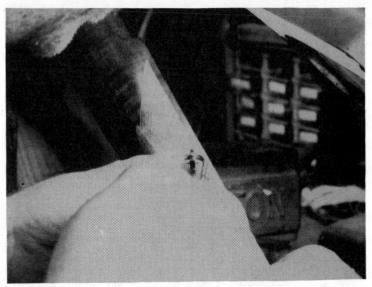

Fig. 9-5. Use both hands to guide the cutter in a straight line.

Some people like to use three- and four-line cutters as much as possible because these cutters offer more lines to guide by. Regardless of the grain of the wood, lines can be cut exactly where they should be with less chance of slipping (Fig. 9-6).

Never try to cut the lines to their full depth the first time over; cut them down approximately halfway. When all of the

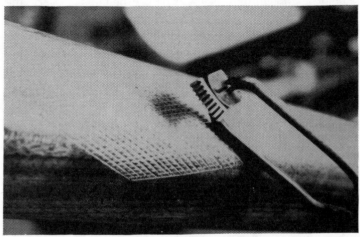

Fig. 9-6. Multiline cutters for checkering make tracking guidelines easier.

lines are cut this way, go back over the job a couple of times and work the lines down to where they are about 85 to 95 percent complete. Then use a 75-degree or 90-degree single-line finishing cutter to bring all of these diamounds to a sharp point.

Don't rush the job. When a line is cut, be sure that it is done right, regardless of how long it takes to do it. Over anxious beginners sometimes have to learn that avoidable mistakes can be made in a few seconds and may take hours to correct. Nevertheless, with good checkering tools and a little patience at the start, many do an excellent job on their first try.

BUILD A CHECKERING CRADLE

Some people may be able to checker a gun stock by using a bench vise to hold it. If the checkering designs are to be perfect, you will need a checkering cradle, like the one in Fig. 9-7. With such a cradle, the stock can be easily rotated as you move across the pattern, keeping the work area at the most comfortable, controlled position at all times. A checkering cradle is also useful for stock inletting, sanding, staining and finishing. Most bolt directly to a work bench or lock into a sturdy vise. Brownells Incorporated, Montezuma, Iowa has a very nice checkering cradle for around $10.

You can also build your own checkering cradle, but it should be thoughtfully planned before beginning. Since the average rifle stock is between 30 and 35 inches, a frame 44 inches in length will accommodate practically any gunstock you plan to work on, with the possible exception of the Mannlicher type—the type that runs to the end of the barrel. If Mannlicher stocks will also be worked on, the checkering cradle frame should be about 52 inches long.

The two upright brackets may be made of wood or metal, with two adjustable cup-pointed screws which will hold the stock between centers.

PRACTICAL APPLICATION

Let's assume that your first checkering job is going to be a rifle stock similar to the ones shown in Fig. 9-8. Here are the steps necessary for a professional job.

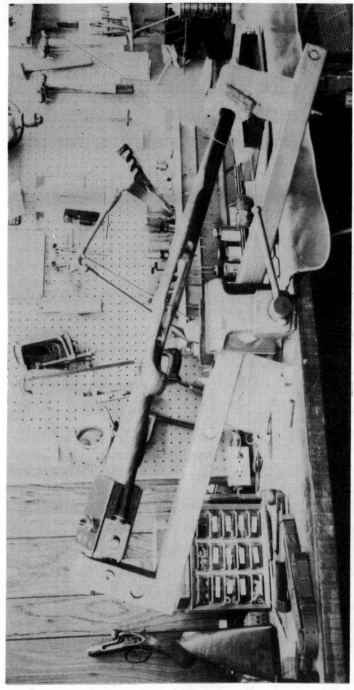

Fig. 9-7. Custom made checkering cradle used at Harold's Gun Shoppe in Waynesboro, Pennsylvania.

Step 1 Completely finish the gun stock as discussed earlier in this chapter (see Fig. 9-8).. The oil finish on the stock should have dried for at least 24 hours prior to checkering.

Step 2 Secure the stock in a checkering cradle if available. A stock can be checkered clamped to a bench or secured in a bench vise with padded jaws, but this requires that the cutting tools be rotated over the curved surface of the stock. When in a checkering cradle, the stock may be rotated while the cutting tool is advanced in a straight path.

Step 3 Layout the fore-end pattern. This may be carefully drawn or scribed on the fore-end from a pattern. More and more professionals and amateurs alike are using decal patterns for checkering or carving their gun stocks. Stan De Treville, Box 33021, San Diego, California 92103 has over twenty decal designs to satisfy practically every gun owner's taste. Here are some of the advantages of decals over designs drawn from a template or traced from a paper pattern:

- A decal may be slid around on the stock and positioned more readily than a design drawn from a template or traced from a paper pattern
- Unlike most pattern materials the decal pattern will adhere to a compound curved surface without forming wrinkles which distort the design
- The thinness of the decal material—about 0.001 inch—permits checkering right through the pattern without dulling the tools or tearing the pattern
- Printed in a dark brown on a contrasting background of yellow, decal designs show up clearly, preventing possible errors in cutting the design

To install the fore-arm decal, measure the outer surface of the stock to where it joins the barrel to determine the centerline of the stock. Now cut the patterns (decals) apart on the dotted lines. Soak the decal in warm water until the decal comes freely from the backing sheet. Align the centerline of the decal on the centerline of the gun stock. Press it in place with a cloth. Make sure the decal is perfectly aligned and free of wrinkles.

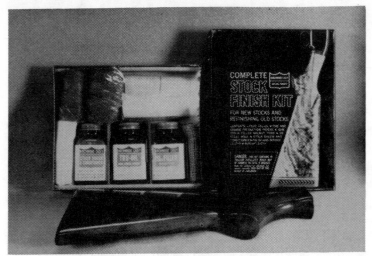

Fig. 9-8. Birchwood Casey's complete stock refinishing kit.

Step 4 Layout the design on the pistol grip which should follow the general theme of the fore-end design. If a decal is used, use the same procedures described in step 3.

Step 5 After the decals are in place, score the master guide lines with a scriber or knife. These lines should not be too deep and it is essential that these initial lines be perfectly straight. Use a flexible straightedge as a guide when making these initial cuts.

Step 6 Make the initial cuts of the master guide and border lines with a V-shaped cutting tool, using great care to follow the pattern exactly and to make straight lines parallel to the rule. These lines are cut on both the fore-end piece and pistol grip. Do not cut these to full depth.

Step 7 Next use a two-cutter (spacing tool) tool in the master guideline and cut a new line with the left edge. Apply just enough pressure to keep the cutting edges centered. Advance the tool with a push-pull motion keeping the arm close to the body to maintain straight lines. Keep the grooves free of dust by blowing or brushing.

Step 8 Proceed to cut all grooves parallel to one master guideline; again, not full depth as you will go over the grooves later with a single line finishing cutter to bring the diamonds to a sharp point.

Step 9 Now cut along the second master guideline on each decal. You will now notice flat diamonds appearing. Continue cutting the grooves in this direction to the border to complete the pattern with care so as not to break the diamonds.

Step 10 Deepen the entire pattern by going over your work a couple of times using the double-edge cutting tool; then finish the grooves with a V-shaped single cutting tool. Proceed slowly until you have gained experience. Finish all grooves to a smooth finish.

Step 11 Finish the job by sealing the checkering area with a stock preparation. This may be applied with an old toothbrush.

The checkering of gunstocks can be an interesting and profitable hobby that will greatly add to the pleasure you derive from your guns. With a little skill and patience you can transform an inexpensive, plain looking gun into one that you will be proud to show your friends.

Checkering is functional too, for in addition to adding that custom look to your guns, it provides a non-slip grip for your hands. This is important in target shooting and absolutely necessary in hunting, where a split-second delay may mean the loss of your game or even injury to you.

INLETTING

A master gunsmith can take an ugly piece of wood and turn out an excellent looking gun stock that will make even the most particular shooter proud. However, for the amateur or hobbyist, a semifinished stock blank is a more sensible way to restock a rifle or shotgun.

Most manufacturers of semifinished gun stocks offer their products for a standard model gun, inletting the barrel channel roughly. The final inletting for the barrel action is a relatively simple matter, and if approached with a little care even the most inexperienced craftsman can achieve professional results.

In general, inletting consists of constant fitting of the metal parts to the wood with slow and careful removal of the excess wood to achieve the desired results. To make this operation simpler an inletting black compound should be used

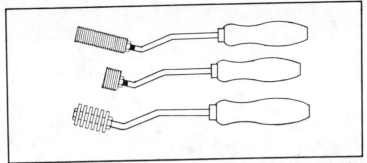

Fig. 9-9. Winton barrel inletting tools available from Frank Mittermeier, Inc. Wilton tools come in two types, solid reversible and adjustable. The solid cutters are available in two lengths and several diameters. They can be used for push or draw cutting. Adjustable cutters come in one length and three diameters.

to map out where the excess wood must be removed. Inletting black is available on the market and most brands give a good, clean impression, do not smear or penetrate too deeply into the wood and are easy to wipe off and to clean your hands. If you want to make your own inletting black, mix regular Vaseline with lamp black oil paint, obtainable at any hardware store.

Only a few tools are required for inletting a rifle stock blank. The barrel inletting rasp (see Fig. 9-9) will be used to clean out the barrel, as will chisels and gouges. Final touch-up and cleaning is accomplished with a bottoming file as shown in Fig. 9-10. Always tackle an inletting job with caution. Remove only a very little amount of wood at a time.

To begin the inletting of a semifinished rifle stock (Fig. 9-11), place the barrel action into the stock and gently tap all metal parts with a wood or plastic mallet. This will secure impressions on the wood. Remove the barreled action and examine the gun stock. Examine the impressions in the stock carefully; then coat the action and underside of the barrel with

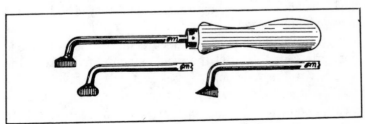

Fig. 9-10. Bottoming files available through Frank Mittermeier, Inc.

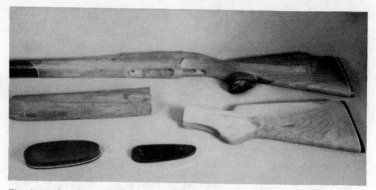

Fig. 9-11. Semifinished stocks are available through most gun shops. Shown here are several along with a butt plate and recoil pad.

inletting black. Again, place the metal parts back into the stock, press firmly and remove. Where high spots are present, light and heavy smudge marks will appear on the wood. These points should be removed with an inletting chisel (Fig. 9-12) using careful peeling cuts.

The main concern during inletting a barrel and action is to prevent slips of the chisel. Each cut must be carefully planned, removing the wood only where impressions have been made with the inletting black. For example, if the chisel is held at too great an angle, a larger chip than intended will probably be removed and once the wood is gone, it cannot be replaced. On your first attempt at inletting an action into a gun stock, the work should progress very slowly. As experience is gained the pace will gradually pick up, and what at first took hours to accomplish will only take minutes.

GLASS BEDDING

For the ultimate fit between wood and metal parts, that is, barreled action to the rifle stock, glass bedding is utilized. Such a bedding normally improves the accuracy of both old and new guns. Glass bedding is also used to repair broken stocks and grips, fill in gorges and deep dents, attach fore-end tips, grip caps, etc. But the main reason is to improve the accuracy of the weapon.

Brownells, Inc. supply a kit called Acraglas. This kit is ideal for bedding, inletting, repairing, etc. To use this kit, 1/16 to ⅛ inch of clearance should be allowed in the barrel channel and behind the recoil lug. The wood should be left rough rather than sanded smoothly as this will add strength to the wood once the glass bedding is applied as it creates more exposed wood surface.

Mix the components according to the instructions with the kit; then spread the prepared mixture in a ridge down the center of the barrel channel to prevent air being trapped when the barrel is seated. Also fill the recoil lug recess sufficiently to completely fill the recess when the action is fitted. Firmly press in the barrel and action to the desired depth.

When the mixture shows signs of hardening, remove any surplus with a dull knife or spatula, being careful not to scratch any of the metal parts. Leave a very small bead of the glass compound above the wood between the stock and metal to be sanded to contours of stock after the final curing.

Under normal conditions, the barreled action can be removed from the stock within 24 to 36 hours. In cases of extremely tight fits, the careful use of a soft rubber mallet will help to get the metal apart from the stock.

Should voids be discovered between the metal and glass once the barrel and action have been removed, a fresh mixture may be applied. Be sure all voids are filled completely and that these voids are free of the release agent, described in the instructions, before filling with the fresh mixture.

Other uses of epoxy compound are as follows:

- Shimming scope mounts which do not properly fit the gun's receiver.
- Filling gaps between butt plates and grip caps.
- Permanently attaching fore end tips, grip caps, inlays, etc.

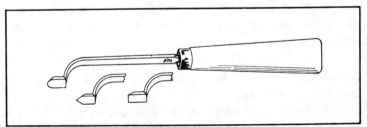

Fig. 9-12. Bottoming chisels used by Europe's master gunsmiths, available through Frank Mittermeier, Inc.

- Repairing anything aluminum—gun parts, camping equipment, boats.
- Making form fitting holding jigs, barrel vise jaws, clamp faces.
- As buildup shims for leveling equipment and machinery.
- To build up eyes in hammer or axe heads to give long lasting fit.
- Repairing enlarged sling swivel screw holes.
- As a pressure point in partially free floating fore stocks.
- Strengthening weak wooden fore stocks by cutting groove or grooves in barrel channel and filling with glass compound.

Carry some of the compound with you when going on extended trips into the back country. You never know when your having it along with you will make it possible to change what could have been a camp disaster into nothing more or less than a minor camp repair job.

REFINISHING MILITARY STOCKS

Stocks for most sporting weapons are relatively easy to finish since the hard finish prevents oils from penetrating into the wood, and this finish can be removed with a good grade of varnish remover. On military stocks, it is an entirely different story. The wood is often grainy, the wood is soaked with dark oils, bore cleaner, and so forth. Most have also seen hard use in the field, showing many nicks and scratches all over the wood area.

To overcome these problems with military stocks, it has been the practice in the past to restock these weapons with a new sporting stock; however, the value of military rifles has increased tremendously and it is recommended that their original components not be altered. Rifles should be refinished as nearly as possible to their original appearance. So, we are once again stuck with the problem of refinishing poor-looking and beat up military stocks (see Fig. 9-13).

To refinish a military stock, first disassemble the rifle completely. A disassembled Grande, .30 cal. M1, is shown in Fig. 9-14. All of these pieces must be carefully stored so they

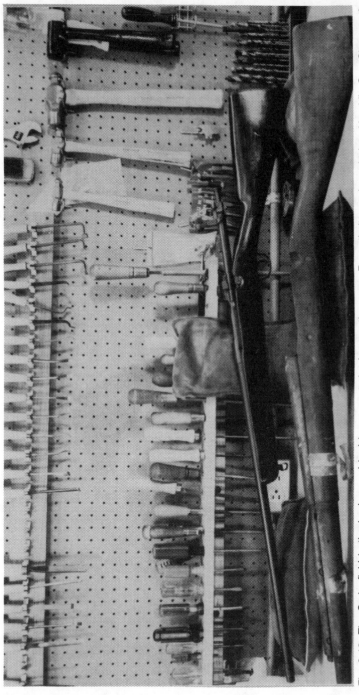

Fig. 9-13. The Springfield in the background had been sporterized some time ago. Recently it was brought into Harold's Gun Shoppe of Waynesboro, Pennsylvania to be fitted with an original military full-length stock, shown in the foreground.

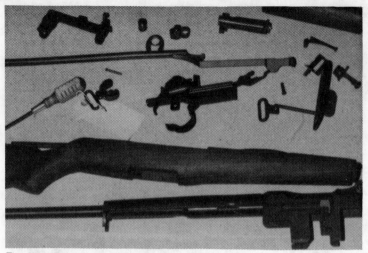

Fig. 9-14. Disassembled Grande .30-caliber M1.

will not become lost. Place the small parts, such as screws, pins, etc., in a plastic bag and tightly tie off the end. These bags, along with the other metal parts, should then be stored in some type of container, such as a cardboard box.

To illustrate what you will run into on military stocks, look at the wood grain of the stock in Fig. 9-15. Note the rough surface of this stock and imagine the amount of time required to smooth it down. The pistol grip in Fig. 9-16 is also typical of military stock you will encounter in gun repair work. Much reshaping and sanding are required. You will also find many dents like ones on the fore end in Fig. 9-17.

Once all of the metal parts are removed from the wood, mix a solution consisting of ½ cup of liquid bleach and 1 cup of Mr. Clean, or similar cleaning agent, to 2 gallons of water. Then with a stiff cleaning brush scrub the stock well for about 10 minutes as shown in Fig. 9-18. Then use a gas burner (Fig. 9-19), hot plate, or heat lamps to heat the stock. This will raise the grain, bringing oil and other finishes to the surface. The solution mentioned previously will also tend to lighten the wood, which most of the time is very dark from the soaked-in oil.

The heat will dry the solution quickly as shown in Fig. 9-20, but be sure not to let the stock get too hot and char. If this occurs, you really will be in trouble.

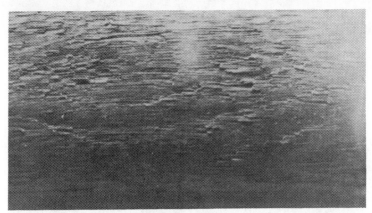

Fig. 9-15. Closeup of the wood grain on military stocks. You've got your work cut out for you refinishing something similar to this.

After the wood is completely dry, use a medium grade of steel wool and go over the complete stock. Do not use sandpaper at this time. During the heating process, the wood whiskers will rise to the surface and the steel wool will cut them off even with the stock surface. Sandpaper will mash them down into the wood, which will rise again and again. You

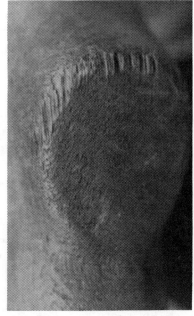

Fig. 9-16. Closeup of pistol grip with very rough grain. Military stocks show a lot of battle scars.

175

Fig. 9-17. This view of an end with dents is typical of what you will run across when refinishing military stocks.

want to remove these whiskers. Once the wood has been completely gone over with the steel wool, sand the surface a few minutes with medium grit sandpaper. Then repeat the process; that is, scrub the wood with the bleach-cleaner solution, heat the wood, then smooth down.

It may take as many as 15 times of scrubbing, heating and sanding to get the surface in good shape for refinishing, maybe more! Once most of the oil is removed, you will always have a few spots that want to be difficult. These spots will usually occur around the butt plate, the trigger guard and action. Rather than scrubbing the entire stock, hold these spots over a heat source until the oil begins to bubble to the surface of the stock. Then immediately wipe the oil off with a rag. Repeat this operation until all of the oil is raised to the surface.

To facilitate the removing of the oil, you might want to purchase a small can of plain whiting at your local hardware store and some type of grease solvent like chlorothene. Put a few ounces of whiting in a small jar and stir in just enough solvent so that the mixture can be spread on the wood with a paint brush. Now heat the stubborn spots again and when the oil bubbles to the surface, coat the area with the whiting-chlorothene mixture. The chlorothene will penetrate deeply into the wood and dissolve most of the oil and grease it

Fig. 9-18. Method of cleaning military stock before refinishing. Mix a half-cup of Clorox and a cup of Mr Clean with 2 gallons of water; then scrub the stock for at least 10 minutes.

encounters. As it evaporates, it brings the oil and grease to the surface of the wood, which are absorbed by the whiting on the surface.

When all of the old finish is removed, use several grades of sandpaper to smooth the surface. Start with a medium grade and work down to very fine.

Fig. 9-19. Heating the stock after cleaning to raise the grain. This brings oil and old finishes to the surface.

Fig. 9-20. Heating the stock using the method shown will dry out the wood very quickly. Be careful not to overheat the stock.

Small dents may be removed by soaking a small cloth with water (a wash cloth is fine), placing the wet cloth over the dent, then heating the cloth with an iron or soldering gun. The steam produced by the heat on the cloth will raise the dent. Repeat until the dent is flush with the surrounding area.

For bad dents and gouges, smooth them flush with the remaining surfaces with a piece of broken glass; or fill in the dents as discussed elsewhere in this book.

Once the wood surface is ready for finishing, finish as described previously in this chapter. One type of good commercial stock finisher for military stock is a product called Dem-Bart Stock Finish and Sealer-Filler. This waterproof oil finish seals and hardens the wood, having a desirable low sheen, London-type finish. It is not quite as quick as some of the finishes on the market, but the fine results are well worth the extra effort. Additional coats of the finish may be applied at any later date to refinish a stock that has been scratched from normal field use.

The sealer-filler is used prior to the stock finish when working with open grain wood. It seals and protects the wood against moisture, prepares the stock for finish with minimum effort. It dries ready for sanding in 15 minutes.

Chapter 10

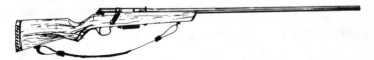

Practical Trigger Repairs

All experienced shooters know that a correct trigger pull is essential for good accuracy in any type of rifle. In general, this correct trigger pull consists of a short, 3-pound pull. Any trigger pull that is much more than 3 pounds will not enable the shooter to control his or her shots as well. Any pull less than 3 pounds is normally too light for hunting, although most bench rest shooters use set triggers with much less than a 3-pound trigger pull. The reason for the ultralight trigger pull for target shooting is that such a pull eliminates the neccessity of the shooter taking his or her mind off the subject of aiming. Also the light trigger pull prevents fatigue of the arm and finger muscles when a number of shots are fired.

TRIGGER MECHANISMS

There are nearly as many different trigger mechanisms as there are guns. Some are designed for target shooting, some are used on hunting rifles, while others were designed for military use. Some are naturally better than others, but in all cases there is always a point of contact between the striking mechanism, the hammer or tumbler that strikes the firing pin, and a sear.

Figure 10-1 illustrates a typical trigger mechanism. To adjust a trigger pull, all parts should be polished first to decrease drag on the moving parts. All sear contact faces or notches must be clean and square with sharp edges. If not, they must be honed with an Arkansas or slip stone, but this is not an easy task without rounding the edges. Remember, the edges must be square for a creepless, crisp letoff.

One aid in stoning a notch to shape is to line up two pieces of 1/16-inch flat stock with the sear notches and stone across them. You will perhaps need a jeweler's eyeglass of medium power to inspect the contacting surfaces to detect any unevenness or deep tool marks made by the stoning. Then stone just enough to eliminate the amount of drag or creep desired.

IMPROVING MILITARY TRIGGERS

Trigger mechanisms on Springfield, Enfield, Mauser, Jap, Krag and other military rifles are always a problem. Any amount of stoning will do little good and most of the time, the sear top or the bottom of the cocking piece will have to be cut down.

Viggo Miller, P.O. Box 4181, Omaha, Nebraska sells a simple device to eliminate the military takeup and to adjust the depth of the trigger sear engagement. Figure 10-2 shows this device applied to several types of military trigger mechanisms.

Referring to Fig. 10-2, the following tells how to install the trigger device on various types of military rifles.

Springfield Rifles

Place adjusting screw bracket E with the stop on the bracket against the stop on the trigger. There is no lip F on the Springfield attachment. Remove screw A from clamp D. Back out set screw B so it is flush with inside of clamp. Slip clamp D over bracket E and trigger with set screw B next to receiver. Be sure upper edge of clamp is in notch on bracket. Insert screw A and screw in snugly. *Don't tighten*. Tighten set screw B; then tighten screw A. Now screw adjusting screw C in or out to obtain the desired trigger pull.

In the event the stock does not have clearance enough around the trigger mechanism, some wood must be removed to accommodate the attachment. Also when the regular issue Springfield stock is used, the screw that passes through the

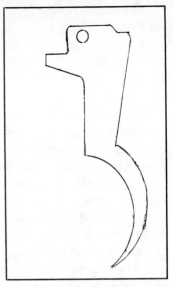

Fig. 10-1. Typical trigger mechanism.

stock just ahead of the trigger must be removed. By cutting ½ inch out of the middle of the screw shank then dipping the two end pieces in glue, they can be used to plug the screw hole.

Sometimes a very thin trigger is encountered on these Springfield rifles. If this is the case, point F of detail 2 Fig. 10-2 may be bent upward closing the gap to fit the trigger.

Enfield Rifles

When installing this trigger attachment to the Enfield Model 1917 rifle, a small amount of material must be removed from point H in detail 1 of Fig. 10-2. This point on the sear prevents the trigger being pulled until the bolt is completely closed. If it is desired to retain this Enfield feature, proceed as follows:

Remove the action from the stock, and remove the bolt from the receiver. Hook the adjusting screw bracket over trigger stop as shown in detail 2 of Fig. 10-2. Now force point G back against trigger. There is some variation in the thickness of the Enfield trigger stops. If your trigger stop is thin be sure point F of detail 2 in Fig. 10-2 is against trigger stop when tightening set screw B. If the trigger stop is too thick, force point G back against trigger with a pair of pliers. This will spread the hook to fit the trigger stop.

Remove screw A from clamp D. Slip clamp D over bracket E and trigger, leaving about 1/16 inch of bracket E extending above the clamp. Be sure set screw B does not protrude inside the clamp. Now insert screw A and screw in snugly—*don't tighten*. Now tighten set screw B, then tighten screw A.

Adjust the trigger with adjusting screw C so the first or lightest stage of the pull is eliminated. Insert the bolt in receiver and observe if point H in detail 1 of Fig. 10-2 of sear obstructs or drags on bolt. If it does, remove trigger and sear assembly by pushing out the pin that attaches the sear and trigger assembly to the receiver. Remove a small amount of material from point H in detail 1 by grinding or with a file. Replace the assembly to try the bolt again. If care is exercised in grinding this point, the trigger cannot be pulled unless the bolt is completely closed.

Many do not care for this feature because the Enfield is just as safe without it as many other rifles which do not have it. In the event you feel this safety is not needed, remove about 1/32 inch from point H in detail 1 and save time on the installation. Some wood may have to be removed from the stock around the trigger. In most cases mortising out for a distance about ½ inch ahead of trigger, ¼ inch deep, is all that is required.

Mauser Rifles

The first step on the Mauser rifle is to remove the action from the stock. Hook adjusting screw bracket E under the stop on the trigger. Remove screw A from clamp D. Back out screw B until flush with inside of clamp D. Then slip clamp over bracket and trigger, with set screw B next to the receiver. Insert screw A in bracket; screw in snugly. *Don't tighten*. Be sure the upper part of clamp D is below or in the notch on adjusting screw bracket E.

Tighten set screw B then tighten screw A. Now screw adjusting screw C in or out to obtain the desired trigger pull. In the event your stock does not have clearance enough around the trigger, a little wood must be removed to accommodate the attachment.

When this attachment is being used on the Models 93, 94 and 95 Mausers, follow Enfield instructions relating to altering point H of detail 1 in Fig. 10-2.

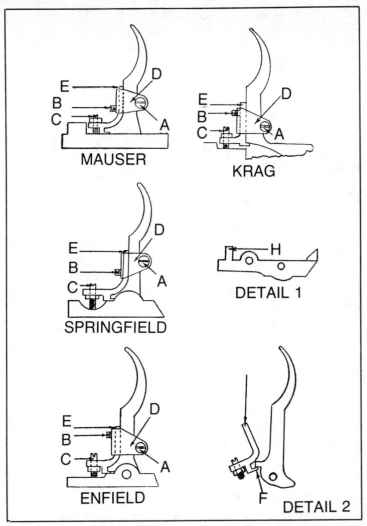

MAUSER

KRAG

SPRINGFIELD

DETAIL 1

ENFIELD

DETAIL 2

Fig. 10-2. Viggo Miller's simple device to improve trigger pulls in military weapons.

Krag Rifles

The stock or Krag rifles must be removed from the action. Hook adjusting screw bracket E into slot at base of the trigger. Back set screw B out until it is flush with inside of clamp D. Remove screw A. Push clamp D over bracket E and trigger; replace screw A. The trigger is tapered and if the clamp is at the upper part of the taper it will be easier to insert screw A. Then push the clamp down on the taper, being sure lip C of detail 2 in Fig. 10-2 on the bracket remains tight against the base of the trigger. Now tighten set screw B, then screw A.

Now adjust the trigger by turning adjusting screw C in or out as needed to obtain the desired trigger pull; lock adjusting screw C with the lock nut.

Your stock may not have clearance enough around the trigger to accommodate the attachment. If this is the case, remove a little of the wood ahead of the trigger.

TRIGGER REPLACEMENT

For ultimate speed, safety and accuracy in a converted military weapon, it is usually best to replace the issue trigger with an all new easily adjustable trigger mechanism. These mechanisms are available on the market for $25.00 or less. In most cases no alterations are required to replace the issue trigger with the more modern one.

Dayton-Traister Company, for example, manufactures an all-steel trigger with case hardened operating parts, expertly honed to deliver crisp, uniform trigger pulls every time. The tempered, treated and blued springs resist corrosion and fatigue and the grooved finger area helps provide a non-slip finger grip. Trigger mechanisms are commonly available for Enfield, Springfield, Mauser, Japanese and other military weapons as well as most sporting arms.

Custom triggers are normally adjustable from 2 to 6 pounds to give a converted military rifle faster lock time and increased accuracy with a uniform, crisp trigger pull.

For target or bench rest shooters, a double-set trigger mechanism is often installed. Double-set triggers, as the name implies, give two advantages to the shooter with the front trigger serving two purposes:

- To fire the gun at a normal trigger pull weight as set by the installer at the time of installation.
- Letoff at a true hair-trigger setting when cocked by the rear trigger.

The front or hair trigger on most mechanisms is fully adjustable for letoff pull weight from ounces to several pounds. Such a trigger mechanism is especially suitable for unusually long shots when even the faintest pull when firing the gun could cause a complete miss. Such triggers have long been popular with serious varmint shooters, bench rest shooters and other precision shooters.

Most double-set trigger mechanisms are easily installed on weapons with conventional mechanisms. Slight alterations are normally required to the trigger guard slot and some stock wood where the existing trigger protrudes.

TRIGGER SHOES

Wide, serrated trigger shoes are available for nearly all rifles, handguns and shotguns (Table 10-1). Their function is to evenly spread trigger release pressure over the ball of the trigger finger. With the evenly spread pressure, the trigger pull seems lighter and gives the shooter that delicate feel so necessary for controlled letoff for the best possible accuracy. Obviously, trigger shoes are very pouplar among competitive rifle, pistol and shotgun shooters and also anyone wanting to make a favorite gun perform better.

When trigger shoes are installed, the user should be aware that the added weight of a trigger shoe may contribute to the accidental firing of a gun if it is dropped. Furthermore, the seemingly less pull may cause the shooter to accidentally fire a round before he or she is ready.

TOOLS FOR TRIGGER WORK

The tools required for good trigger work—even in the professional gun shops—are few and relatively inexpensive. A description of the most needed ones follows.

Trigger Pull Gauges

Trigger pull gauges are available in two different types. One is a direct reading type that measures trigger pull in both ounces and grams. Such gauges normally have a finger-tab adjustment of the gauge face to give a positive zero setting. To use, the weapon is placed with the stock butt against a solid object, the pull gauge hook is then rested against the trigger, and the gauge ring is held in the hand of the operator. Pressure is applied, all the while noticing the calibrations and pointer on the scale, until the hammer snaps. The reading at the time of the snapping is the trigger pull weight.

The other type of gauge uses weights in place of a gauge, but its use is very similar. Where ultimate accuracy in trigger pull is needed, this is the best gauge to use as weights are carefully calibrated for accurate checking of trigger pulls from 2 pounds to 4½ pounds, in 4-ounce increments.

To use this type, the weapon to be checked must be held vertically with the muzzle up and the trigger cocked. The trigger weight, resting on the floor or bench, must have the trigger arm placed against the trigger with no tension whatever. The gun is then raised vertically, lifting the weight with the center of the trigger straight up. If the trigger does not release the bolt or hammer, the operation is repeated, this time with an additional 4-ounce weight.

This operation is repeated until the hammer or striking piece is released. The total amount of weights on the apparatus at the time of trigger release is the amount of trigger pull. In using this method of trigger pull measuring, remember that the weapon must be raised very gradually. One way to help in providing a gradual raising of the weapon without any tension is to rest the trigger weights on a thick rectangular sponge or similar yielding surface. This allows the trigger to receive the weight tension very slowly, as the weapon is lifted.

Stones For Trigger Work

Hard Arkansas oil stones are necessary for precision trigger and sear work. These oil stones are superior to metal files as the latter will scratch the stock. Here are some of the most common type in use.

- ■ **Square Stone**—used for cleaning corners or where some material is to be removed without scratching.
- ■ **Triangular Stone**—for the same kind of work as the square shapes but used on jobs having sharp or deep grooves.
- ■ **Round Stone**—widely used for lapping round holes and for stoning and cleaning. Also used on many curved edges.

Table 10-1. Ace trigger shoes.

Model	Code
Anschutz 22	12
Anschutz Target Rifle	24
Anschutz 64 Target	2
Beretta	20
Blackhawk	9
British 303	22
Browning Auto (old)	6
Browning Auto (new)	23
Browning Super Light	21
Browning F. N.	12
Browning O/U	5
Browning 9m/m Pistol	6
BSA Rifle	1
Browning 22 Cal.	2
Canjar Trigger	13
BSA Monarch	23

COLT

Model	Code
Agent	10
25 Auto	3
32 & 380 Auto	20
38 Super Auto	20
45 Auto (late model)	3
45 Auto (old model—long trigger)	20
57 Deluxe	13
.357 Mag.	8
Bankers Special	10
Challenger	5
Cobra	10
Commander	20
Commando	2
Centenial	8
Courier	10
Detective Special	10
New Service	17
New 1956 Match	23
OM Target Match	8
OM Target Special (new model)	8
OP	8
Pre-War Woodsman	18
Police Positive	10
Python	8
Scout	24
Sentinel	8
Shooting Master	17
Single Action	24
Sports & Target Woodsman	23
Terrier	14
Trooper	8
Woodsman (late model)	5
Dayton Traister Trigger	13
Enfield Model 1917	22
Esquire	16
Finnbear	12
F. N. (reg. & 300 series)	13
400 Series FN	11
Franchi	14
GEW 41	10
Great Western Single Action	24
High Standard (most models)	4
High Standard Sentinal	22
HVA	12
H&R Double 9	23
Huntsman	23
Ithaca 37	3
Jap 6.5	7
Jap 7.7	1
Jaeger (old model)	12
Jaeger (new model)	13
JCH Model 88	8
Krag	24
LAMA 380	3

MARLIN

Model	Code
39A, 336, 56	6
222	9
Mannlicher Sch.	12
Marshall	1
Mashburn Trigger	12
Matador	2
Mauser 98	12
M1 Carbine	6
M1 Garand	11
Model 999	23

Model	Code
46B Mossberg 144 LS	14
Mossberg 300 B	13
Ortgies	20

REMINGTON

Model	Code
581	6
11-48	3
30	22
31	6
34	14
37	16
58 Auto	20
121	6
141	7
510, 511, 512, 513, 513T, 512X	9
514, 521	9
572	3
760 (old)	3
760 (new)	24
721 722 (old model)	7
740, 742	9
700 ADL	23
870	24
1100	3
40X	23
Ruger Mark I & Mark II Auto.	15
Ruger Single Six	24
Ruger M77	3
Ruger 1 (single shot)	17

SAVAGE

Model	Code
23D	9
99	19
101	9
110	16
340-B & C	23
219 B	11
Sako L57 (old model)	9
Sako L579 (new), L46	11
Sako L461	12
Schultz & Larsen	12
Springfield 03, 03A3, 22	11
Stevens Walnut Hill	17
Stevens M416	17
Stevens 54 A	11

SMITH & WESSON

Model	Code
1917	17
1950, .357 Mag, 38/44, Airflite	1
Airweight	14
Bodyguard	14
Chief Special	14
DA Army Special	1
K-22 (old model), K-38	1
Kit Gun	14
M. & P., Patrolman	1
Timney	11
Walther P. P.	23
Wby Mark V	2
Whitney Wolverine	7
Kreigoff O/U, Star Auto	20

WINCHESTER

Model	Code
12, 21, 42	6
43	2
50	6
52 (old model), 52B	21
54	2
61	5
69, 70	2
71	17
72A	2
74	5
75	2
77, 88	10
94	19
97	6
100	10
101	12
HI & Low Wall	6
New 70 Win.	23
Win. 1400, Win. 250	6
Charles Daly	2
1200	3

- **Half-Round Stone**—for trigger mechanisms having both straight and curved edges.

Some of the other shapes include taper round stones, knife blade, bench stones and similar combinations.

Always use a good stone of the proper cutting grade for the particular job at hand. Natural Arkansas stones are the only stones in the world that polish as they sharpen, and these remarkable stones are known the world over for their ability to put superior cutting edges on knives, chisels and other precision cutting tools. The purchase of a set of Arkansas stones will not be limited to trigger work alone.

Arkansas stones are separated into four distinct grades: Washita, soft Arkansas, hard Arkansas and black hard Arkansas. Each grade has a special sharpening application as recommended below:

- **Washita** This is the most rapid cutting stone of the lot. It is used to start edges on knives for all who desire a keen edge in the minimum of time. It will sharpen a knife for shaving purposes.
- **Soft Arkansas** This is probably the best general-purpose stone as it produces and maintains very sharp polished edges on all knives and tools.
- **Hard Arkansas** This type of stone is used for touching up and final polishing of an already sharp edge. It does not sharpen as quickly as the softer stone, but for a truly polished, razor-sharp edge, the time is well worth the effort.
- **Black Hard Arkansas** Again, this type of stone is used only on the already sharp blades. It will give the ultimate finish.

Honing oil is used with all sharpening stones to keep them cutting faster and to prevent metal particles from clogging the pores. Other types of stones include India stones, which are used primarily for sharpening extremely hard metals, and Ruby stones, which will cut any tool, steel, hardened steel and tungsten carbide.

NEEDLE FILES

Needle files are unsurpassed for use in tight areas and on odd-shaped pieces. They will find much use in fitting trigger mechanisms, safeties, trigger shoes and many other items. Needle files will be found on every professional gunsmith's bench. They will also find many uses for work done by the hobbyist.

Chapter 11

Hints of Value

The home gunsmith will more than likely be using metal drill bits frequently and for best results and to eliminate breakage, they should be kept sharp at all times. The data contained herein is designed to aid the gunsmith—professional and hobbyist alike—in caring for metal-cutting drills.

Elimination of drill breakage depends to a very great extent on the correct point grinding of the drill. When the drill is worn down by use, it must be ground or breakage will result. Not only must a drill be ground, but it must be properly ground in order to insure maximum drilling life. It has been estimated that 90 percent of all drill breakage is caused by incorrect grinding. For this reason, too much emphasis cannot be laid on the importance of this operation.

Point grinding by hand requires great skill and care on the part of the operator. Whenever skilled help is not available, the use of a point-grinding machine is recommended.

When pointing a drill, four things must be carefully considered: (1) lip clearance, (2) point angle, (3) cutting edges, (4) point thinning.

Lip Clearance Lip clearance is one of the most important features of the drill point. The angle of lip clearance should be within 12 to 15 degrees, measured at the circumference of the drill. If the angle is greater it weakens the cutting edge; if smaller, there is not sufficient clearance to allow the cutting lip to enter the work, and the usual result is that the drill splits up the center.

Point Angle The angle of a drill point is measured to the axis of the drill. The proper point angle of a drill depends upon the material being drilled. All standard drills are furnished with 59-degree points, as this angle has proven to be the most suitable for the average class of work. In general, it can be said that the harder the material the greater the point angle should be. For example, a point angle of 75 degrees is recommended for manganese steel, while for wood, fiber, and similar materials, a point angle of 30 degrees is recommended.

Cutting Edges The cutting edges of a drill must make exactly the same angle with the center line of the drill. In other words, while the 59-degree angle may vary a trifle one way or the other, the variation must be uniform in both cutting edges. A difference in angle will cause one edge to cut differently from the other, thus putting an unequal strain on the two edges.

If the cutting edges are of unequal length, the result is that the point or chisel point is off-center even though the point angle may be uniform on both edges. This condition will cause the drill to cut oversize.

If the point angle is changed from 59 degrees, as originally made it will be found that, due to this change, the cutting edges are no longer straight but have become either convex or concave. If the point angle is changed appreciably, it may be necessary to grind the flutes of the drill in order to produce straight cutting edges.

Point Thinning The web of a drill increases in thickness toward the shank and a web-thinning operation becomes necessary when the drill has been shortened by repeated grindings. This operation is essential in order to minimize the pressure required to make the drill penetrate. The point-thinning operation must be carried out equally on both sides of the web, otherwise the web will be off-center and the drill will produce an oversize hole. Care must also be taken to see that the thinning operation is not carried too far up the web, thus weakening the point of the drill. As a general rule, a web thickness at the point of approximately 12½ percent (⅛) of the drill diameter, is recommended.

GRINDING WHEELS FOR HIGH-SPEED DRILLS

A soft medium-grain wheel approximately 12 inches by 2 inches should be used. Drills should be ground on the face and not on the side of wheels. The face of the wheel should be trued by proper dressing before drills are ground, otherwise correct results cannot be obtained. The drill should be held at an approximate angle of 45 degrees to the vertical. All point grinding must be done dry.

If during grinding the drill is accidentally allowed to get too hot, it should never be cooled in water but should be allowed to cool of its own accord. A sudden cooling is almost sure to produce grinding checks. If the drill has been re-pointed, it should be examined in order to make sure that the margin shows no sign of wear, particularly at the extreme corners of the drill point.

CRANKSHAFT DRILLS

A crankshaft drill is made with a very heavy web that must be thinned or changed in shape at each grinding. This operation is somewhat different from that ordinarily followed when point grinding standard drills.

In the first operation, the drill is pointed with a 59-degree point angle, about a 9-degree lip clearance and a 125-degree angle chisel edge. The wheel to use is a 12- by 2- by 1-inch size grade 36L. It is important that the cutting lips be of equal angle and length.

The drill is then taken to another wheel for the web-thinning operation. This procedure might be correctly termed an additional pointing operation since two new cutting edges are produced. Some users prefer to rough down this part of the point on the wheel, then finish as described in the process that follows. Others prefer to do all the web thinning on a separate wheel. Either procedure may be followed. These two new cutting edges should be ground to the center of original chisel edge, reducing the non cutting chisel edge to practically a point.

The drill is held at an angle of about 30 degrees with the vertical and touches the wheel periphery at a point just below its center line. The wheel to use is a 6- # 2 by 1- by ½-inch size, grade 60N, dressed to a sharp corner. It is essential that the grinding wheel has a sharp square corner and that it runs with minimum vibration or bearing play. The drill point must be brought up to the wheel very carefully so that the original chisel edge is not ground out.

LATHE OPERATION

Most home gunsmiths will seldom have enough work to warrant purchasing an expensive metal-cutting lathe. Nevertheless, those who do gun repair as a part or full-time living will find such a tool indispensable. The paragraphs to follow in this section generally describe the operation of a metal-cutting lathe.

Before starting a new lathe, the operator should carefully study the action of the various parts and become thoroughly familiar with the operation of all control levers and knobs.

The principal parts of a lathe will usually be shown in the owner's manual accompanying the tool. Become familiar with the name of each part as they will be referred to frequently in details of operation.

Do not operate the lathe under power until it is properly set up and leveled. Also make sure that all bearings have been oiled and the belt tension, between the motor and the lathe pulley, is correct. Always give the lathe pulley a twist by hand to make sure the lathe runs freely before starting a lathe under power.

Spindle speeds are usually changed by shifting the belt from one slot of the pulley to another and by engaging or disengaging the back gears.

Lathes can sometimes be reversed by reversing the electric drive motor. Nevertheless, most lathes have a feed reverse lever on the headstock that has three positions: up, central and down. The central position is neutral, and when in this position all power carry feeds are disconnected. When the lever is in the up position or down position, the power carry feeds will be in operation.

To operate the lathe carriage and apron, the apron hand-wheel is turned to move the carriage along the lathe bed, and the cross feed knob and compound rest knob are turned to move the tool rest in and out. The carriage lock screw is used to lock the carriage to the lathe bed. This screw should never be tightened except for facing or cutting-off operations.

Lathes equipped with an automatic feed friction clutch have the advantage of controlling the operation of both the automatic longitudinal power feed and the automatic power cross feed. To engage the clutch, turn the clutch knob to the right; to disengage, turn to the left. The direction of the feed is controlled by the position of the reverse lever on the headstock.

Most feed change levers have three positions: up for longitudinal feeds, down for cross feeds, and center for neutral position. The half-nut lever is used only for thread cutting. The feed change lever must be in the center or neutral position before the half-nuts can be engaged with the lead screw.

The tailstock slides along the lathe bed and may be locked in any position by tightening clamp bolt nut. To lock the tailstock spindle, tighten the binding lever by pulling it forward.

A wide range of power longitudinal feeds and power cross feeds is available on all quick change gear lathes. To obtain any desired feed it is only necessary to arrange the levers on the gear box according to the direct reading index chart shown on most lathes.

Standard change gear lathes are equipped with a set of independent change gears for cutting screw threads and obtaining various power longitudinal feeds and power cross feeds. A large screw gear should be placed on the lead screw and a small stud gear on the reverse stud. These two gears should be connected with a compound idler gear. To obtain finer or coarser feeds, smaller or larger stud gear is used.

LATHE TOOLS & THEIR APPLICATION

In order to machine metal accurately and efficiently, it is necessary to have the correct type of lathe tool with a sharp, well-supported cutting edge, ground for the particular kind of metal being machined, and set at the correct height. High-speed steel cutter bits mounted in forged steel holders are the most popular type of lathe tools.

The boring tool, cutting-off tool, threading tool and knurling tool are required for various classes of work that cannot be readily accomplished with the regular turning tool.

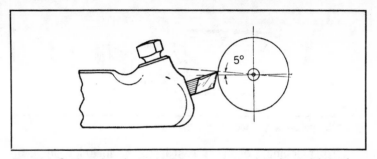

Fig. 11-1. Cutting edge of cutter bit 5 degrees above center for straight turning.

The cutting edge of the cutter bit should be about 5 degrees above center, or 3/64 inch per inch in diameter of the work, as shown in Fig. 11-1 for ordinary straight turning. The position of the cutter bit must be taken into consideration when grinding the various angles, as the height of the cutter bit determines the amount of front clearance necessary to permit free cutting.

The cutting edge of the cutter bit should always be placed exactly on center, as shown in Fig. 11-2 for all types of taper turning and boring, for cutting screw threads and for turning brass, copper and other tenacious metals.

The included angle of the cutting edge of a cutter bit is known as the tool angle or angle of keenness and varies with the texture of the work to be machined. For example, when turning soft steel a rather acute angle should be used. But for machining hard steel or cast iron the cutting edge must be well supported; therefore, the angle is less acute.

It has been found that an included angle of 61 degrees is the most efficient tool angle for machining soft steel. This is the angle of the cutter bit as shown in Fig. 11-3.

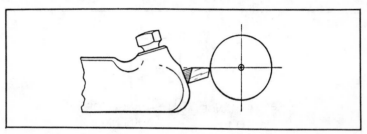

Fig. 11-2. Cutting edge of cutter bit exactly on center for thread cutting, taper turning, machining brass, copper, etc.

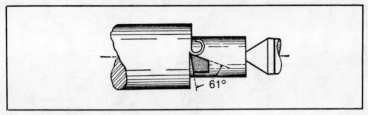

Fig. 11-3. Tool angle for machining soft steel.

For machining ordinary cast iron, the included angle of the cutting edge should be approximately 71 degrees as shown in Fig. 11-4. For machining chilled iron or very hard grades of cast iron, the tool angle may be as great as 85 degrees.

The angle of the cutter bit with the bottom of the tool holder must be taken into consideration when grinding cutter bits.

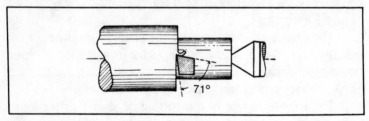

Fig. 11-4. Tool angle for machining cast iron.

Side clearance (Fig. 11-5) is to permit the cutting edge to advance freely without the heel of the tool rubbing against the work. Front clearance (Fig. 11-6) is to permit the cutting edge to cut freely as the tool is fed to the work. Too much clearance will weaken the cutting edge so that it will break; however, insufficient clearance will prevent the tool from cutting.

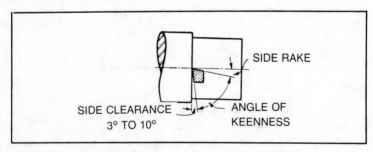

Fig. 11-5. Correct side clearance and side rake of cutter bit.

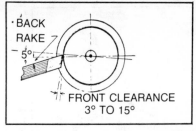

Fig. 11-6. Correct front clearance and back rake of cutter bit.

Side rake and back rake (Figs. 11-5 and 11-6) also facilitate free cutting. For cast iron, hard bronze and hard steel very little side rake or back rake is required. Angle of keenness (Fig. 11-5) may vary from 60 degrees for soft steel to nearly 90 degrees for cast iron, hard steel, bronze, etc.

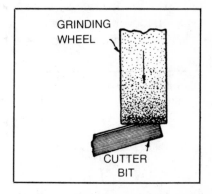

Fig. 11-7. Grinding left side of cutter bit.

Figures 11-7 to 11-11, inclusive, show the various steps in grinding a cutter bit for general machine work. Honing the cutting edge (Fig. 11-12) will improve the quality of the finish and lengthen the life of the tool.

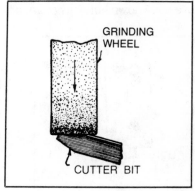

Fig. 11-8. Grinding right side of cutter bit.

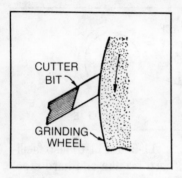

Fig. 11-9. Grinding front of cutter bit.

Figures 11-13 and 11-14 illustrate an excellent tool for taking heavy roughing cuts to reduce the diameter of a steel shaft to the approximate size desired. This tool will cut freely but does not produce a very smooth finish. When using this type of tool it is advisable to leave sufficient stock for a finishing cut with a round-nosed tool.

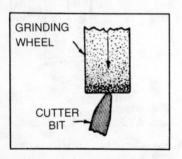

Fig. 11-10. Rounding end of cutter bit.

The cutting edge of the tool is straight and the point is only slightly rounded. A very small radius at the point (approximately 1/64 inch) will prevent the point of the tool from breaking down but will not impair the free-cutting quality of the

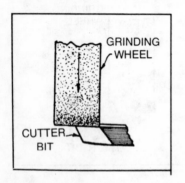

Fig. 11-11. Grinding side rake and back rake.

198

Fig. 11-12. Honing the cutting edge of cutter bit with an oil stone.

tool. Tool angle or included angle of the cutting edge of this tool should be approximately 61 degrees.

Hone the cutting edge of the tool with a small oil stone. This will lengthen the life of the tool and it will cut better.

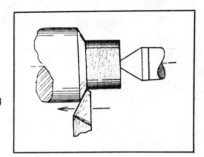

Fig. 11-13. Application of roughing tool.

Figures 11-15 and 11-16 illustrate a round-nosed turning tool for taking finishing cuts. The tool is very much the same shape as the more pointed tool for rough turning shown in Figs. 11-14 and 11-15, except that the point of the tool is rounded with approximately a 1/32-inch to 1/16-inch radius.

This tool will produce a very smooth finish if, after grinding, the cutting edge is well honed with an oil stone and a fine automatic power carriage feed is used.

Fig. 11-14. Detail of roughing tool.

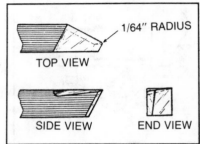

1/64″ RADIUS

TOP VIEW

SIDE VIEW   END VIEW

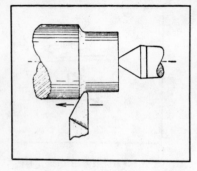

Fig. 11-15. Application of finishing tool.

The round-nosed turning tool shown in Figs. 11-17 and 11-18 is ground flat on top so that the tool may be fed in either direction, as indicated by the arrows in Fig. 11-17. This is a very convenient tool for reducing the diameter of a shaft in the center. The shape of the cutter bit is shown in Fig. 11-17. The

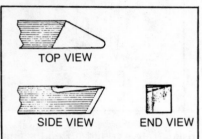

TOP VIEW

SIDE VIEW   END VIEW

Fig. 11-16. Detail of finishing tool.

correct angle for the front clearance and side clearance can be obtained by referring to Figs. 11-5 and 11-6.

The right-hand turning tool shown in Figs. 11-19 and 11-20 is the most common type of tool for general all-around machine work. This tool is used for machining work from right

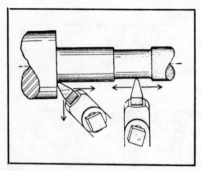

Fig. 11-17. Application of round-nosed tool.

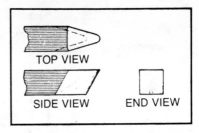

Fig. 11-18. Detail of round-nosed tool bit.

to left, as indicated by the arrow in Fig. 11-19. The shape of the cutter bit is shown in Fig. 11-20.

The left-hand turning tool illustrated in Figs. 11-21 and 11-22 is just the opposite of the right-hand turning tool shown in Figs. 11-19 and 11-20. This tool is designed for machining work from left to right.

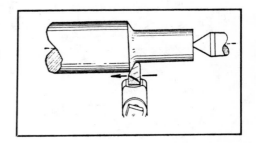

Fig. 11-19. Application of right-hand turning tool.

The right-hand side tool shown in Figs. 11-23 and 11-24 is intended for facing the ends of shafts and for machining work on the right side of a shoulder. This tool should be fed outward from the center, as indicated by the arrow in Fig. 11-23. The point of the tool is sharp and is ground to an angle of 58 degrees to prevent interference with the tailstock center. When using this cutter bit care should be taken not to bump the end of the tool against the lathe center, as this will break the point.

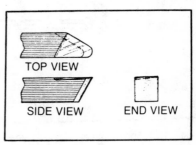

Fig. 11-20. Detail of right-hand turning tool.

201

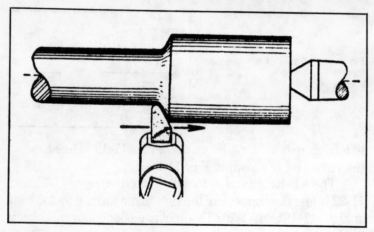

Fig. 11-21. Application of left-hand turning tool.

The left-hand side tool shown in Figs. 11-25 and 11-26 is just the reverse of the right-hand side tool shown in Figs.

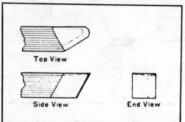

Fig. 11-22. Detail of left-hand turning tool.

11-23 and 11-24. This tool is used for facing the left side of the work, as shown in Fig. 11-25.

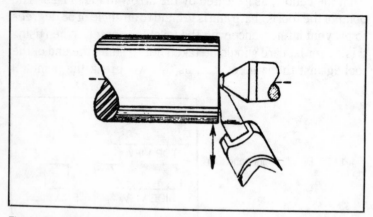

Fig. 11-23. Application of right-hand side tool.

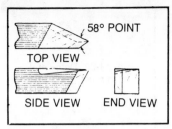

Fig. 11-24. Detail of right-hand side tool.

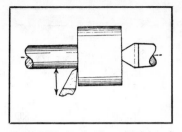

Fig. 11-25. Application of left-hand side tool.

Figures 11-26 and 11-27 show the standard type of cutter bit for cutting United States or American National screw threads. The cutter bit is usually ground flat on top, as shown in Fig. 11-26, and the point of the tool must be ground to an included angle of 60 degrees, as shown in Fig. 11-27. Careful grinding and setting of this cutter bit will result in perfectly formed screw threads. When using this cutter bit to cut screw threads in steel, always keep the work flooded with lard oil in order to obtain a smooth thread. Machine oil may be used if no lard oil is available.

The brass turning tool shown in Figs. 11-29 and 11-30 is similar to the round-nosed turning tool illustrated in Figs. 11-17 and 11-18, except that the top of the tool is ground flat so that there is no side rake or back rake. This is to prevent the tool from digging into the work and chattering.

The cutting-off tool should always be set exactly on center, as shown in Fig. 11-31. This type of tool may be sharpened by grinding the end of the cutter blade to an angle of 5 degrees as shown in Fig. 11-32. The sides of the blade have sufficient taper to provide side clearance, so do not need to be

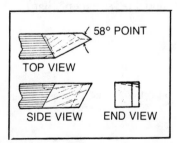

Fig. 11-26. Detail of left-hand side tool.

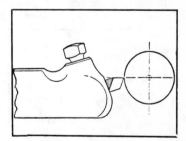

Fig. 11-27. Application of screw thread cutting tool.

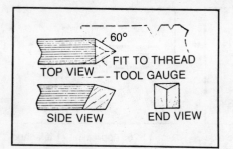

60°
FIT TO THREAD
TOP VIEW — TOOL GAUGE

SIDE VIEW   END VIEW

Fig. 11-28. Detail of thread cutting tool.

ground. When cutting off steel always keep the work flooded with oil. No oil is necessary when cutting off cast iron.

The boring tool in Figs. 11-33 and 11-34 is ground exactly the same as the left-hand turning tool shown in Figs. 11-21 and

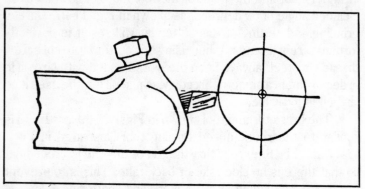

Fig. 11-29. Application of brass turning tool.

11-22, except the front clearance of boring tool must be ground at a slightly greater angle so that the heel of the tool will not rub in the hole of the work. The inside-threading tool shown in Fig. 11-35 is ground the same as the screw thread cutting tool shown in Figs. 11-26 and 11-27, except that the

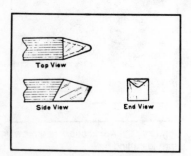

Top View

Side View   End View

Fig. 11-30. Detail of brass turning tool.

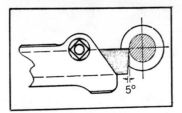

Fig. 11-31. Application of cutting-off tool.

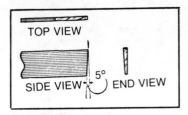

Fig. 11-32. Detail of cutting-off tool.

front clearance must be increased for the same reason as for the boring tool.

HOW TO TAKE ACCURATE MEASUREMENTS

The ability to take accurate measurements can be acquired only by practice and experience. Careful and accurate measurements are essential to good gunsmithing work. All measurements should be made with an accurately graduated steel scale or a micrometer. Never use a cheap steel scale or a wood ruler, as they are likely to be inaccurate and may cause spoiled work.

An experienced gunsmith can take measurements with a steel scale and calipers to a surprising degree of accuracy. This is accomplished by developing a sensitive "caliper feel" and by carefully setting the calipers so that they split the line graduated on the scale.

An experienced gunsmith can take measurements with a steel scale and calipers to a surprising degree of accuracy. This is accomplished by developing a sensitive "caliper feel" and by carefully setting the calipers so that they split the line graduated on the scale.

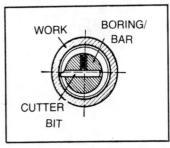

Fig. 11-33. Application of boring tool.

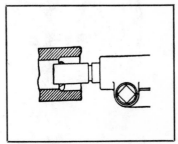

Fig. 11-34. Detail of boring tool.

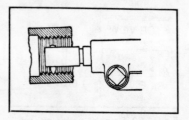

Fig. 11-35. Inside threading tool.

A good method for setting an outside caliper to a steel scale is shown in Fig. 11-36. The scale is held in the left hand and the caliper is held against the end of the scale and is supported by the finger of the left hand, while the adjustment is made with the thumb and first finger of the right hand.

The proper application of the outside caliper when measuring the diameter of a cylinder or a shaft is shown in Fig. 11-37. The caliper is held exactly at right angles to the center line of the work and is pushed gently back and forth across the diameter of the cylinder to be measured. When the caliper is adjusted properly, it should easily slip over the shaft due to its

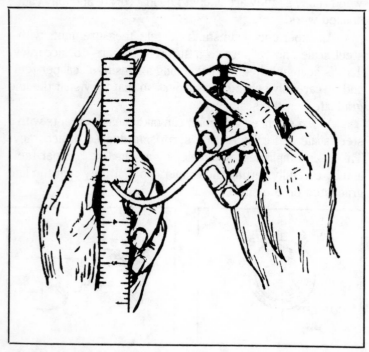

Fig. 11-36. Setting an outside caliper.

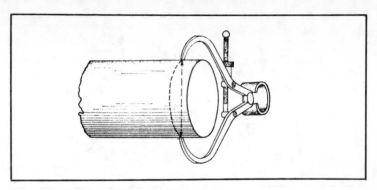

Fig. 11-37. Measuring with an outside caliper.

own weight. Never force a caliper or it will deform the instrument and the measurement will not be accurate.

To set an inside caliper for a definite dimension, place the end of the scale against a flat surface and the end of the caliper

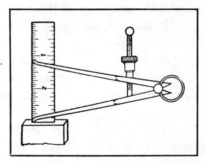

Fig. 11-38. Setting an inside caliper.

at the edge and end of the scale as shown in Fig. 11-38. Hold the scale square with the flat surface. Adjust the other end of the caliper to the required dimension.

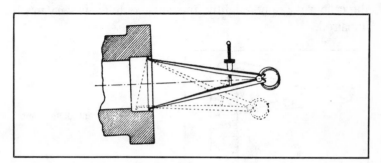

Fig. 11-39. Measuring with inside caliper.

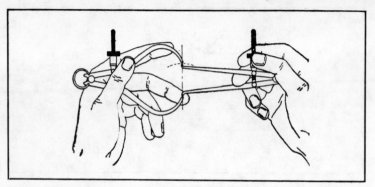

Fig. 11-40. Transferring a measurement from an inside caliper to an outside caliper.

To measure an inside diameter, place the caliper in the hole as shown on the dotted line in Fig. 11-39 and raise your hand slowly. Adjust the caliper until it will slip into the hole with a very slight drag. Be sure to hold the caliper square across the diameter of the hole.

In transferring measurement from an outside caliper to an inside caliper, the point of one leg of the inside caliper rests on a similar point of the outside caliper, as shown in Fig. 11-40. Using this contact point as a pivot, move the inside caliper along the dotted line shown in illustration, and adjust with the thumb screw until you feel your measurement is right.

The hermaphrodite caliper shown in Fig. 11-41 is set from the end of the scale exactly the same as the outside caliper.

The accuracy of all contact measurements is dependent upon the sense of touch or feel. The caliper should be delicately and lightly held in the finger tips, not gripped tightly. If the caliper is gripped tightly, the sense of touch is very much impaired.

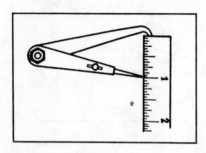

Fig. 11-41. Hermaphrodite caliper.

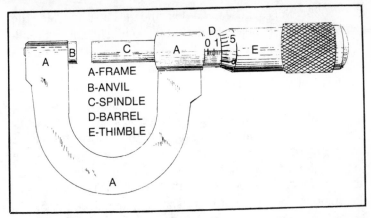

Fig. 11-42. An outside micrometer caliper for English measurements reading in thousandths of an inch.

HOW TO READ A MICROMETER

Each graduation on the micrometer barrel D in Fig. 11-42 represents one turn of the spindle or 0.025 inch. Every fourth graduation is numbered and the figures represent tenths of an inch since 4 ×0.025 =0.100 inch or 1/10 of an inch.

Thimble E has 25 graduations, each of which represents 0.001 inch. Every fifth graduation is numbered, from 5 to 25.

The micrometer reading is the sum of the readings of the graduations on the barrel and the thimble. For example, there are 7 graduations visible on the barrel in Fig. 11-42. Since each graduation represents 0.025 inches, the reading on the barrel

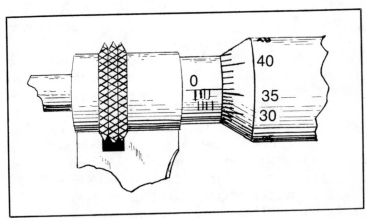

Fig. 11-43. Metric micrometer.

is 7×.025= 0.175 inches. To this amount must be added the reading on the thimble which is 0.003 inch. The correct reading is the sum of these two figures or 0.175 +0.003=0.178 inch. It should be clear then this micrometer is set for a diameter of 0.178 inch.

Micrometers for measuring in the metric system are graduated to read in hundreths of a millimeter as shown in Fig. 11-43. For each complete revolution the spindle travels ½ millimeter or 0.50 millimeter. Two complete revolutions are required for 1.00 millimeters. Each of the upper set of graduations on the barrel represents 1 millimeter, two revolutions of the spindle, and every fifth graduation is numbered 0, 5, 10, 15, etc. The lower set of graduations subdivides each millimeter division into two parts.

The beveled edge of the thimble is divided into 50 graduations, each of which represents 0.01 millimeter.

The micrometer reading is the sum of the readings on the barrel and the thimble. For example, in Fig. 11-43 there are three millimeter graduations visible on the barrel, also a ½-millimeter graduation. The reading on the thimble is 36 millimeters. Therefore, the reading is 3.00+0.50+0.36=3.86 millimeters.

CUTTING SCREW THREADS

Cutting screw threads on a lathe is accomplished by connecting the headstock spindle of the lathe with the lead screw by a series of gears so that a positive carriage feed is obtained. The lead screw is driven at the required speed with relation to the headstock spindle.

Gearing between the headstock spindle and lead screw may be arranged so that any desired pitch of the thread may be cut. For example, if the lead screw has eight threads per inch and the gears are arranged so that the headstock spindle revolves four times while the lead screw revolves once, the thread cut will be four times as fine as the thread on the lead screw or thirty-two threads per inch.

The cutting tool is ground to the shape required for the form of the thread to be cut, that is, American National Fine V, Acme, Square, Whitworth, International metric, etc.

Either right-hand or left-hand threads may be cut by reversing the direction of rotation of the lead screw. This may be accomplished by shifting the reverse lever on the headstock.

TERMS RELATING TO SCREW THREADS

- **Screw thread**—A ridge of uniform section in the form of a helix on the surface of a cylinder or cone.
- **External & Internal Threads**—An external thread is a thread on the outside of a member. Example: a threaded plug. An internal thread is a thread on the inside of a member. Example: a threaded hole.
- **Major diameter**—The largest diameter of the thread of the screw or nut. The term major diameter replaces the term outside diameter as applied to the thread of a screw and also the term full diameter as applied to the thread of a nut.
- **Minor diameter**—The smallest diameter of the thread of the screw or nut. The term minor diameter replaces the term core diameter as applied to the thread of a screw and also the term inside diameter as applied to the thread of a nut.
- **Pitch diameter**—On a straight screw thread, the diameter of an imaginary cylinder, the surface of which would pass through the threads at such points as to make equal the width of the threads and the width of the spaces cut by the surface of the cylinder.
- **Pitch**—The distance from a point on a screw thread to a corresponding point on the next thread measured parallel to the axis.
- **Lead**—The distance a screw advances axially in one turn. On a single-thread screw, the lead and pitch are identical; on a double-thread screw the lead is twice the pitch; on a triple-thread screw, the lead is three times the pitch, etc.

CUTTING THREADS ON STANDARD LATHES

Screw threads are cut on standard change gear lathes by engaging the apron half-nuts with the lead screw. The pitch of

CHART FOR THREADS AND FEEDS
STANDARD CHANGE GEAR LATHE

THREADS PER INCH	STUD GEAR	IDLER GEAR	SCREW GEAR	AUTO. FEEDS
4	24	FIG. 1	48	
4½	24	FIG. 1	54	
5	16	FIG. 1	40	
5½	16	FIG. 1	44	
6	16	FIG. 1	48	
6½	16	FIG. 1	52	
7	32	FIG. 2	28	
8	32	FIG. 2	32	
9	32	FIG. 2	36	
10	32	FIG. 2	40	
11	32	FIG. 2	44	
11½	32	FIG. 2	46	
12	32	FIG. 2	48	
13	32	FIG. 2	52	
14	32	FIG. 2	56	
16	24	FIG. 2	48	
18	24	FIG. 2	54	
20	16	FIG. 2	40	
22	16	FIG. 2	44	.0156
24	16	FIG. 2	48	.0144
26	16	FIG. 2	52	.0133
27	16	FIG. 2	54	.0128
28	16	FIG. 2	56	.0123
30	16	FIG. 2	60	.0115
32	32	FIG. 3	32	.0108
36	32	FIG. 3	36	.0096
40	32	FIG. 3	40	.0086
44	32	FIG. 3	44	.0078
46	32	FIG. 3	46	.0075
48	32	FIG. 3	48	.0072
52	32	FIG. 3	52	.0066
54	32	FIG. 3	54	.0064
56	32	FIG. 3	56	.0062
60	32	FIG. 3	60	.0057
64	16	FIG. 3	32	.0054
72	16	FIG. 3	36	.0047
80	16	FIG. 3	40	.0043
88	16	FIG. 3	44	.0039
92	16	FIG. 3	46	.0037
96	16	FIG. 3	48	.0036
104	16	FIG. 3	52	.0033
112	16	FIG. 3	56	.0030
	16	FIG. 3	60	.0028
	16	FIG. 3	80	.0021

AUTOMATIC FEEDS THROUGH FRICTION CLUTCH

STUD GEAR — 80T — SCREW GEAR — 72T — 18T — FIG. 1

STUD GEAR — 80T — SCREW GEAR — FIG. 2

STUD GEAR — SCREW GEAR — 72T — 18T — 80T — FIG. 3

AUTOMATIC CROSS FEED = .375 X LONGITUDINAL FEED

Fig. 11-44. Thread cutting chart.

thread to be cut is determined by the number of teeth in the change gears used on the reverse stud and the lead screw, also the compound gears used.

To set up the lathe for cutting a screw thread, first determine the number of threads per inch to be cut. By referring to the change gear chart (Fig. 11-44) attached to the lathe the change gears required can be determined. The thread to be cut should be located in the first column under the heading *Threads Per Inch*. In the second column under the heading *Stud Gear* is listed the number of teeth in the change gear which should be placed on the reverse stud of the lathe. In the third column under the heading *Idler Gear* is listed the figure number on the index chart showing the arrangement of idler gear and compound gears. In the fourth column under the heading *Screw Gear* is listed the number of teeth in the gear to be placed on the lead screw.

After selecting the change gears necessary for cutting the desired thread, place them on the reverse stud and lead screw respectively, and connect them with the idler gear and compound gears.

A thread cutting chart similar to the one in Fig. 11-44 showing the gearing required for various pitches of screw threads and various power tuning feeds is attached to each standard change gear lathe.

CUTTING THREADS ON QUICK CHANGE LATHES

The quick change gear lathe is fitted with a gear box which permits obtaining various pitches of screw threads without the use of loose change gears. A typical screw thread chart attached to the gear box is shown in Fig. 11-45. This chart reads directly in threads per inch. It is only necessary to arrange the levers of the gearbox as indicated on the index plate in order to obtain various screw threads and feeds.

The shape or form of a screw thread cut on the lathe is determined by the shape of the cutter bit, which must be carefully ground and set if an accurate thread form is to be

SOUTH BEND LATHE WORKS						SOUTH BEND, IND., U. S. A.			AUTOMATIC CROSS FEED EQUALS .375 TIMES LONGITUDINAL FEED.
QUICK CHANGE						GEAR LATHE			
SLIDING GEARS	TOP LEVER	SCREW THREADS PER INCH USING HALF NUTS							
IN	LEFT	2	2¼	2½	2¾	2⅞	3	3¼	3½
	CENTER	4	4½	5	5½	5¾	6	6½	7
	RIGHT	8	9	10	11	11½	12	13	14
OUT	LEFT	16	18	20	22	23	24	26	28
	CENTER	32	36	40	44	46	48	52	56
	RIGHT	64	72	80	88	92	96	104	112
	AUTOMATIC FEEDS THROUGH FRICTION CLUTCH								
	LEFT	.0208	.0185	.0166	.0151	.0144	.0138	.0128	.0119
	CENTER	.0104	.0093	.0083	.0075	.0072	.0069	.0064	.0059
	RIGHT	.0052	.0046	.0041	.0037	.0036	.0034	.0032	.0030

Fig. 11-45. A screw thread chart is attached to the gear box.

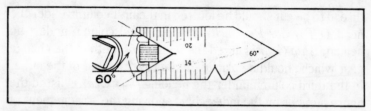

Fig. 11-46. Cutter bit for cutting screw threads is ground to 60-degrees center gauge.

obtained. A gauge should be used for grinding the lathe tool to the required shape for any form of screw thread.

The point of the cutter bit must be ground to an angle of 60 degrees for cutting American National screw threads in the lathe, as shown in Fig. 11-46. A center gauge having a 60-degree included angle is used for grinding the tool to the exact angle required. The top of the tool is usually ground flat, with no side rake or back rake; however, for cutting threads in steel, side rake is sometimes used.

There must be sufficient front clearance on the cutter bit to permit it to cut freely. Usually the front clearance is sufficient to prevent the tool from dragging in the helix angle of the thread so that except for very coarse pitches the helix angle may be ignored.

A formed threading tool is sometimes used if considerable threading is to be done. The formed threading tool requires grinding on top only to sharpen, and therefore always remains true to form and correct angle.

A gauge for grinding threading tools to the exact shape required for various pitches of American National screw threads is shown in Fig. 11-47.

For American National screw threads finer than 10 per inch, the point of the tool is usually left sharp or with a very small flat. But, for coarser pitches of threads and when maximum strength is desired, the flat on the point of the tool should be one-eighth of the pitch.

The top of the threading tool should be placed exactly on center, as shown in Fig. 11-48 for cutting external screw threads. Note that the top of the tool is ground flat and is in exact alignment with the lathe center. This is necessary to obtain the correct angle of the thread.

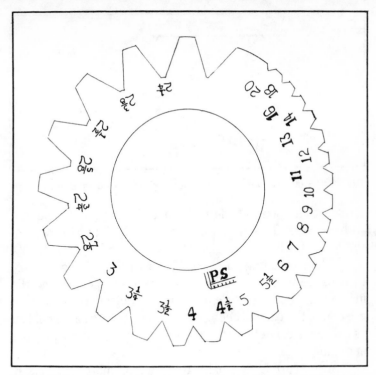

Fig. 11-47. Standard screw thread tool gauge for grinding thread cutting tools.

The threading tool must be set square with the work, as shown in Fig. 11-49. The center gauge is used to adjust the point of the threading tool, and if the tool is carefully set a perfect thread will result. Of course, if the threading tool is not set perfectly square with the work, the angle of the thread will be incorrect.

The point of the threading tool is also placed exactly on center, as shown in Fig. 11-50 for cutting internal screw

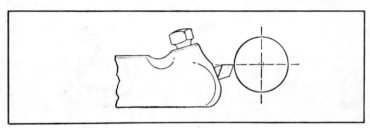

Fig. 11-48. Top of cutter bit set on center for cutting screw threads.

215

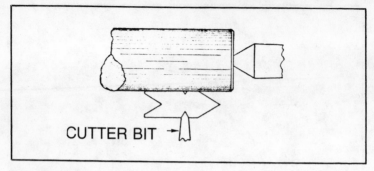

CUTTER BIT

Fig. 11-49. Cutter bit set square with work for cutting external screw threads.

threads. The point of the tool must be set perfectly square with the work. This may be accomplished by fitting the point of the tool into the center gauge, as shown in Fig. 11-51.

When adjusting the threading tool for cutting internal threads, allow sufficient clearance between the tool and the inside diameter of the hole to permit backing out the tool when the end of the cut has been reached. The boring bar should be as large in diameter and as short as possible to prevent springing.

When cutting internal screw threads more front clearance is required to prevent the heel of the tool from rubbing than when cutting external threads.

Due to the lost motion caused by the play necessary for smooth operation of the change gears, lead screw, half-nuts, etc., the thread cutting tool must be withdrawn quickly at the end of each cut, before the lathe spindle is reversed to return the tool to the starting point. If this is not done, the point of the tool will dig into the thread and may be broken off. The stop may be used for regulating the depth of each successive chip.

Fig. 11-50. For cutting internal screw threads, top of cutter bit should be set exactly on center.

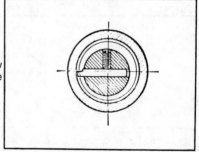

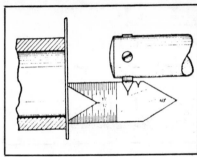

Fig. 11-51. Cutter bit set square with work for cutting internal screw threads.

The point of the tool should first be set so that it just touches the work; then lock the thread cutting stop and turn the thread cutting stop screw until the shoulder is tight against the stop. When ready to take the first chip run the toolrest back by turning the cross feed screw the thread is to start. Then turn the cross feed screw to the right until the thread cutting stop screw strikes the thread cutting stop. The tool rest is now in the original position, and by turning the compound rest feed screw in 0.002 inch or 0.003 inch the tool will be in a position to take the first cut.

The micrometer collar on the cross feed screw of the lathe may be used in place of the thread cutting stop if desired. To do this, first bring the point of threading tool up so that it just touches the work; then adjust the micrometer collar on the cross feed screw to zero.

All adjusting for obtaining the desired depth of cut should be done with the compound rest screw. Withdraw the tool at the end of each cut by turning the cross feed screw to the left one complete turn, return the tool to the starting point and turn the cross feed screw to the right one turn, stopping at

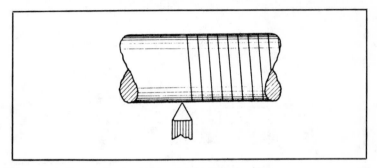

Fig. 11-52. Trial cut to check the setup for thread cutting.

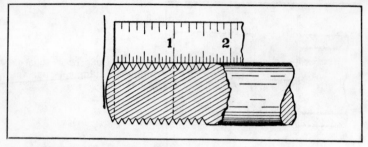

Fig. 11-53. Measuring screw threads.

zero. The compound rest feed screw may then be adjusted for any desired depth of chip.

After setting up the lathe, as explained on the preceding pages, take a very light trial cut just deep enough to scribe a line on the surface of the work, as shown in Fig. 11-52. The purpose of this trial cut is to make sure the lathe is arranged for cutting the desired pitch of thread.

To check the number of threads per inch, place a scale against the work, as shown in Fig. 11-53, so that the end of the scale rests on the point of the thread or on one of the scribed lines. Count the spaces between the end of the scale and the first inch mark. This will give you the number of threads per inch. Figure 11-53 shows eight threads per inch.

A screw thread gauge as illustrated in Fig. 11-54 is very convenient for checking the finer pitches of screw threads. This gauge consists of a number of sheet metal plates in which are cut the exact form of the various pitches of threads.

The final check for both the diameter and pitch of the thread may be made with the nut that is to be used or with a

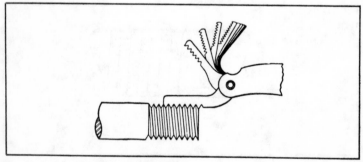

Fig. 11-54. Screw thread pitch gauge.

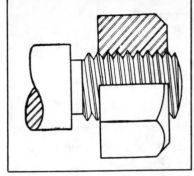

Fig. 11-55. Screw thread fitted to a nut.

ring thread gauge, if one is available. Figure 11-55 shows how the nut may be used for checking the thread. The nut should fit snugly without play or shake but should not bind on the thread at any point.

If the angle of the thread is correct and the thread is cut to the correct depth it will fit the nut perfectly. If the angle of the thread is incorrect, the thread may appear to fit the nut but will only be touching at a few points. For this reason, the thread should be checked by other methods in addition to the nut or ring gauge.

If for any reason it is necessary to remove the thread cutting tool before the thread has been completed, the tool must be carefully adjusted so that it will follow the original groove when it is replaced in the lathe. Before adjusting the tool, take up all the lost motion by pulling the belt forward by hand.

The compound rest top should be set at an angle. By adjusting the cross feed screw and compound rest feed screw

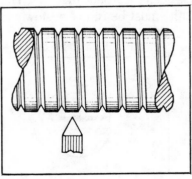

Fig. 11-56. Adjusting point of threading tool to conform with thread.

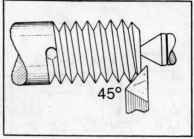

Fig. 11-57. Finish end of thread with 45-degree chamfer.

simultaneously the point of the tool can be made to enter exactly into the original groove. (Fig. 11-56).

The end of the thread may be finished by any one of several methods. The 45-degree chamber on the end of the thread, as shown in Fig. 11-57, is commonly used for bolts, cap screws, etc. For machine parts and special screws the end is often finished by rounding with a forming tool, as shown in Fig. 11-58.

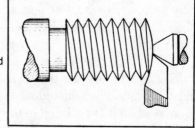

Fig. 11-58. Finishing end of thread with forming tool.

It is difficult to stop the threading tool abruptly; so some provision is usually made for clearance at the end of the cut. In Fig. 11-57 a hole has been drilled in the end of the shaft, and in Fig. 11-58 a neck or groove has been cut around the shaft. The groove is preferable as the lathe must be run very slowly in order to obtain satisfactory results with the drilled hole.

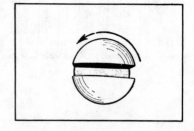

Fig. 11-59. A left-hand screw advances when turned counterclockwise.

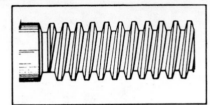

Fig. 11-60. A left-hand screw thread.

A left-hand screw is one that turns counter-clockwise when advancing, looking at head of screw, as shown in Fig. 11-59. This is just the opposite of a right-hand screw. An example of a left-hand screw thread is shown in Fig. 11-60. In cutting left-hand screw threads the lathe is set up exactly the same as for cutting right-hand screw threads, except that the lathe must be arranged to feed the tool from left to right, instead of from right to left, when the spindle is revolving forward.

Chapter 12

How to Get Your
Federal Firearms License

Anyone who works on a firearm, other than your own, must obtain a Federal Firearms License. This includes even cleaning or oiling a weapon. You will also need a license if you personally buy guns or ammunition for resale to others at wholesale or retail if you reload ammunition for others and if you want to buy, sell and benefit from substantial trade discounts from manufacturers and distributors of guns and related products. To qualify for a Federal Firearms License, you:

- Must be 21 years of age or over.
- Must not (1) be under indictment for or have been convicted of a crime punishable by imprisonment for a term exceeding 1 year (not including business offenses or misdemeanors not involving a firearm or explosive that are punishable by a term of imprisonment for 2 years or less) (2) be a fugitive from justice (3) be an unlawful user or addicted to marijuana or any depressant, stimulant, or narcotic drug or (4) have been adjudicated as a mental defective or been commited to a mental institution.
- Must not be an alien, unlawfully or illegally, in the United States.

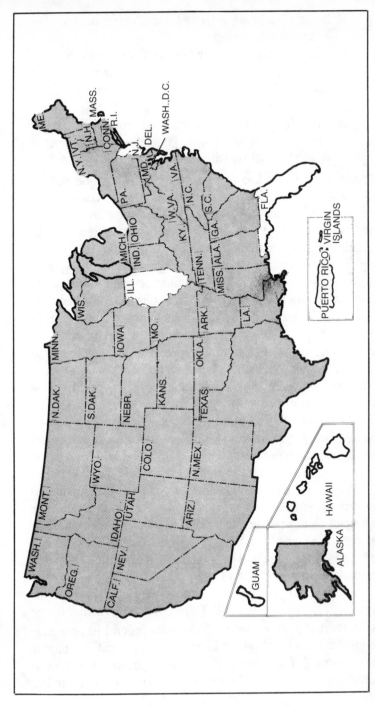

Fig. 12-1. Contiguous state enabling legislation indicated by shaded areas.

- Must not, being a United States citizen, have renounced citizenship.
- Must not have willfully filed to disclose any material information or made any false statement as to any material fact in connection with an application for a Federal Dealer's License.
- Must have premises from which you conduct your business or from which you intend to conduct a dealer's business within a reasonable period of time.

A Federal Firearms License entitles you to buy and sell, at wholesale or retail, firearms and ammunition to residents of your state. You may also, depending on state laws, sell to residents of contiguous, or adjoining states. (See map of states permitting contiguous sales shown in Fig. 12-1.) You may operate out of your home, a garage, an outbuilding, or a regular place of business, but you must be open to the public during the hours you specify on your application. Remember, however, that some local zoning laws may prohibit you from operating any business out of your home or may prohibit the manufacture or storage of ammunition. Be sure you look into your local requirements for a business license to operate from your home before making application for a Federal Firearms License if you intend to be open to the public.

When you specify open-to-the-public on your application, you need only open your doors from 6 to 8 pm weekdays and from 9 to noon weekends. This is perfectly legal, as long as those hours are listed on your application and then observed.

A Dealer's License also entitles you to do gun repairs on the same premises, providing this phase of your business is also open to the public during the hours listed for nonrepair services. The cost for a Dealer's License entitling you to buy, sell, and repair guns is $10 annually, covering the 12-month period following issuance of the license.

To apply for your license, write to the Department of the Treasury, Bureau of Alcohol, Tobacco, and Firearms, to the same address you use when filing your federal income tax. Request an "Application for License Under U.S.C. Chapter 44, Firearms." You will then receive an application like the one shown in Fig. 12-2. This figure also explains how to fill out the

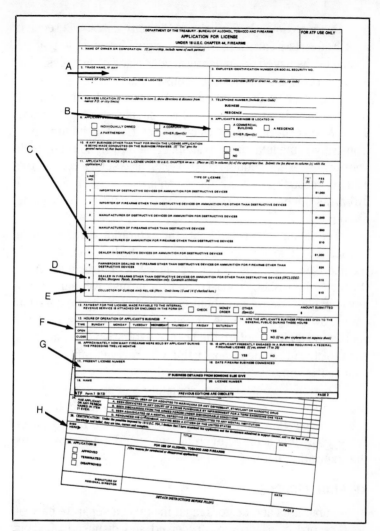

Fig. 12-2. Federal Firearms License application. (A) If you'll use a fictitious firm name, a name for your business other than your own, such as Acme Gun Sales, Bonanza Guns, etc., enter here. (B) Be specific. If out of your garage, basement or outbuilding, say so here. (C) If you want your Ammunition Making License now, check line 5. (D) Dealer only? Gun repair only? Will you handle both sales and service? For either or both of these activities, check line 8. (E) Don't fill in unless you'll collect guns only. (F) Sideline or full time? State the hours you'll be open, weekends included. (G) Doesn't apply unless you were previously licensed. (H) Back of form is simple, self-explanatory. Be sure to sign here.

application. If you want only a Dealer's License, enclose a check or a money order for $10. If you want both a Dealer's license and an Ammo-Maker's License, enclose $20.

In approximately 6 weeks to 2 months, you will receive your Federal Firearms License if you qualify, and the original should be displayed prominently in your place of business. You will also receive a copy of the license; this is to be used when ordering firearms and ammunition. Have a few dozen copies of this copy made at your local office supply store or library. Then when ordering firearms or ammunition for the first time from a given manufacturer or supplier, send a signed copy with your order. When requesting catalogs, also send a copy of the license because most suppliers require a copy of a Federal Firearms License as proof that you're entitled to a trade discount.

Your license is in effect until the expiration date shown on the license. It covers operations only at the location shown on the license. When it is time for renewal of your license, ATF (Bureau of Alcohol, Tobacco and Firearms) will send a renewal application to you about 60 days before the expiration date shown on your license. If you don't receive your renewal application 30 days before the license expiration date, and you want to stay in business, notify the ATF regional office serving your state immediately.

To renew your license, complete and send the application, with the fee attached, to your IRS center before the license expiration date. Then you may operate until you receive your new license, even though you don't receive it by the expiration date.

KEEPING RECORDS

Gunsmiths and dealers must maintain a separate permanent record of all firearms received and disposed of. This includes firearms received in pawn, curios and relics, and firearms received for repair.

Firearms must be logged in when received and logged out as they are disposed of using a Firearms Acquisition and Disposition Record as shown in Fig. 12-3. Figures 12-4 and 12-5 explain how to enter acquisitions and dispositions of firearms.

You will have to prepare Form 4473 (Fig. 12-6), Firearms Transaction Record, covering the transfer of each firearm to a

FIREARMS ACQUISITION AND DISPOSITION RECORD

Manufacturer and/or Importer	Model	Serial Number	Type of Action	Caliber or Gauge	From Whom Received (Name and Address or Name and License Number)	Date	Name	Date	Address or License Number (if Licensee) OR FORM 4473 Serial No (if non Licensee) (For Numerically)
1) Ithaca	102100 4	6607386	Pump	20	John's Fine Guns Inc. FFL #42-987	3/2/75	James House	11/29/76	Form 4473 #2
2) Smith & Wesson	10	M60512	Revolver	.38	Swap Shop FFL #PC-3988	8/4/75			
3) Western Field	10504	691467	Pump	20	John's Fine Guns Inc. FFL #42-987	8/4/75	Jim Michaels	11/2/76	Form 4473 #6P
4) Winchester	94	382906	Lever	.30-30	Al Green Fire Ther GAP Forrest Hill	11/4/75	Bill Bounce	9/1/76	Form 4473 #50
5) Remington	870	4932	Pump	16	Tom Problem 605 E. Colonial Pine Bluff 66057	6/14/76	Fix it or Melt it Inc.	6/20/76	FFL #46-3988
6) Remington	540X	3R268V	single	.22	Joan Rcala for FFL #PC-9477	1/3/76	Brian Smith	7/4/76	Form 4473 #35
7) Browning	1200	38679	Auto	.45	John Doe 637 Pine St. 66057	8/24/76	John Doe	7/1/77	Form 4473 #36
8) Western Field	10504	691467	Pump	20	Jim Michaels 189 Mich 2 ? 66058	11/24/76	Stolen – Reported to Police on 12/2/76		
9) Smith Wesson	34-1	M60562	Auto	.22	Brian Smith (owner) 611 Willow Pine Bluff, Ill. 66057	12/1/76	Jake Jones, Metro Police	12/2/76	305 Wilking Blvd. Atchison, Kansas 70504 See certification letter mailed at F 4473
10) Remington	870	4932	Pump	16	Fix it or Melt it Inc. FFL #46-3988	12/2/76	Tom Problem	12/2/76	605 East Colonial Pine Bluff, Ill. 66057

Fig. 12-3. Firearms Acquisition and Disposition Record.

227

Line

1 Shows purchase of a firearm from a licensed dealer — you must record their license number. In order for Brian to obtain this firearm, he had to submit a current copy of his FFL to John's Fine Guns (178.94). When Brian received the firearm, he entered it into this book immediately. (For variation see 178.125(f).)

4 Purchase of firearm from an unlicensed person.

5 Gun is brought in for repair. If firearm can be fixed and returned to owner on same business day, no entry need be made. However, if firearm cannot be returned that day, it must be entered as an acquisition even though it is not a purchase. Gunsmithing transactions such as this may be recorded in a separate bound book.

7 John Doe has brought in a gun for sale on consignment. Make entry on date of receipt.

8 Michaels originally purchased the gun on 11/2/76 (line 3). He does not like it and returns it on 11/24/76. The firearm must be reentered showing date of receipt and from whom received. (It was received from Michaels on 11/24/76.) The original entry on line 3 remains unchanged.

9 Brian Smith, owner of the licensed business, has a personal firearm he wants to sell. Enter firearm in book and show acquisition date as the date it was put up for sale.

10 Firearm sent to Fix It or Melt It Inc. for repair on 6/20/76 is returned to Smith's shop and reentered on 12/2/76.

Hand-ruled paper with the same column arrangement, same column headings, and the same language notations as the illustration above, may be used.

Line numbers are given for illustration purposes only.

Fig. 12-4. Explanation of acquisition when filling out the Firearms Acquisition and Disposition Record.

Line

1 Sale to an unlicensed person. The buyer's name is inserted directly across from the firearm purchased. Brian's Sport Shop files Form 4473 numerically (see 178.124(b) for options) and lists the form number in place of the address. Number "2" is the serial number of the Form 4473 that Mr. House filled out.

2 This firearm has not been traded, sold, loaned, stolen or transferred out. It should be on hand and available for inspection.

4 Bounce borrows a gun. It is not a sale but it is a disposition. Form 4473 must be filled out. (See 178.97 for loans and rentals by clubs). When Bounce returns the gun, it must be shown as an acquisition.

5 Brian is unable to fix the firearm brought in by Mr. Problem and sends it to a gunsmith for repair. Gunsmiths must be licensed and Brian's Sport Shop must obtain a current certified copy of Fix It or Melt It Inc. license prior to delivery of the firearm.

6 Brian Smith, owner of the store, takes a firearm from inventory for his own personal firearm. Since this will be a personal firearm, Smith must fill out Form 4473 for himself. When this happens, it must be either removed from the business premises, or, if kept on the business premises, must be identified as not being part of his business inventory. (Such as by a tag reading "NOT FOR SALE.")

7 Gun brought in by John Doe for sale on consignment was not sold. Form 4473 must be filled out by John Doe when the gun is returned to him.

8 The firearm is stolen — show disposition of firearm as "stolen" and show date the theft was reported to the local authorities. If the police case number is available, please report it here.

9 Firearms were sold to out-of-State policeman for official use, as evidenced by certification letter. See instructions on sale to law enforcement officers.

10 Mr. Problem gets his repaired gun back. He does not need to fill out Form 4473. The gun was returned to the same person who brought the gun in for repair. If someone picked the gun up for Mr. Problem a Form 4473 would then have to be filled out by that person (178.124(a)).

Fig. 12-5. Explanation of disposition when filling out the Firearms Acquisition and Disposition Record.

DEPARTMENT OF THE TREASURY – BUREAU OF ALCOHOL, TOBACCO AND FIREARMS

FIREARMS TRANSACTION RECORD
PART I – INTRA-STATE OVER-THE-COUNTER

TRANSFEROR'S TRANSACTION NO.

NOTE: Prepare in original only. All entries other than signatures must be typed or clearly printed in ink. All signatures on this form must be in ink.

SECTION A – MUST BE COMPLETED PERSONALLY BY TRANSFEREE (BUYER) *(See Notice and Instructions on reverse.)*

1. TRANSFEREE'S *(Buyer's)* NAME *(Last, First, Middle)* *(Mr., Mrs., Miss)*		2. HEIGHT	3. WEIGHT	4. RACE

5. RESIDENCE ADDRESS *(No., Street, City, State, Zip code)*	6. DATE OF BIRTH	7. PLACE OF BIRTH

8. CERTIFICATION OF TRANSFEREE *(Buyer)* – An untruthful answer may subject you to criminal prosecution. Each question must be answered with a "yes" or a "no" inserted in the box at the right of the question:

a. Are you under indictment or information in any court for a crime punishable by imprisonment for a term exceeding one year?

b. Have you been convicted in any court of a crime punishable by imprisonment for a term exceeding one year? *(Note: The actual sentence given by the judge does not matter—a yes answer is necessary if the judge could have given a sentence of more than one year. Also, a "yes" answer is required if a conviction has been discharged, set aside, or dismissed pursuant to an expungement of rehabilitation statute.)*

c. Are you a fugitive from justice?

d. Are you an unlawful user of, or addicted to, marijuana, or a depressant, stimulant, or narcotic drug?

e. Have you ever been adjudicated mentally defective or have you ever been committed to a mental institution?

f. Have you been discharged from the Armed Forces under dishonorable conditions?

g. Are you an alien illegally in the United States?

h. Are you a person who, having been a citizen of the United States, has renounced his citizenship?

I hereby certify that the answers to the above are true and correct. I understand that a person who answers any of the above questions in the affirmative is prohibited by Federal law from purchasing and/or possessing a firearm. I also understand that the making of any false oral or written statement or the exhibiting of any false or misrepresented identification with respect to this transaction is a crime punishable as a felony.

TRANSFEREE'S (*Buyer's*) SIGNATURE | DATE

SECTION B – TO BE COMPLETED BY TRANSFEROR (SELLER) *(See Notice and Instructions on reverse.)*

THE PERSON DESCRIBED IN SECTION A:
☐ IS KNOWN TO ME
☐ HAS IDENTIFIED HIMSELF TO ME IN THE FOLLOWING MANNER

9. TYPE OF IDENTIFICATION *(Driver's License, etc. Positive identification is required. A Social Security card is not considered positive identification.)*

10. NUMBER ON IDENTIFICATION

On the basis of: (1) the statements in Section A; (2) the verification of identity noted in Section B; and (3) the information in the current list of Published Ordinances, it is my belief that it is not unlawful for me to sell, deliver or otherwise dispose of the firearm described below to the person identified in Section A.

11. TYPE *(Pistol, Revolver, Rifle, Shotgun, etc.)* | 12. MODEL | 13. CALIBER OR GAUGE | 14. SERIAL NO.

15. MANUFACTURER *(and importer, if any)*

16. TRADE/CORPORATE NAME AND ADDRESS OF TRANSFEROR *(Seller)* *(Hand stamp may be used.)* | 17. FEDERAL FIREARMS LICENSE NO.

18. TRANSFEROR'S *(Seller's)* SIGNATURE | 19. TRANSFEROR'S TITLE | 20. TRANSACTION DATE

ATF F 4473 (5300.9) PART I (3-78)   EDITION OF 2/77 MAY BE USED
Fig. 12-6. Firearms Transaction Record, Form 4473.

nonlicensed person. Read this form carefully as it is the most important form or record you will keep. These forms must be kept alphabetically by name of purchaser, chronologically by date of disposition, or numerically by transaction serial number. The yellow Form 4473, Part 1 is used for over-the-counter sales while the green Form 4473, Part 2, is used for either contiguous (bordering) state sales or nonover-the-counter sales.

You must also keep a record of all ammunition received. Filing invoices in an orderly manner is acceptable if they are kept separate from other commerical records. These records must be kept for 2 years.

You do not have to keep a record of the disposition of ammunition for shotguns and ammunition used only in rifles, or component parts of these types of ammunition. However, you must keep a separate, permanent record like the one in Fig. 12-7 of the disposition of handgun ammunition or ammunition that is interchangeable between handguns and rifles, such as .22 caliber.

TRANSFERS BETWEEN LICENSEES

In general, licensees may freely buy and sell firearms and ammunition among themselves. They do not have to prepare Form 4473 on transfers to other licensees, but these transactions must be recorded in the bound record book. The licensee to receive the firearms or ammunition must furnish a copy of his or her license to the licensee selling or otherwise disposing of the firearms or ammunition prior to making the transaction. Licensees may also ship interstate to other licensees.

Dealers may take orders for firearms and ammunition at any location, but the orders must be filled only at your licensed premises.

KNOW YOUR CUSTOMER

Identify the buyer by name, age and residence address before delivering any firearm or ammunition. Under federal law, the minimum age for purchasers of firearms and ammunition may be either 18 or 21 years, depending on the item being purchased. For example, you may not sell a handgun or handgun ammunition to persons under 21 years of age. You may

DEPARTMENT OF THE TREASURY – BUREAU OF ALCOHOL, TOBACCO AND FIREARMS
DISPOSITION RECORD OF INTERCHANGEABLE AMMUNITION AND HANDGUN AMMUNITION

MUST BE RETAINED FOR 2 YEARS AFTER DATE OF LAST ENTRY ON PAGE

DATE	MANUFACTURER	22 CALIBER RIMFIRE*	OTHER		PURCHASER			IDENTIFICATION (Enter A (✓) in the "Known" column if purchaser is personally known to you. Otherwise establish the purchaser's identification)		
1976			Caliber, Gauge or Type of Component	No. of Boxes	Name	Address	Date of Birth	Known (✓)	Driver's License Number	Other (Specify)
12/1	Winchester	✓			Spencer Gatling	400 Wesley Drive Richards, Illinois	3/1/31		B100-0011-1010	
12/2	Remington		.25	3	Marlin Stevens	58 Sauer St. Bullard, Illinois	4/8/40	✓		
12/3	Winchester		.30-30	5	Guedes Reformado	44 Sharps Blvd. Creedmoor, Illinois	6/7/41		C410-1000-0005	
12/4	Smith and Wesson		.30	4	Maynard Trounds	95 Peabody St. Borchardt, Illinois	12/4/58		D003-3000-0101	

For this entry, Mr. Trounds is 18 years old and the ammunition is intended for use in a rifle (178.125(c)).

SAMPLE COPY
FOR USE OF
COMMERCIAL PRINTERS

You may obtain a copy of this form, for reproduction by a commercial printer, from the ATF Distribution Center, 3800 S. Four Mile Run Drive, Arlington, Va. 22206.

Hand-ruled paper with the same column arrangement, same column headings, and the same language notations as this sample, may be used.

*Enter only A (✓) if 10 boxes or less. If more than 10 boxes enter the number of boxes.

ATF F 5300.2 (11-77) COMMERCIAL SAMPLE

Fig. 12-7. Ammunition disposition record for types that can be used in handguns.

not sell shotguns or rifles, or shotgun and rifle ammunition to persons under 18 years of age. You may sell ammunition that is interchangeable between rifles and handguns to a purchaser who is at least 18 years of age if you are satisfied that he or she will use the ammunition in a rifle.

If you sell or deliver a handgun to a nonlicensed person, that person must be a resident of the state in which your licensed premises is located. If you sell or deliver a rifle or shotgun to a nonlicensed person, that person must be a resident of the state in which your business is located or a resident of a contiguous (bordering) state. This latter condition is valid only if the buyer's state has enacted legislation allowing such a sale or delivery. The sale conforms to legal requirements in both states, the appropriate law enforcement officer in the buyer's home State has been notified as required and the waiting period requirement has been satisifed.

In addition to these requirements, you may not lawfully sell or dispose of any firearm or ammunition to certain types of persons; that is, convicted felons, etc. If any of your customers would violate any state law or local ordinance that applies at the place where you sell or deliver, by purchasing or possessing any firearm or ammunition, then, under federal law, you may not lawfully sell or deliver any firearms or ammunition to that customer.

If firearms are lost or stolen, you should immediately contact your local law enforcement authorities. Also, if you deliver more than one handgun to the same individual non-licensee within 5 consecutive business days, this must be reported to ATF on Form 3310.4. The original of Form 3310.4 must be mailed to the ATF Criminal Enforcement office for your area at the end of the business day that the sale occurs. A list of these offices and their addresses follows:

Alabama
> Special Agent in Charge (ATF)
> 2121 8th Avenue North, Room 1025
> Birmingham, AL 35203
> Phone: 205/254-1205

Alaska

Resident Agent in Charge (ATF)
Room G-79, U.S. Court House
Anchorage, AK 99501
Phone: 907/279-7914

California, Arizona, Nevada,Utah

Special Agent in Charge (ATF)
PO Box 1991
Main Post Office
Los Angeles, CA 90053 (serves Arizona)

Special Agent in Charge (ATF)
525 Market St, 25th Floor
San Francisco, CA (serves Nevada and Utah)
Phone: 415/556-6769

Connecticut, Maine,
New Hampshire, Rhode Island, Vermont

Special Agent in Charge (ATF)
135 High Street, Rooms 105-108
P.O. Box 25
Hartford, CT 06101
Phone: 203/244-3642

Florida

Special Agent in Charge (ATF)
5205 Northwest 84th Ave. Suite 108
Miami, FL 33166
Phone: 305/592-9968

Georgia

Special Agent in Charge (ATF)
1 West Court Square, Suite 265
Decatur, GA 30030
Phone: 404/221-6526

Guam

U.S. Attorney
District of Guam
Corn Trading House Building
Aspinall Avenue and West Soledad
P.O. Box Z
Agana, GU 96910
Phone: Overseas 772-6458

Hawaii, Guam

Resident Agent in Charge (ATF)
300 Ala Moana Blvd.
PO Box 50103
Honolulu, HI 96850
Phone: 808/546-3196

Illinois

Special Agent in Charge (ATF)
Butterfield Office Plaza
2625 Butterfield Road
Oak Brook, IL 60521
Phone: 312/325-8620

Kentucky, Indiana

Special Agent in Charge (ATF)
600 Federal Place, Room 872-D
P.O. Box 1707, 40201
Louisville, KY 40202
Phone: 502/582-5211

Louisiana, Arkansas

Special Agent in Charge (ATF)
500 Camp Street, Room 330
PO Box 30776, 70190
New Orleans, LA 70130
Phone: 504/589-2048

Massachusetts

Special Agent in Charge (ATF)
John F. Kennedy Government Center, 19th Floor
P.O. Box 9115, John F. Kennedy Post Office
Boston, MA 02114
Phone: 617/233-3187

Michigan

Special Agent Charge (ATF)
231 West LaFayette Blvd. Room 371
P.O. Box 1897
Detroit, MI 48226
Phone: 313/226-7300

Minnesota, North Dakota, South Dakota, Wisconsin
Special Agent in Charge (ATF)
316 North Robert St. Room 156
St. Paul, MN 55101
Phone: 612/725-7092

Mississippi
Special Agent in Charge (ATF)
301 N. Lamar St. Room 506
Jackson, MS 39202
Phone: 601/969-4200

Missouri, Iowa, Kansas, Nebraska
Special Agent in Charge (ATF)
1150 Grand Avenue, 2nd Floor
Kansas City, MO 64106 (serves Iowa, Kansas,
Nebraska)
Phone: 816/374-3886

Special Agent in Charge (ATF)
1114 Market Street, Room 611
St. Louis, MO 63101
Phone: 314/425-5560

New Jersey
Special Agent in Charge (ATF)
2401 Morris Avenue, 2nd Floor
Union, NJ 07083
Phone: 201/687-6100

New York
Special Agent in Charge (ATF)
90 Church Street
P.O. Box 3482, Church Street Station, 10008
New York, NY 10007
Phone: 212/264-4658

North Carolina
Special Agent in Charge (ATF)
5821 Park Road, Suite 504
Charlotte, NC 28209
Phone: 704/372-0711/7425

Ohio, West Virginia

Special Agent in Charge (ATF)
U.S. Post Office and Courthouse Bldg. Room 304
Cincinnati, OH 45202 (serves West Virginia)
Phone: 513/684-3756
Special Agent in Charge (ATF)
Federal Office Building
1240 E. 9th Street
Cleveland, OH 44129
Phone: 216/522-3080

Oklahoma, Colorado, Wyoming

Special Agent in Charge (ATF)
200 Northwest 5th, Room 960
Oklahoma City, OK 73102
Phone: 405/231-4877/4841

Pennsylvania

Special Agent in Charge (ATF)
U.S. Custom House, Room 504
2nd and Chestnut Streets
Philadelphia, PA 19106
Phone: 215/597-7266

Puerto Rico

Special Agent in Charge (ATF)
U.S. Courthouse and Federal Bldg.
Avenida Carlow Chardon, Room 354
PO Box 111
Hato Rey, PR 00919
Phone: 809/753-4084

South Carolina

Special Agent in Charge (ATF)
901 Sumter St. Room 501
Columbia, SC 29201
Phone: 803/765-5541/42/43

Tennessee

Special Agent in Charge (ATF)
4004 Hillsboro Road, Room 210
Nashville, TN 37215
Phone: 615/251-5412

Texas, New Mexico
Special Agent in Charge (ATF)
1200 Min Tower, Room 330
Dallas, TX 75202 (serves New Mexico)
Phone: 214/767-2250
Special Agent in Charge (ATF)
3910 Kirby Drive, Suite 260
Houston, TX 77098
Phone: 713/226-5405

Virginia, Delaware, District of Columbia, Maryland
Special Agent in Charge (ATF)
701 West Broad St. Room 206
Falls Church, VA 22046 (serves Delaware, D.C., Maryland)
Phone: 703/557-1766
Special Agent in Charge (ATF)
400 North 8th St. Room 6008
PO Box 10068
Richmond, VA 23240
Phone: 804/782-2871

Washington, Idaho, Montana, Oregon
Special Agent in Charge (ATF)
915 2nd Avenue, Room 806
Seattle, WA 98174
Phone: 206/442-4485

Licensed collectors may buy curios and relics from any source, and they may be disposed of to another licensee anywhere or to nonlicensed residents in the collector's state. A collector must maintain the same records as other licensees. A collector's license entitles him or her to conduct transactions in curios and relics only. In other words, a licensed collector has the same status as a nonlicensee in any transactions involving firearms and ammunition other than curios and relics.

CHANGE OF ADDRESS

If a licensee moved the business location, the regional regulatory administrator must be notified at least 10 days before moving the firearms and ammunition to a new address.

GOING OUT OF BUSINESS

Within 30 days after the licensee sells or otherwise discontinues the firearms or ammunition business, written notice must be given of this change in status to the regional regulatory administrator. If the licensee sells or discontinues the firearms or ammunition business and is succeded by a new licensee, the firearm dealer records should be marked to show this fact and must be delivered to the successor.

You must deliver all of your firearms to your ATF regional regulatory administrator within 30 days of going completely out of the firearms or ammunition business.

FIREARM SALE TO LAW ENFORCEMENT OFFICERS

Section 925 (a) (1) of the Gun Control Act exempts law enforcement agencies from the transportation, shipment, receipt, or importation controls of the act when firearms are to be used for the official business of the agency.

If a law enforcement officer is issued a certification letter on the agency's letterhead signed by a person in authority within the agency stating that the officer will use the firearms in performance of official duties, then that officer specified in the certification may purchase a firearm from you regardless of the state in which he or she resides or in which the agency is located. The seller is not required to prepare a Form 4473 covering such a sale: however, the transaction must be entered in the permanent record. The certification letter from the officer must be kept in your files.

The Bureau considers the following as persons having authority to make certifications that the law enforcement officer purchasing the firearms will use the firearms in performance of official duties.

- In a city or county police department, the director of public safety or the chief or commissioner of police.
- In a sheriff's office, the sheriff.
- In a state police or highway patrol department, the superintendent or the supervisor in charge of the office to which the state officer or employee is assigned.

- In federal law enforcement offices, the supervisor in charge of the office to which the federal officer or employee is assigned.

The Bureau would also recognize someone signing on behalf of a person of authority provided there is a proper delegation of authority and overall responsibility has not changed in any way.

QUESTIONS AND ANSWERS

The following questions and answers are intended to help you understand federal laws and regulations which pertain to firearms and ammunition. Although this listing is by no means all inclusive, it contains a selection of those questions that ATF receives frequently.

These questions and answers relate only to Federal Laws and Regulations. Numerous states, counties, and municipalities have enacted their own requirements concerning firearms and ammunition. State laws and local published ordinances which are relevant to the enforcement of the Gun Control Act of 1968 are contained in ATF Publication 5300.5.

General Questions

Does the law regulate who can be in the gun business?

Yes. The Gun Control Act (GCA), administered by the Bureau of Alcohol, Tobacco and Firearms (ATF) of the Department of the Treasury, contains Federal licensing standards for various firearms-related businesses—manufacturers, importers and dealers. Two examples of such standards are the applicant must have a business premises and must be open to the public.

Who can get a licenses?

ATF will approve the application if the applicant is 21 years or more of age, is not prohibited from shipping or receiving firearms or ammunition in interstate commerce, has not willfully violated the GCA or its regulations, has not willfully failed to disclose required material information or willfully made false statements concerning material facts in connection with his application and has premises for conducting business or collecting.

Do antique firearms come within the purview of the GCA?

No. As defined in Title 1 and Title 11, they are excluded.

Are all kinds of ammunition covered by the GCA?

Yes, all ammunition, including components such as cartridge cases, primers, bullets and propellant powder for use in modern firearms, is covered by the GCA. Items not covered include blank ammunition, tear gas ammunition, pellets, non-metallic shotgun hulls and casings without primers.

Does the GCA control the sale of firearms parts?

No, except frames or receivers. They are firearms as defined in the law and subject to the same controls as complete firearms.

Does the GCA prohibit anyone from making a handgun, shotgun or rifle?

No, provided it is not for sale and is not a firearm as defined in the Nation Firearms Act.

Are suppliers who deal in black powder required to be licensed as ammunition dealers under the GCA?

No. However, black powder dealers are subject to the provisions of 27 CFR Part 181, Commerce in Explosives, which provides, in part, that a dealer in any quantity of black powder must have a license as a dealer in explosives. Contact your nearest ATF office for further information.

Licensing

How does one get a license?

Submit ATF Form 7, with the appropriate fee as listed on the form, to the IRS Service Center in your area. These forms may be obtained through your local ATF office.

Can one license cover several locations?

No. A separate license must be obtained for each location. Storage facilities are not required to be covered by a license.

Does an importer or manufacturer also need a dealer's license?

No, as long as he or she is engaged in business at the licensed premises in the same type of firearms and ammunition authorized by his or her license to be imported or manufactured.

If a person timely files an application for the renewal of a license and the present license expires prior to receipt of the license so applied for, may the person continue to conduct the business covered by the expired license?

Yes, a person who timely files an application for the renewal of a license may continue such operations as were authorized by the expired license until the application is finally acted upon. An application is timely filed when it is executed and filed with the Internal Revenue Service Center prior to the expiration date of the license being renewed. If a person does not timely file an application for the renewal of a license and the license expires, that person must file ATF Form 7, Application for License, and obtain the required license before continuing business activity.

Must a licensee's records be surrendered to ATF if the licensee discontinues business?

Unless there is a successor to the business, a licensee must close out his or her records and send them to the Regional Regulatory Administrator, ATF, within 30 days. If someone is taking over the business, then the licensee will deliver the Firearms Transaction Forms and the *bound book* to the successor.

Can a successor owner of a business entity, other than one who is a successor under the provisions of 27CFR 178.56 (for example, the surviving spouse or child, or a receiver or trustee in bankruptcy), commence a firearms or ammunition business prior to receiving a Federal Firearms License in his or her name?

No. Each person intending to engage in business as a firearms or ammunition dealer, importer, or manufacturer must obtain the required Federal Firearms License prior to commencing such business.

How is an unlicensed person affected by the Gun Control Act?

He or she can only buy or sell a firearm within his or her own state, with the following exceptions: he or she (1) may sell firearms to a licensee in any state (2) may buy a rifle or shotgun from a licensee in a contiguous state provided that the purchaser's state of residence permits such sale or delivery and the purchase and sale comply fully with the laws of both states and (3) may buy a rifle or shotgun from a licensee in another state under the circumstances described in 27 CFR.

In addition, when an unlicensed person purchases a firearm from a licensed dealer, that person will be required to furnish sufficient identification to the dealer to establish name, address, and age, and must complete Section A of Form 4473 and sign the form certifying that he or she is not prohibited by federal law from purchasing or possessing a firearm.

May an unlicensed person obtain a firearm from an out-of-state source if that person arranges to obtain the firearm through a licensed dealer in purchaser's own state?

A person not licensed under the Act and who is not prohibited by the Act from purchasing firearms and ammunition may buy ammunition in any state and transport it into the purchaser's home state. However, a licensed importer, manufacturer, dealer or collector will not be able to ship ammunition in interstate commerce to anyone other than another licensee.

Are there certain persons who can't send or get guns under any circumstances?

Yes. Under the provisions of Title 1 of the Gun Control Act, a person who (1) is under indictment or convicted of a crime punishable by more than a year's imprisonment, or (2) is a fugitive from justice, or (3) is a marijuana or narcotics user or addict, or (4) has been adjudicated as a mental defective or committed to a mental institution cannot ship or receive, in interstate commerce, any firearms or ammunition. Under Title VII of the Omnibus Crime Control and Safe Streets Act of

1968, a person who (1) is a convicted felon, or (2) has been discharged from the Armed Forces under dishonorable conditions, or (3) has been adjudicated as being mentally imcompetent, or (4) having been a citizen of the United States has renounced his or her citizenship, or (5) being an alien, is illegally or unlawfully in the United States, cannot receive, possess or transport a firearm in commerce or affecting commerce.

Convicted felons may apply for relief from the firearms disabilities imposed by federal law.

May a nonlicensee transport firearms interstate for sporting purposes?

Generally, yes. However, the Gun Control Act makes it unlawful for certain persons, such as felons, to engage in the interstate transportation of any firearms or ammunition.

Is there a federal permit or license which allows an individual to take personal firearms into another state or carry them locally?

No. Any requirement in this area is the responsibility of state and local authorities.

Can a nonlicensee ship a firearm out of state?

Yes, provided the addressee is a firearms licensee.

Who may ship firearms through the mails?

Rifles and shotguns may be mailed by nonlicensees. Handguns may be mailed only by licensed firearms dealers and other specified categories of persons. All shipments must be in conformity with U.S. Postal Service laws and regulations.

Can a person who is relocating out of state move firearms with other household goods?

Yes, a person may transport Title I firearms if that person is not prohibited by the GCA or Title VII. Certain Title II firearms, must have the director's prior approval before they may be legally moved. The person must notify the mover that a firearm is being transported. That person should also check state and local laws where he is relocating to insure that the movement into the new state does not violate any state law or local ordinance.

Can someone who isn't in the gun business make a sale to a person in another state?

No. A person who is not licensed may not transfer a firearm by any means to someone in another state who is not a licensee.

Can someone who isn't in the gun business sell a firearm to another person who resides in the same state as the seller?

Yes. There is nothing in the Gun Control Act which prohibits such a sale between residents of the same state provided the sale is not in violation of the state or local ordinances and the purchaser is not prohibited by any provision of the GCA from acquiring or possessing a firearm. In general, a single sale, unattended by other circumstances, does not require that a person be licensed.

What constitutes residency in a state?

The state of residence is the state in which an individual regularly resides or maintains a home. A member of the armed forces on active duty is a resident of the state in which his permanent duty station is located. If a member of the armed forces maintains a home in one state and a permanent duty station in another nearby state to which he commutes each day, then he may purchase a firearm in either the state where stationed or where that person maintains a home.

Can a person who resides in one state and owns property in another state purchase a firearm in either state?

If the person maintains a home in both states and resides in both states for certain periods of the year, he may, while residing in each particular state, purchase a firearm in that state. But simply owning property in another state does not qualify the person to purchase a firearm in that state.

May foreign visitors buy firearms?

Yes, provided they meet the residency requirement. An alien who is in this country legally and has resided in a particular state for a period of at least 90 days can be considered a resident of that state and thus may be able to purchase a firearm providing he or she is not otherwise prohibited. Or, a legal alien who is in a state in which his or her embassy or consulate is located and who has been authorized in writing by the principal officer of the embassy or consulate to purchase a firearm would be considered a resident of that state for purposes of purchasing a firearm. For ammunition purchases, foreign visitors must meet the same requirements as United States citizens.

Since underaged persons cannot buy firearms or ammunition from dealers, how can they obtain them?

A parent or guardian may purchase firearms and ammunition for a juvenile. GCA age restrictions are intended only to prevent juveniles from acting without their parents' or guardian's knowledge.

Firearms Transaction Record Form 4473

Where can a dealer get Forms 4473?

They are available free from the Bureau of Alcohol, Tobacco and Firearms Distribution Center, 3800 S. Four Mile Run Drive, Arlington, Virginia 22206.

Is a Form 4473 needed in the private sale of firearms by a nonlicensee?

No. Form 4473 is required only for sales by a licensee.

Does a dealer have to execute Form 4473 to take a weapon out of saleable inventory for his or her own use?

Yes, such a transfer is treated as any other transfer to a nonlicensed person.

Who signs Form 4473 for the seller?

Form 4473 must be signed by the person who verified the identity of the buyer.

Is a Social Security card a proper means of identification?

No. The seller must verify the purchaser's age and place of residence. A Social Security card cannot be used for this purpose because it does not contain the person's date of birth or address.

When must the Form 4473 be signed?

Form 4473 (Part I) must be signed at the time the physical possession of the firearm is transferred from the licensee to the recipient. Form 4473 Part II is to be signed as required in 27 CFR 178.124.

What is a bound book?

A bound book should be a permanently bound book, or an orderly arrangement of loose-leaf pages which must be maintained on the business premises. In either event, the format must follow that is prescribed in the regulations, and the pages must be numbered consecutively.

May a dealer keep more than one bound book at the same time?

Yes. A dealer in firearms and ammunition is required to maintain two separate bound books—one for firearms and one for ammunition. It may also be convenient for a dealer to account for different brands or types of firearms in separate bound books.

Does the government sell a record book for licensees to use in recording their receipt and disposition of firearms and ammunition?

No. Certain trade associations have them available at nominal cost. Your supplier should be able to tell you about this.

What is the dealer's responsibility where a variation from normal regulatory practice has been authorized?

The Regional Regulatory Administrator's letter authorizing the variation must be kept at the licensed premises and available for inspection. For businesses with more than a single licensed outlet, each outlet covered by the variation must have a copy of the letter authorizing the change.

How much time does a dealer have to record acquistions and dispositions of firearms in his bound book?

Provided commercial records are kept containing the information required on Form 4473, and provided these records are kept available for inspection and separate from other commercial documents, dealers have seven days from the time of receipt or disposition to record said receipt or disposition.

Receipts not covered by such records must be entered in the bound book by the close of the next business day after the acquistion or purchase. If a disposition is made before the acquistion has been entered in the bound book, the acquistion entry must be made at the same time as the disposition entry.

Are the ammunition record-keeping requirements the same as for firearms?

No. Ammunition purchase invoices are records of receipt and do not have to be entered in a bound book. They should be filed separately in an orderly manner to allow inspection, and they should be retained on the licensed premises of the dealer for not less than 2 years following the date of acquisition. The dealer must maintain records of all ammunition he receives for the purposes of sale or distribution, including rifle ammunition and shotgun ammunition.

Retail sales of shotgun ammunition and rifle ammunition need not be recorded. But sales of ammunition which is interchangeable between rifles and handguns and all handgun ammunition must be recorded in the bound book. Rimfire .22 caliber ammunititon is an example of interchangeable ammunition subject to the bound book entry requirement. Unlike firearms which must be retained permanently, these records must be retained for not less than 2 years following the date of sale or disposition.

Are rental firearms subject to record-keeping control?

Yes, but the control is not imposed on the loan or rental of firearms for use on the premises by clubs, associations or similar organizations.

Conduct of Business—Licensees

Does the federal firearms law require that licensees comply with state laws and local published ordinances which are relevant to the enforcement of the Gun Cntrol Act?

Yes. It is unlawful for any licensed importer, licensed manufacturer, licensed dealer, or licensed collector to sell or deliver any firearm or ammunition to any person if the person's purchase or possession would be in violation of any state law or local published ordinance applicable at the place of sale or delivery.

When may a contiguous state sale be permitted?

Contiguous State sales are not permissible until enabling legislation has been enacted by the state so involved. This means that a state has to pass a law which specifically permits its residents to purchase a shotgun or a rifle from a licensee in an adjoining state before those residents may go into the adjoining state and make such a purchase. Of course, all such sales must conform to the requirements of law in the place of sale or delivery.

Can a licensed dealer sell a firearm to a nonlicensee who is a resident of another state?

Generally, no. However, there are two exceptions. In many states, contiguous state sales of rifles and shotguns are permitted. Additionally, a licensed dealer may sell a rifle or shotgun to a resident of another state if the purchaser gives a sworn statement, as required, that his rifle or shotgun has been lost, stolen or has become inoperative during a hunting trip or organized rifle or shotgun match or contest. In all other cases, a licensee may not make direct sales to a nonresident. The dealer may, however, ship the firearm to a licensed dealer whose business is in the purchaser's state of residence. The purchaser could then pick up the firearm after completing Form 4473.

May a dealer sell firearms and ammunition to law enforcement agencies and individual officers in another state?

Yes. Sales and deliveries of firearms and ammunition to police and sheriff departments are not prohibited by the GCA. A dealer may also sell or ship a Title I firearm or ammunition to an individual law officer, regardless of age, if he has a signed statement from an authorized official of the agency for which the officer works stating that the item is to be used in the buyer's official duties. Form 4473 need not be executed; however, the bound book must be properly notated.

May an agent of a licensed dealer, such as a manager or clerk, who is under 21 years of age, sell handguns and ammunition suitable for use in handguns for the licensee?

Yes. As an agent of the dealer, he is not restricted by the GCA because of age. Form 4473, in all cases, should be signed for the seller by the person who verifies the identity of the buyer.

Must a buyer sign for ammunition?

The Gun Control Act doesn't require this, but local or state law or some businesses may.

Does a customer have to be a certain age to buy firearms and ammunition from a licensee?

Yes. Long guns and long gun ammunition may be sold only to persons 18 years of age or older. Sales of handguns and handgun ammunition are limited to persons 21 years of age and older. Although some state and local ordinances have lower age requirements, dealers are bound by the minimum age requirements established by the GCA. If state or local ordinances establish a higher minimum age, dealers must observe those higher age requirements.

May a licensee sell interchangeable ammunition such as .22 caliber rimfire to a person less than 21 years old?

Yes, provided the buyer is 18 years of age or older, and the dealer is satisifed that it is for use in a rifle. If the ammunition is intended for use in a handgun, the 21-year-old minimum age requirement is applicable. In any case, the sale must be recorded.

In transactions between licensees, how is the seller assured that a purchaser of the firearms is a licensed firearm dealer?

Verification shall be established by the transferee furnishing to the transferor a signed certified copy of the transferee's license and by such other means as the transferor deems necessary.

Must a multilicensed business submit a certified copy of each of its licenses when acquiring firearms or ammunition?

No. It need submit to the seller only a list, certified to be true, correct and complete, containing the name, address, license number and expiration date for each location.

May a licensee continue to deliver to a business whose license has expired?

Yes, for a period of 45 days following the expiration date of the license.

After the 45-day period the transferor licensee is required to again verify the licensed status of the transferee. If the transferee's license renewal application is still pending, in order to continue shipments, the transferor licensee must obtain evidence from the regional director to the effect that a license renewal has been timely filed by the transferee and is still pending.

Are gun clubs also considered to be in the business of selling ammunition?

Generally, no. A club with facilities for shooting, gun handling classes, etc., furnishing ammunition for on premises use, is not engaged in the business.

If such clubs desire, they may be licensed as a firearms dealer, and authorized to sell for off-premises use. All ammunition sold for off-premises use must be recorded in the manner prescribed for ordinary ammunition sales.

May firearms and ammunition be sold at a gun show?

Yes, within the following framework, provided local ordinances are not violated and excepting NFA weapons.
A licensed firearms dealer may:

1. Display and take orders for firearms and ammunition. Orders must be filled only at the dealer's licensed premises.
2. Buy firearms and ammunition from a licensed collector and any nonlicensee.

A nonlicensed resident of the state in which the show is being held may:

1. Make an occasional sale of a firearm to another nonlicensee residing in his state, as long as that person is not *engaging in the business*
2. Buy firearms from a nonlicensee residing in his or her state

A licensed collector may:

1. Buy curios and relics from any source.
2. Dispose of curios and relics to another licensed collector or to nonlicensee residents in his or her state.

Gunsmiths

Is a license needed to engrave, customize, refinish or repair a firearm?

Yes. A person conducting such activity is considered to be a gunsmith within the definition of a dealer.

Does a gunsmith need to enter in his permanent bound book record every firearm which is received for adjustment or repair?

Yes. However, if a firearm is brought in for repairs and the owner waits while it is being repaired or if the gunsmith is able to return the firearm to the owner during the same business day, it is not necessary to list the gun in the records as an acquisiton. If the gunsmith has possession of the firearm from one business day to another or longer, it must be recorded in the permanent bound book records.

Is Form 4473 required when a gunsmith returns a repaired firearm?

No, provided the firearm is returned to the person from whom received.

Can a gunsmith make immediate repairs at locations other than the established place of business?

Yes.

Is one who reloads ammunition required to be licensed?

Yes, if he sells or distributes the reloads. No, if reloading only for personal use.

Chapter 13

The National Rifle Association

For more than a century, or since 1871 when the organization was founded in New York State by a group of National Guard officers, the National Rifle Association (NRA) has fought for the right of reputable American citizens to own and enjoy firearms. Wherever antigun legislation is proposed limiting that right, in Congress or small town council, the NRA leads the fight against it.

The headquarters of the NRA is now located at 1600 Rhode Island Ave., Washington, D.C. 20036. The organization is owned and operated by its members—a group of people who have been brought together by a mutual desire to enhance their ability with and knowledge of firearms, and to improve the lot of American shooters through organization.

Its chief goal is to help legislative bodies draft intelligent laws which will be effective in discouraging the use of firearms by the criminal element and yet not hinder the rights of reputable citizens. But it does more. In the field of national defense, the NRA has had much to do with the development of the small arms training program of the armed forces of the United States. It has made shooting into a well-organized national sport.

NRA membership does not entail any obligation to qualify for a marksmanship rating or to compete in shooting matches.

In fact, thousands of NRA members don't even own a gun, but are just interested in furthering the broad program of the Association.

Adult membership in the NRA is open to U.S. citizens over 18 years of age, and includes a subscription to *The American Rifleman*—the organization's official monthly publication. The current membership fee is $15 per year, $40 for 3 years, $60 for 5 years. Life membership is also available and includes the privileges of active affiliation for life, plus a lifetime subscription to *The American Rifleman*. The current life membership fee is $300.

NRA POLICY ON FIREARMS CONTROLS

The National Rifle Association believes that the *illegal use* and not the *ownership* of a firearm should be the subject of legislative control.

The National Rifle Association believes that the efforts of government should be directed toward the enforcement of existing laws rather than further regulation of the purchase and possession of firearms.

The NRA believes in more effective enforcement of present laws directed against criminal conduct. It wants to assure more speedy trials unencumbered by technicalities, to forbid plea bargaining in cases of violent crimes, to impose safeguards against unwarranted probation and parole of convicted persons and to initiate reforms of our penal system.

The NRA opposes any legislation directed against the firearm rather than against its criminal use.

The NRA is against the efforts towards legislation to outlaw certain kinds of handguns—legislation which it feels will be ineffective in the prevention of crime and which ignores the crime deterrent effect of the possession of firearms by law-abiding people.

The NRA believes that calls for additional gun controls do a great disservice to the cause of effective and substantial law enforcement by distracting attention from the causes of crime and diverting funds and energy from solutions. Crime is the product of differing conditions from place to place, and the factors that affect the volume and type of crime as indicated in the FBI Uniform Crime Reports annually are as follows:

- Density and size of the community population and the metropolitan area of which it is a part
- Composition of the population with reference particularly to age, sex and race
- Economic status and mores of the population
- Stability of population, including commuters, seasonal and other transient types
- Climate, including seasonal weather conditions
- Educational, recreational and religious characteristics
- Effective strength of the police force
- Policies of the prosecuting officials
- Attitudes and policies of the courts and corrections
- Relationships and attitudes of law enforcement and the community
- Administrative and investigative efficiency of law enforcement, including degree of adherence to crime reporting standards
- Organization and cooperation of adjoining and overlapping police jurisdictions

The NRA has long supported a broad framework of regulation of the sale, purchase, use and importation of firearms. NRA-supported controls range from the imposition of mandatory penalties for the possession of a firearm or a firearm facsimile in crime, and the prohibition of the possession of firearms by certain undesirable persons, to the licensing of manufacturers, dealers, importers and pawnbrokers and their keeping of records.

Basic Policy Statement

The following statement of policy was adopted by the NRA Board of Directors in April 1958. This policy remains the basic position of the NRA on firearms regulation.

Among the objectives of the NRA of America are the following: to promote public safety, law and order, and the national defense; to educate and train citizens of good repute in the safe and efficient handling of small arms, and in the technique of design, production and group instruction; to increase the knowledge of small arms and promote efficiency in the use of such arms on the part of members of law enforcement agencies, of the armed forces, and of citizens who would be subject to service in the event of war; and generally to encourage the lawful ownership and use of small arms by citizens of good repute.

A. The NRA believes that firearms legislation is of insufficient value in the prevention of crime to justify the inevitable restrictions which such legislation places upon law-abiding citizens. In those cases where legislative bodies, nevertheless, determine that some firearms control legislation is necessary, the position of the NRA is as follows:

1. The NRA is opposed to control measures which levy discriminatory or punitive taxes or fees on the purchase, ownership or use of rifles, shotguns, pistols and revolvers.

2. The NRA is opposed to proposals to license the possession or purchase of a rifle, shotgun, pistol or revolver. The inevitable result of such a licensing regulation is to vest the arbitrary power to say who may and who may not own a gun in the hands of an appointed or elected official. It is the illegal use and not the ownership of a firearm which should be subject of legislative control.

3. The NRA is opposed to the theory that a target shooter, hunter or collector, in order to transport a handgun for lawful purposes, should be required to meet the conditions for a permit to carry a weapon concealed on his person.

4. The NRA is opposed to the registration on any level of government of the ownership of rifles, shotguns, pistols or revolvers for any purpose whatever. Regardless of professed intent, there can be only one outcome of registration, and that is to make possible the seizure of such weapons by political authorities, or by persons seeking to overthrow the government by force. Registration will not keep guns out of the hands of undesirable persons, and few people seriously claim that it will.

5. The NRA is opposed to legislation which denies, or interferes with, individual rights of our citizens or is designed purely for the convenience of law enforcement officers or for the purpose of circumventing due process of law in order to obtain convictions more easily. The desire to see our laws adequately enforced is not justification for any law which can make a prudent, law-abiding citizen an unwitting violator, or which denies the right of self-defense.

B. The National Rifle Association of America does not initiate any gun control legislation at any level of government. When, nevertheless, firearms legislation is enacted, it should not exceed any of the following four provisions:

1. Legislation designed to prohibit the possession of firearms by persons who have been finally convicted of a crime of violence, fugitives from justice, mental incompetents, drug addicts and persons while adjudicated an habitual drunkard.

2. Legislation providing severe additional penalties for the use of a dangerous weapon in the commission of a crime.

3. Legislation making the sale of firearms to juveniles subject to parental consent and the use of firearms in public by juveniles subject to adequate supervision.

4. Legislation regulating the carrying of concealed handguns should be reasonable and the requirements for such carrying should be clearly set forth in the law. The conditions having been met, the issuance of a license to carry should be mandatory and should license the act of carrying, not the handgun itself.

Amplification of Basic Policy

The NRA Board of Directors in November 1971 adopted the following eight points which are a positive restatement and reflection of NRA policy.

■ Prohibit firearms sales by dealers to persons under voting age.

- Require adequate supervision for use of firearms by juveniles.
- Require mandatory penalties for the possession of a firearm or facsimile in the commission of a crime.
- Control the importation of all firearms and their component parts.
- Prohibit possession of firearms by convicted felons, drug addicts, habitual drunkards, fugitives from justice, metal incompetents and juvenile delinquents.
- Control all machine guns and destructive devices.
- Require licensing of manufacturers, importers, dealers and pawnbrokers, and their keeping of records.
- Assure citizens of good repute the continuing right to own and use firearms for sport and self-defense.

Against Crime Rather Than Firearms

The NRA Executive Committee adopted the following statement in July 1974 on the ineffectiveness of legislation directed against firearms rather than the unlawful use of firearms:

There are many thousands of firearms laws in force at federal, state and local levels throughout the United States. Numerous additional laws are proposed and some are enacted every year. The majority of such laws are intended to prevent or reduce the incidence of violent crime. However, virtually all such laws are directed toward the inanimate object used in the crime—the firearm—rather than toward the deterrence and punishment of the criminal misuse of firearms. The widespread increase in violent crime throughout the United States and in many other nations clearly demonstrates that such firearms legislation cannot successfully prevent or reduce violent crime.

Accordingly, the NRA opposes any proposed legislation, at any level of government, which is directed against the inanimate firearm rather than against the criminal misuse of firearms.

The NRA also takes the position that the attempt, whether by legislation or regulation, to outlaw certain kinds of handguns by employing size, metallurgical or similar standards or characteristics is arbitrary and unsound. Such legislation is ineffective in the prevention or reduction of crime and ignores the crime deterrent effect of the possession of firearms by law-abiding owners.

The NRA is wholly dedicated to the reduction and prevention of crime, but legislation against firearms rather than the criminal misuse of firearms is both unneeded and counterproductive. Such firearms legislation further burdens the vast majority of law-abiding firearms owners, and results in immense waste of resources and diverts public attention and support from truly effective crime control efforts.

Glossary

action—main mechanism in a modern rifle.

barrel—holds the powder charge, wading and bullet before firing and acts as a guide for the bullet upon firing.

black powder—mixture of charcoal, sulphur and saltpeter; grains are coated with graphite.

blow-back—a type of recoil-powered semiautomatic action where the shell casing blows back against the breech block causing it to open.

bluing—process done to metal parts on firearms to dull the bright steel color of exposed metal parts and also helps prevent rust.

bolt-action—operates by a bolt which locks the cartridge in the chamber of the barrel and also ejects the cartridges when the bolt is open.

break-open shotgun—action where the gun opens at the breech, tipping the rear of the barrel upward where the shells are then placed in the chamber; barrels then lift up until locked in place.

browning—process similar to bluing but gives the traditional brown finish found on Damascus barrels.

button rifling—method of rifling where a special button, similar in shape to a bullet, is drawn through a barrel blank to create the grooves.

caliber—refers to the size of the barrel bore in a rifle.

checkering—process of cutting a pattern into pistol grips and forearms on gun stocks.

checkering cradle—used to secure the gun stock during checkering so it can be easily rotated as you move across the pattern; also useful for stock inletting, sanding, staining and finishing.

checkering tools—used for fine-line checkering on stocks and forearms.

chilled shot—shot formed with an alloy of lead and antimony different from that used in drop shot.

choke—classification determined by the amount of constriction created at the end of the barrel. Amount of choke is dependent on the number of shot that actually hits the target in comparison with the number that leaves the end of the barrel. Measured in terms of points.

chrome-molybdenum steel—type of steel which withstands high pressure well; used for making barrels.

copperized shot—shot covered with copper by an electrolytic process, making the shot harder and more resistant to deformation.

Damascus barrels—twist steel barrels whose manufacture resulted in the grain of the metal appearing on the outside of the barrel in the form of irregular links or spirals creating intricate patterns; unsafe to use with smokeless powder.

double-action revolver—cocks and fires the pistol with a single pull of the trigger.

double-kick—jolts experienced from the two-part recoil of the long-recoil shotgun. One kick is felt when the shell is fired; the other when the barrel and breech slam home.

drooped wire brush—heavy brush made of bronze that removes hard fouling and rust from barrels with ease.

drop shot—shot formed when molten lead is mixed with a small amount of arsenic.

Enfield rifling—type of rifling with a square shape that twists through the length of the rifle barrel.

Federal Firearms License—must be held by anyone who works on a firearm other than his own.

Firearms Transaction Record—federal form covering the transfer of a firearm to a nonlicensed person.

flexible brass jag tip—type of tip for cleaning firearms; patch wraps around the jag causing the patch to press evenly on the bore squeezing oil into the pores of the steel.

florentine finish—gun engraving made by cutting crossed sets of lines.

gas-operated action—method of powering a semiautomatic action where the rifle operates off the gases generated by the expansion of gun powder.

gauge—refers to the size of the barrel bore in a shotgun.

glass bedding—used to fit the barreled action to the rifle stock to improve accuracy; also used for repairs.

Gun Control Act—regulates firearms-related businesses.

gun sling—provides a comfortable means of carrying a firearm and helps steady a weapon while firing.

hammer rifling— method of rifling where the rifle barrel is pounded over a special mandrel to make the grooves.

inletting—process for making a rifle stock from a blank by inserting the metal parts and chipping away excess wood.

leading—metal fouling from lead bullets; caused by a rough or pitted barrel.

leather polisher tips—type of tip for cleaning firearms using buff leather disks; recommended since no metal touches the bore.

lever action—rapid-firing, repeating rifles using a magazine to feed ammunition.

lock—main mechanism on a muzzle-loading rifle that controls the ignition of powder in the barrel.

loop—upper portion of the gun sling; should be adjusted to come within two inches of the butt swivel.

Kentucky rifle—one of the first rifles using spiral grooves in the barrel resulting in more accuracy.

Mannlicher stocks—forearm extends to the muzzle of the barrel; barrel lengths commonly 18 to 20 inches.

metal fouling—comes from a deposit of metal left by the bullet in the bore; can cause poor accuracy.

micrometer reading—sum of the readings of the graduations on the barrel and the thimble.

muzzle brake—installed on the barrel to reduce recoil; most use a prequick outlet for surplus gas to escape.

National Rifle Association—organization formed to lobby for gun legislation that will not hinder the rights of citizens to own firearms.

ordinance steel—steel with high tensile strength and easy to machine; used for making barrels.

pattern—percentage of shot that hits within a circular target at a specified range.

plain jag tip—type of tip used for cleaning firearms which gives a uniform cleaning action and reverses inside the barrel.

point—refers to 0.001 inch difference between the muzzle diameter and the bore diameter; measurement of choke.

pump action—mechanism allows the shooter to cycle cartridges through without having to remove the trigger finger.

recoil—method for powering semiautomatic actions.

recoil pads—cushions the gun's recoiling kick as the gun is fired; can be used to extend the stock's length for better fit.

revolver—a cylinder rotates one chamber at a time allowing 6 to 9 discharges.

rifling—spiral grooves in a barrel that impart spin to a bullet as it traverses the length of the barrel.

roll jag tip—type of tip for cleaning firearms; permits rolled or wrapped patches to be used; good for cleaning rifles that have to be wiped out from the muzzle end.

rolling-block action—single-shot action where the breech block pivots and rolls back to eject the fired cartridge and insert a new one.

semiautomatic—requires the trigger be pulled each time a shot is made.

shotgun—smoothbored gun; modern shotguns are loaded at the breech instead of through the muzzle.

single-action revolver—hammer has to be pulled back after the trigger has been pulled before the pistol can be fired again.

single slotted tip—type of tip for cleaning firearms; holds the patch under all conditions.

solder—used to join sight ramps, sight bases and other firearm accessories; use conventional 50% tin and 50% lead solder without an acid core.

sporter stock—most common type of rifle stock.

stock—wooden member in which the lock and barrel are imbedded.

target stocks—area of the forearm and action is somewhat wider than on the sporting stock.

tinning—coating an area of a firearm by soft soldering.

tip-up action—type of single-shot action where the breech end of the barrel tips up and fires.

trigger shoe—evenly spreads trigger release pressure over the ball of the trigger finger.

twist—amount of pitch in a rifle barrel's rifling; determines rate of spin a bullet will have when it leaves the end of the rifle barrel.

wool mop tips—type of tip used for cleaning firearms; good for oiling the bores of rifles and shotguns; must be kept clean.

Appendix A

Sources of Supply

Alamo Heat Treating Co.
Box 55345
Houston , TX 77055

Albright Prod. Co.
P.O. Box 1144
Portola, CA 96122
(trap butt plates)

Alley Supply Co.
Carson Valley Industrial Park
Gardnerville, NV 89410

Ames Precision Machine Works
5270 Geddes Rd.
Ann Arbor, MI 48105
(portable hardness tester)

Anderson & Co.
1203 Broadway
Yakima, WA 98902
(tang safe)

Armite Labs
1845 Randolph St.
Los Angeles, CA 90001
(pen oiler)

B-Square Co.)
Box 11281
Fort Worth, TX 76110

Jim Baiar
Rt. 1-B Box 352
Columbia Falls, MT 59912
(hex screws)

Al Biesen
W. 2039 Sinto Ave.
Spokane, WA 99201
(grip caps, butt plates)

Bonanza Sports Mfg. Co.
412 Western Ave.
Faribault, MN 55021

Brown & Sharpe Mfg. Co.
Presision Park
No. Kingston, RI 02852

Brownells, Inc
200 South Front Street
Montezuma, IA 50171

W.E. Brownell
1852 Alessandro Trail
Vista, CA 92083
(checkering tools)

Maynard P. Buehler, Inc.
17 Orinda Hwy.
Orinda, CA 94563
(Rocol lube)

Burgess Vibrocrafters, Inc.
Rt. 83
Grayslake, IL 60030
M.H. Canjar
500 E. 45th
Denver, CO 80216
(triggers, etc.)

Chapman Mfg. Co.
Rt. 17 at Saw Mill Rd.
Durham, CT 06422
Chase Chemical Corp.
3527 Smallman St.
Pittsburgh, PA 15201
(Chubb Multigauge)
Chicago Wheel & Mfg. Co.
1101 W. Monroe St.
Chicago, IL 60607
(Handee grinders)
Christy Gun Works
875-57th St.
Sacramento, CA 95819
Clover Mfg. Co.
139 Woodward Ave.
Norwalk, CT 06856
(Clover compound)
Clymer Mfg. Co.
14241 W. 11 Mile Rd.
Oak Park, Mi 48237
(reamers)
Colbert Industries
10107 Adella
South Gate, CA 90280
(PanaVise)
A. Constantine & Son
2050 Eastchester Rd.
Bronx, NY 10461
(wood)
Dave Cook
720 Hancock Ave.
Hancock, MI 49930
(metalsmithing only)
Cougar & Hunter
G 6398 W. Pierson Rd.
Flushing, MI 48433
(scope jigs)

Alvin L. Davidson
1215 Branson
Las Cruses, NM 88001
(action sleeves)
Dayton-Traister Co.
P.O Box 593
Oak Harbor, WA 98277
(triggers)
Dem-Bart Electric Checkering Tools
117-5th St.
Edmonds, WA 98020
Ditto Industries
527 N. Alexandria
Los Angeles, CA 90004
(clamp tool)
Dixie Diamond Tool Co., Inc.
6875 S.W. 81st St.
Miami, FL 33143
(marking pencils)
Dremel Mfg. Co.
4915-21st St.
Racine, WI 53406
(grinders)
Charles E. Duffy
Williams Lane
West Hurley, NY 12491

E-Z Tool Co.
P.O. Box 3186
Des Moines, IA 50313
(lathe taper attachment)
Edmund Scientific Co.
101 E. Glouster Pike
Barrington, NJ 08077
F.K. Elliot
Box 785
Ramona, CA 92065
(reamers)

Forster Products, Inc.
82 E. Lanark Ave.
Lanark, IL 61046
Keith Francis
P.O. Box 537
Talent, OR 97540
(reamers)

G.R.S. Corp.
Box 1157
Boulder, CO 80302
(Gravemeister)
Gager Gage and Tool Co.
27509 Industrial Blvd.
Hayward, CA 94545
(speedlock triggers for Rem.
1100 & 870 pumps)
Gilmore Pattern Works
P.O. Box 50231
Tulsa, OK 74150
Gold Lode, Inc.
181 Gary Ave.
Wheaton, IL 60187
(gold inlay kit)
Gopher Shooter's Supply
Box 278
Garibault, MN 55021
(screwdrivers, etc.)
Grace Metal Prod.
115 Ames St.
Elk Rapids, MI 49629
(screwdrivers, drifts)
Gunline Tools Inc.
719 No. East St.
Anaheim, CA 92805

H & M
24062 Orchard Lake Rd.
Box 258
Farmington, MI 48024
(reamers)
Half Moon Rifle Shop
Rt. 1B, Box 352
Columbia Falls, MT 59912
(hex screws)
Hartford Reamer Co.
Box 134
Lathrup Village, MI 48075

Paul Jaeger Inc.
211 Leedom St.
Jenkintown, PA 19046

Jeffredo Gunsight Co.
1629 Via Monserate
Fallbrook, CA 92028
(trap butt plate)

Kasenite Co., Inc.
3 King St.
Mahwah, NJ 07430
(surface hardening compound)

LanDav Custom Guns
7213 Lee Highway
Falls Church, VA 22046
John G. Lawson
1802 E. Columbia Ave.
Tacoma, WA 98404
Lea Mfg. Co.
237 E. Aurora St.
Waterbury, CT 06720
Lock's Phila. Gun Exchange
6700 Rowland Ave.
Philadelphia, PA 19149

Marker Machine Co.
Box 426
Charleston, IL 61920

Michaels of Oregon Co.
P.O.Box 13010
Portland, OR 97213

Viggo Miller
P.O. Box 4181
Omaha, NE 68104
(trigger attachment)

Miller Single Trigger Mfg. Co.
R.D. on Rt. 209
Millersburt, PA 17061

Frank Mittermeier, Inc.
3577 E. Tremont
Bronx, NY 10465

Modern Tools Corp.
Box 407 Dept. GD
Woodside, NY 11377

N&J Sales
Lime Kiln Rd.
Northford, CT 06472
(screwdrivers)

Karl A. Neise, Inc.
5602 Roosevelt Ave.
Woodside, NY 11377

Palmgren
8383 South Chicago Ave.
Chicago, IL 60167
(vises, etc.)

PanaVise, Colbert Industries
10107 Adelia Ave.
South Gate, CA 90280

C.R. Pedersen & Son
Ludington, MI 49431

Ponderay Lab
210 W. Prasch
Yakima, WA 98902
(epoxy glass bedding)

Redford Reamer Co.
Box 40604
Redford Hts. Sta.
Detroit, MI 48240

Richland Arms Co.
321 W. Adraian St.
Blissfield, MI 49228

Riley's Supply Co.
121 No. Main St.
Avilla, IN 46710
(Niedner butt plates, caps)

Ruhr-American Corp.
So. Hwy. #5
Glenwood, MN 56334
A.G. Russell
1705 Hiway 71N
Springdale, AR 72764
(Arkansas oilstones)

Schaffner Mfg. Co.
Emsworth, Pittsburgh, PA 15202
(polishing kits)

Schuetzen Gun Works
Rt. 12
Olympia, WA 98503

Shaw's
Rt. 4 Box 407-L
Escondido, CA 92025

A.D. Soucy Co.
Box 191
Fort Kent, ME 04743
(ADSCO stock finish)

L.S. Starrett Co.
Athol, MA 01331

Texas Platers Supply Co.
2453 W. Five Mile Parkway
Dallas, TX 75233
(plating kit)

Timney Mfg. Co.
2847 E. Siesta Lane
Phoenix, AZ 85024

Stan de Treville
Box 33021
San Diego, CA 92103
(checkering patterns)

Twin City Steel Treating Co., Ins.
1114 S. 3rd.
Minneapolis, MN 55415
(heat treating)

Ward Mfg. Co.
500 Ford Blvd.
Hamilton, OH 45011

Will-burt Co.
P.O. Box 160
Orrville, OH 44667
(vises)

Williams Gun Sight Co.
7389 Lapeer Rd.
Davison, MI 48423

Wilson Arms Co.
63 Leetes Island Rd.
Branford, CT 06405

W.C. Wolff Co.
Box 232
Ardmore, PA 19003
(springs)

Woodcraft Supply Corp.
313 Montvale
Woburn, MA 01801

Appendix B

Gunsmithing: Continuing Education

If you are thinking of going into the gun repair business or of practicing gunsmithing on a full-time basis, you may want to look into formal training. The following schools offer courses in gunsmithing.

Trade Schools

Colorado School of Trades
1545 Hoyt
Lakewood, CO 80215

Lassen Community College
P.O. Box 3000
Susanville, CA 96130

Oregon Institute of Technology
Small Arms Dept.
Klamath Falls, OR 97601

Penn. Gunsmith School
812 Ohio River Blvd. Avalon
Pittsburgh, PA 15202

Trinidad State Junior College
Trinidad, CO 81082

Correspondence Courses

Modern School of Gunsmithing
4225 North Brown Ave.
Scottsdale, AZ 85251

North American School of Firearms
4401 Birch St.
Newport Beach, CA 92663

Appendix C

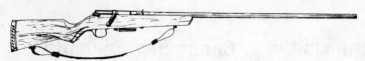

Charts & Formulas

Gunsmithing work, along with any other mechanical trade, requires a certain amount of calculations, such as laying out and cutting screw threads. In addition a knowledge of formulas for performing such operations as gun bluing or mixing one's own bore cleaner is required. Charts and formulas found here should prove useful to the hobbyist and professional alike.

Table C-1. Metric English Conversion.

Measures of Length

1 millimeter (mm) = 0.03937 inch
1 centimeter (cm) = 0.39370 inch
1 meter (m) = 39.37008 inches
              = 3.2808 feet
              = 1.0936 yards
1 kilometer (km) = 0.6214 mile
1 inch = 25.4 millimeters (mm)
        = 2.54 centimeters (cm)
1 foot = 304.8 millimeters (mm)
        = 0.3048 meter (m)
1 yard = 0.9144 meter (m)
1 mile = 1.609 kilometers (km)

Measures of Area

1 square millimeter = 0.00155 square inch
1 square centimeter = 0.155 square inch
1 square meter = 10.764 square feet
               = 1.196 square yards
1 square kilometer = 0.3861 square mile
1 square inch = 645.2 square millimeters
              = 6.452 square centimeters
1 square foot = 929 square centimeters
              = 0.0929 square meter
1 square yard = 0.836 square meter
1 square mile = 2.5899 square kilometers

Measures of Capacity (Dry)

1 cubic centimeter (cm³) = 0.061 cubic inch
1 liter = 0.0353 cubic foot
        = 61.023 cubic inches
1 cubic meter (m³) = 35.315 cubic feet
                   = 1.308 cubic yards
1 cubic inch = 16.38706 cubic centimeters (cm³)
1 cubic foot = 0.02832 cubic meter (m³)
             = 28.317 liters
1 cubic yard = 0.7646 cubic meter (m³)

Measures of Capacity (Liquid)

1 liter = 1.0567 U.S. quarts
        = 0.2642 U.S. gallon
        = 0.2200 Imperial gallon
1 cubic meter (m³) = 264.2 U.S. gallons
                   = 219.969 Imperial gallons
1 U.S. quart = 0.946 liter
1 Imperial quart = 1.136 liters
1 U.S. gallon = 3.785 liters
1 Imperial gallon = 4.546 liters

Measures of Weight

1 gram (g) = 15.432 grains
           = 0.03215 ounce troy
           = 0.03527 ounce avoirdupois
1 kilogram (kg) = 35.274 ounces avoirdupois
                = 2.2046 pounds
1000 kilograms (kg) = 1 metric ton (t)
                    = 1.1023 tons of 2000 pounds
                    = 0.9842 ton of 2240 pounds
1 ounce avoirdupois = 28.35 grams (g)
1 ounce troy = 31.103 grams
1 pound = 453.6 grams
        = 0.4536 kilogram (kg)
1 ton of 2240 pounds = 1016 kilograms (kg)
                     = 1.016 metric tons
1 grain = 0.0648 gram (g)
1 metric ton = 0.9842 ton of 2240 pounds
             = 2204.6 pounds

Table C-2. English to Metric Conversion Table.

Decimals to Millimeters

Decimal	mm	Decimal	mm
0.001	0.0254	0.500	12.7000
0.002	0.0508	0.510	12.9540
0.003	0.0762	0.520	13.2080
0.004	0.1016	0.530	13.4620
0.005	0.1270	0.540	13.7160
0.006	0.1524	0.550	13.9700
0.007	0.1778	0.560	14.2240
0.008	0.2032	0.570	14.4780
0.009	0.2286	0.580	14.7320
0.010	0.2540	0.590	14.9860
0.020	0.5080		
0.030	0.7620		
0.040	1.0160	0.600	15.2400
0.050	1.2700	0.610	15.4940
0.060	1.5240	0.620	15.7480
0.070	1.7780	0.630	16.0020
0.080	2.0320	0.640	16.2560
0.090	2.2860	0.650	16.5100
0.100	2.5400	0.660	16.7640
0.110	2.7940	0.670	17.0180
0.120	3.0480	0.680	17.2720
0.130	3.3020	0.690	17.5260
0.140	3.5560		
0.150	3.8100		
0.160	4.0640	0.700	17.7800
0.170	4.3180	0.710	18.0340
0.180	4.5720	0.720	18.2880
0.190	4.8260	0.730	18.5420
0.200	5.0800	0.740	18.7960
0.210	5.3340	0.750	19.0500
0.220	5.5880	0.760	19.3040
0.230	5.8420	0.770	19.5580
0.240	6.0960	0.780	19.8120
0.250	6.3500	0.790	20.0660
0.260	6.6040		
0.270	6.8580		
0.280	7.1120	0.800	20.3200
0.290	7.3660	0.810	20.5740
0.300	7.6200	0.820	20.8280
0.310	7.8740	0.830	21.0820
0.320	8.1280	0.840	21.3360
0.330	8.3820	0.850	21.5900
0.340	8.6360	0.860	21.8440
0.350	8.9000	0.870	22.0980
0.360	9.1440	0.880	22.3520
0.370	9.3980	0.890	22.6060
0.380	9.6520		
0.390	9.9060	0.900	22.8600
0.400	10.1600	0.910	23.1140
0.410	10.4140	0.920	23.3680
0.420	10.6680	0.930	23.6220
0.430	10.9220	0.940	23.8760
0.440	11.1760	0.950	24.1300
0.450	11.4300	0.960	24.3840
0.460	11.6840	0.970	24.6380
0.470	11.9380	0.980	24.8920
0.480	12.1920	0.990	25.1460
0.490	12.4460	1.000	25.4000

Fractions to Decimals to Millimeters

Fraction	Decimal	mm	Fraction	Decimal	mm
1/64	0.0156	0.3969	33/64	0.5156	13.0969
1/32	0.0312	0.7938	17/32	0.5312	13.4938
3/64	0.0469	1.1906	35/64	0.5469	13.8906
1/16	0.0625	1.5875	9/16	0.5625	14.2875
5/64	0.0781	1.9844	37/64	0.5781	14.6844
3/32	0.0938	2.3812	19/32	0.5938	15.0812
7/64	0.1094	2.7781	39/64	0.6094	15.4781
1/8	0.1250	3.1750	5/8	0.6250	15.8750
9/64	0.1406	3.5719	41/64	0.6406	16.2719
5/32	0.1562	3.9688	21/32	0.6562	16.6688
11/64	0.1719	4.3656	43/64	0.6719	17.0656
3/16	0.1875	4.7625	11/16	0.6875	17.4625
13/64	0.2031	5.1594	45/64	0.7031	17.8594
7/32	0.2188	5.5562	23/32	0.7188	18.2562
15/64	0.2344	5.9531	47/64	0.7344	18.6531
1/4	0.2500	6.3500	3/4	0.7500	19.0500
17/64	0.2656	6.7469	49/64	0.7656	19.4469
9/32	0.2812	7.1438	25/32	0.7812	19.8438
19/64	0.2969	7.5406	51/64	0.7969	20.2406
5/16	0.3125	7.9375	13/16	0.8125	20.6375
21/64	0.3281	8.3344	53/64	0.8281	21.0344
11/32	0.3438	8.7312	27/32	0.8438	21.4312
23/64	0.3594	9.1281	55/64	0.8594	21.8281
3/8	0.3750	9.5250	7/8	0.8750	22.2250
25/64	0.3906	9.9219	57/64	0.8906	22.6219
13/32	0.4062	10.3188	29/32	0.9062	23.0188
27/64	0.4219	10.7156	59/64	0.9219	23.4156
7/16	0.4375	11.1125	15/16	0.9375	23.8125
29/64	0.4531	11.5094	61/64	0.9531	24.2094
15/32	0.4688	11.9062	31/32	0.9688	24.6062
31/64	0.4844	12.3031	63/64	0.9844	25.0031
1/2	0.5000	12.7000	I	1.0000	25.4000

Table C-3. Metric to English Conversion Table.

mm	Decimal	mm	Decimal	mm	Decimal	mm	Decimal	mm	Decimal
0.01	.00039	0.41	.01614	0.81	.03189	21	.82677	61	2.40157
0.02	.00079	0.42	.01654	0.82	.03228	22	.86614	62	2.44094
0.03	.00118	0.43	.01693	0.83	.03268	23	.90551	63	2.48031
0.04	.00157	0.44	.01732	0.84	.03307	24	.94488	64	2.51969
0.05	.00197	0.45	.01772	0.85	.03346	25	.98425	65	2.55906
0.06	.00236	0.46	.01811	0.86	.03386	26	1.02362	66	2.59843
0.07	.00276	0.47	.01850	0.87	.03425	27	1.06299	67	2.63780
0.08	.00315	0.48	.01890	0.88	.03465	28	1.10236	68	2.67717
0.09	.00354	0.49	.01929	0.89	.03504	29	1.14173	69	2.71654
0.10	.00394	0.50	.01969	0.90	.03543	30	1.18110	70	2.75591
0.11	.00433	0.51	.02008	0.91	.03583	31	1.22047	71	2.79528
0.12	.00472	0.52	.02047	0.92	.03622	32	1.25984	72	2.83465
0.13	.00512	0.53	.02087	0.93	.03661	33	1.29921	73	2.87402
0.14	.00551	0.54	.02126	0.94	.03701	34	1.33858	74	2.91339
0.15	.00591	0.55	.02165	0.95	.03740	35	1.37795	75	2.95276
0.16	.00630	0.56	.02205	0.96	.03780	36	1.41732	76	2.99213
0.17	.00669	0.57	.02244	0.97	.03819	37	1.45669	77	3.03150
0.18	.00709	0.58	.02283	0.98	.03858	38	1.49606	78	3.07087
0.19	.00748	0.59	.02323	0.99	.03898	39	1.53543	79	3.11024
0.20	.00787	0.60	.02362	1.00	.03937	40	1.57480	80	3.14961
0.21	.00827	0.61	.02402	1	.03937	41	1.61417	81	3.18898
0.22	.00866	0.62	.02441	2	.07874	42	1.65354	82	3.22835
0.23	.00906	0.63	.02480	3	.11811	43	1.69291	83	3.26772
0.24	.00945	0.64	.02520	4	.15748	44	1.73228	84	3.30709
0.25	.00984	0.65	.02559	5	.19685	45	1.77165	85	3.34646
0.26	.01024	0.66	.02598	6	.23622	46	1.81102	86	3.38583
0.27	.01063	0.67	.02638	7	.27559	47	1.85039	87	3.42520
0.28	.01102	0.68	.02677	8	.31496	48	1.88976	88	3.46457
0.29	.01142	0.69	.02717	9	.35433	49	1.92913	89	3.50394
0.30	.01181	0.70	.02756	10	.39370	50	1.96850	90	3.54331
0.31	.01220	0.71	.02795	11	.43307	51	2.00787	91	3.58268
0.32	.01260	0.72	.02835	12	.47244	52	2.04724	92	3.62205
0.33	.01299	0.73	.02874	13	.51181	53	2.08661	93	3.66142
0.34	.01339	0.74	.02913	14	.55118	54	2.12598	94	3.70079
0.35	.01378	0.75	.02953	15	.59055	55	2.16535	95	3.74016
0.36	.01417	0.76	.02992	16	.62992	56	2.20472	96	3.77953
0.37	.01457	0.77	.03032	17	.66929	57	2.24409	97	3.81890
0.38	.01496	0.78	.03071	18	.70866	58	2.28346	98	3.85827
0.39	.01535	0.79	.03110	19	.74803	59	2.32283	99	3.89764
0.40	.01575	0.80	.03150	20	.78740	60	2.36220	100	3.93701

Table C-4. Decimal Equivalents of 8ths, 16ths, 32nds, 64ths.

8ths	32nds	64ths	64ths
$\frac{1}{8}$ = .125	$\frac{1}{32}$ = .03125	$\frac{1}{64}$ = .015625	$\frac{33}{64}$ = .515625
$\frac{1}{4}$ = .250	$\frac{3}{32}$ = .09375	$\frac{3}{64}$ = .046875	$\frac{35}{64}$ = .546875
$\frac{3}{8}$ = .375	$\frac{5}{32}$ = .15625	$\frac{5}{64}$ = .078125	$\frac{37}{64}$ = .578125
$\frac{1}{2}$ = .500	$\frac{7}{32}$ = .21875	$\frac{7}{64}$ = .109375	$\frac{39}{64}$ = .609375
$\frac{5}{8}$ = .625	$\frac{9}{32}$ = .28125	$\frac{9}{64}$ = .140625	$\frac{41}{64}$ = .640625
$\frac{3}{4}$ = .750	$\frac{11}{32}$ = .34375	$\frac{11}{64}$ = .171875	$\frac{43}{64}$ = .671875
$\frac{7}{8}$ = .875	$\frac{13}{32}$ = .40625	$\frac{13}{64}$ = .203125	$\frac{45}{64}$ = .703125
16ths	$\frac{15}{32}$ = .46875	$\frac{15}{64}$ = .234375	$\frac{47}{64}$ = .734375
$\frac{1}{16}$ = .0625	$\frac{17}{32}$ = .53125	$\frac{17}{64}$ = .265625	$\frac{49}{64}$ = .765625
$\frac{3}{16}$ = .1875	$\frac{19}{32}$ = .59375	$\frac{19}{64}$ = .296875	$\frac{51}{64}$ = .796875
$\frac{5}{16}$ = .3125	$\frac{21}{32}$ = .65625	$\frac{21}{64}$ = .328125	$\frac{53}{64}$ = .828125
$\frac{7}{16}$ = .4375	$\frac{23}{32}$ = .71875	$\frac{23}{64}$ = .359375	$\frac{55}{64}$ = .859375
$\frac{9}{16}$ = .5625	$\frac{25}{32}$ = .78125	$\frac{25}{64}$ = .390625	$\frac{57}{64}$ = .890625
$\frac{11}{16}$ = .6875	$\frac{27}{32}$ = .84375	$\frac{27}{64}$ = .421875	$\frac{59}{64}$ = .921875
$\frac{13}{16}$ = .8125	$\frac{29}{32}$ = .90625	$\frac{29}{64}$ = .453125	$\frac{61}{64}$ = .953125
$\frac{15}{16}$ = .9375	$\frac{31}{32}$ = .96875	$\frac{31}{64}$ = .484375	$\frac{63}{64}$ = .984375

Table C-5. Decimal Equivalents of Letter Size Drills.

Letter	Size of Drill in Inches	Letter	Size of Drill in Inches
A	.234	N	.302
B	.238	O	.316
C	.242	P	.323
D	.246	Q	.332
E	.250	R	.339
F	.257	S	.348
G	.261	T	.358
H	.266	U	.368
I	.272	V	.377
J	.277	W	.386
K	.281	X	.397
L	.290	Y	.404
M	.295	Z	.413

Table C-6. Decimal Equivalents of Number Size Drills.

No.	Size of Drill in Inches	No.	Size of Drill in Inches	No.	Size of Drill in Inches	No.	Size of Drill in Inches
1	.2280	21	.1590	41	.0960	61	.0390
2	.2210	22	.1570	42	.0935	62	.0380
3	.2130	23	.1540	43	.0890	63	.0370
4	.2090	24	.1520	44	.0860	64	.0360
5	.2055	25	.1495	45	.0820	65	.0350
6	.2040	26	.1470	46	.0810	66	.0330
7	.2010	27	.1440	47	.0785	67	.0320
8	.1990	28	.1405	48	.0760	68	.0310
9	.1960	29	.1360	49	.0730	69	.0292
10	.1935	30	.1285	50	.0700	70	.0280
11	.1910	31	.1200	51	.0670	71	.0260
12	.1890	32	.1160	52	.0635	72	.0250
13	.1850	33	.1130	53	.0595	73	.0240
14	.1820	34	.1110	54	.0550	74	.0225
15	.1800	35	.1100	55	.0520	75	.0210
16	.1770	36	.1065	56	.0465	76	.0200
17	.1730	37	.1040	57	.0430	77	.0180
18	.1695	38	.1015	58	.0420	78	.0160
19	.1660	39	.0995	59	.0410	79	.0145
20	.1610	40	.0980	60	.0400	80	.0135

Table C-7. American Standard Pipe Thread and Tap Drill Sizes.

Pipe Size Inches	Threads Per Inch	Root Diameter Small End of Pipe and Gage	Tap Drill	
			Taper NPT	Straight NPS
1/8	27	.3339"	Q	11/32"
1/4	18	.4329"	7/16"	7/16"
3/8	18	.5676"	9/16"	37/64"
1/2	14	.7013"	45/64"	23/32"
3/4	14	.9105"	29/32"	59/64"
1	11-1/2	1.1441"	1-9/64"	1-5/32"
1-1/4	11-1/2	1.4876"	1-31/64"	1-1/2"
1-1/2	11-1/2	1.7265"	1-47/64"	1-3/4"
2	11-1/2	2.1995"	2-13/64"	2-7/32"

Table C-8. American National and
Unified Coarse and Fine Thread Dimensions and Tap Drill Sizes.

$p = \text{pitch} = \dfrac{1}{\text{No. thrd. per in.}}$

$d = \text{depth} = p \times .649519$

$f = \text{flat} = \dfrac{p}{8}$

$\text{pitch diameter} = d - \dfrac{.6495}{N}$

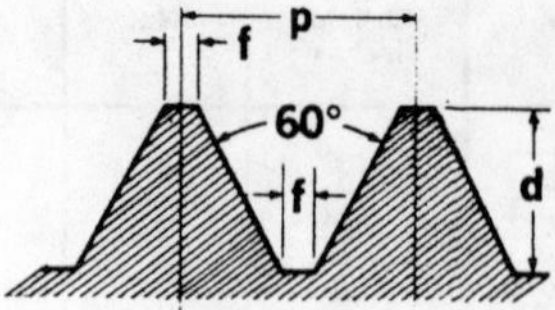

For Nos. 575 and 585 Screw Thread Micrometers

Size	Threads per inch NC UNC	Threads per inch NF UNF	Outside Diameter Inches	Pitch Diameter Inches	Root Diameter Inches	Tap Drill Approx. 75% Full Thread	Decimal Equiv. of Tap Drill
0	..	80	.0600	.0519	.0438	$\frac{3}{64}$	.0469
1	64	..	.0730	.0629	.0527	53	.0595
1	..	72	.0730	.0640	.0550	53	.0595
2	56	..	.0860	.0744	.0628	50	.0700
2	..	64	.0860	.0759	.0657	50	.0700
3	48	..	.0990	.0855	.0719	47	.0785
3	..	56	.0990	.0874	.0758	46	.0810
4	40	..	.1120	.0958	.0795	43	.0890
4	..	48	.1120	.0985	.0849	42	.0935
5	40	..	.1250	.1088	.0925	38	.1015
5	..	44	.1250	.1102	.0955	37	.1040
6	32	..	.1380	.1177	.0974	36	.1065
6	..	40	.1380	.1218	.1055	33	.1130
8	32	..	.1640	.1437	.1234	29	.1360
8	..	36	.1640	.1460	.1279	29	.1360
10	24	..	.1900	.1629	.1359	26	.1470
10	..	32	.1900	.1697	.1494	21	.1590
12	24	..	.2160	.1889	.1619	16	.1770
12	..	28	.2160	.1928	.1696	15	.1800
¼	20	..	.2500	.2175	.1850	7	.2010
¼	..	28	.2500	.2268	.2036	3	.2130
⁵⁄₁₆	18	..	.3125	.2764	.2403	F	.2570
⁵⁄₁₆	..	24	.3125	.2854	.2584	I	.2720
⅜	16	..	.3750	.3344	.2938	$\frac{5}{16}$	.3125
⅜	..	24	.3750	.3479	.3209	Q	.3320
⁷⁄₁₆	14	..	.4375	.3911	.3447	U	.3680
⁷⁄₁₆	..	20	.4375	.4050	.3726	$\frac{25}{64}$	.3906
½	13	..	.5000	.4500	.4001	$\frac{27}{64}$	.4219
½	..	20	.5000	.4675	.4351	$\frac{29}{64}$	.4531
⁹⁄₁₆	12	..	.5625	.5084	.4542	$\frac{31}{64}$	.4844
⁹⁄₁₆	..	18	.5625	.5264	.4903	$\frac{33}{64}$	.5156
⅝	11	..	.6250	.5660	.5069	$\frac{17}{32}$	.5312
⅝	..	18	.6250	.5889	.5528	$\frac{37}{64}$	.5781
¾	10	..	.7500	.6850	.6201	$\frac{21}{32}$	.6562
¾	..	16	.7500	.7094	.6688	$\frac{11}{16}$	.6875
⅞	9	..	.8750	.8028	.7307	$\frac{49}{64}$	.7656
⅞	..	14	.8750	.8286	.7822	$\frac{13}{16}$	.8125

Table C-8. American National and
Unified Coarse and Fine Thread Dimensions and Tap Drill Sizes—Continued.

Size	Threads per inch NC UNC	Threads per inch NF UNF	Outside Diameter Inches	Pitch Diameter Inches	Root Diameter Inches	Tap Drill Approx. 75% Full Thread	Decimal Equiv. of Tap Drill
1	8	..	1.0000	.9188	.8376	⅞	.8750
1	..	12	1.0000	.9459	.8917	59/64	.9219
1⅛	7	..	1.1250	1.0322	.9394	63/64	.9844
1⅛	..	12	1.1250	1.0709	1.0168	1 3/64	1.0469
1¼	7	..	1.2500	1.1572	1.0644	1 7/64	1.1094
1¼	..	12	1.2500	1.1959	1.1418	1 11/64	1.1719
1⅜	6	..	1.3750	1.2667	1.1585	1 7/32	1.2187
1⅜	..	12	1.3750	1.3209	1.2668	1 19/64	1.2969
1½	6	..	1.5000	1.3917	1.2835	1 11/32	1.3437
1½	..	12	1.5000	1.4459	1.3918	1 27/64	1.4219
1¾	5	..	1.7500	1.6201	1.4902	1 9/16	1.5625
2	4½	..	2.0000	1.8557	1.7113	1 25/32	1.7812
2¼	4½	..	2.2500	2.1057	1.9613	2 1/32	2.0313
2½	4	..	2.5000	2.3376	2.1752	2¼	2.2500
2¾	4	..	2.7500	2.5876	2.4252	2½	2.5000
3	4	..	3.0000	3.8376	2.6752	2¾	2.7500
3¼	4	..	3.2500	3.0876	2.9252	3	3.0000
3½	4	..	3.5000	3.3376	3.1752	3¼	3.2500
3¾	4	..	3.7500	3.5876	3.4252	3½	3.5000
4	4	..	4.0000	3.3786	3.6752	3¾	3.7500

Table C-9. Tap Drill Sizes For Fractional
Size Threads Approximately 65% Depth Thread American National Thread Form.

Tap Size	Threads per Inch	Diam. Hole	Drill	Tap Size	Threads per Inch	Diam. Hole	Drill
1/16	72	.049	3/64	1/2	20	.451	29/64
1/16	64	.047	3/64	1/2	13	.425	27/64
1/16	60	.046	56	1/2	12	.419	27/64
5/64	72	.065	52	9/16	27	.526	17/32
5/64	64	.063	1/16	9/16	18	.508	33/64
5/64	60	.062	1/16	9/16	12	.481	31/64
5/64	56	.061	53	5/8	27	.589	19/32
3/32	60	.077	5/64	5/8	18	.571	37/64
3/32	56	.076	48	5/8	12	.544	35/64
3/32	50	.074	49	5/8	11	.536	17/32
3/32	48	.073	49	11/16	16	.627	5/8
7/64	56	.092	42	11/16	11	.599	19/32
7/64	50	.090	43	3/4	27	.714	23/32
7/64	48	.089	43	3/4	16	.689	11/16
1/8	48	.105	36	3/4	12	.669	43/64
1/8	40	.101	38	3/4	10	.653	21/32
1/8	36	.098	40	13/16	12	.731	47/64
1/8	32	.095	3/32	13/16	10	.715	23/32
9/64	40	.116	32	7/8	27	.839	27/32
9/64	36	.114	33	7/8	18	.821	53/64
9/64	32	.110	35	7/8	14	.805	13/16
5/32	40	.132	30	7/8	12	.794	51/64
5/32	36	.129	30	7/8	9	.767	49/64
5/32	32	.126	1/8	15/16	12	.856	55/64
11/64	36	.145	27	15/16	9	.829	53/64
11/64	32	.141	9/64	1	27	.964	31/32
3/16	36	.161	20	1	14	.930	15/16
3/16	32	.157	22	1	12	.919	59/64
3/16	30	.155	23	1	8	.878	7/8
3/16	24	.147	26	1 1/16	8	.941	15/16
13/64	32	.173	17	1 1/8	12	1.044	1 3/64
13/64	30	.171	11/64	1 1/8	7	.986	63/64
13/64	24	.163	20	1 3/16	7	1.048	1 3/64
7/32	32	.188	12	1 1/4	12	1.169	1 11/64
7/32	28	.184	13	1 1/4	7	1.111	1 7/64
7/32	24	.178	16	1 5/16	7	1.173	1 11/64
15/64	32	.204	6	1 3/8	12	1.294	1 19/64
15/64	28	.200	8	1 3/8	6	1.213	1 7/32
15/64	24	.194	10	1 1/2	12	1.419	1 27/64
1/4	32	.220	7/32	1 1/2	6	1.338	1 11/32
1/4	28	.215	3	1 5/8	5 1/2	1.448	1 29/64
1/4	27	.214	3	1 3/4	5	1.555	1 9/16
1/4	24	.209	4	1 7/8	5	1.680	1 11/16
1/4	20	.201	7	2	4 1/2	1.783	1 25/32
5/16	32	.282	9/32	2 1/8	4 1/2	1.909	1 29/32
5/16	27	.276	J	2 1/4	4 1/2	2.034	2 1/32
5/16	24	.272	I	2 3/8	4	2.131	2 1/8
5/16	20	.264	17/64	2 1/2	4	2.256	2 1/4
5/16	18	.258	F	2 5/8	4	2.381	2 3/8
3/8	27	.339	R	2 3/4	4	2.506	2 1/2
3/8	24	.334	Q	2 7/8	3 1/2	2.597	2 19/32
3/8	20	.326	21/64	3	3 1/2	2.722	2 23/32
3/8	16	.314	5/16	3 1/8	3 1/2	2.847	2 27/32
7/16	27	.401	Y	3 1/4	3 1/2	2.972	2 31/32
7/16	24	.397	X	3 3/8	3 1/4	3.075	3 1/8
7/16	20	.389	25/64	3 1/2	3 1/4	3.200	3 3/16
7/16	14	.368	U	3 5/8	3 1/4	3.325	3 5/16
1/2	27	.464	15/32	3 3/4	3	3.425	3 1/16
1/2	24	.460	29/64	4	3	3.675	3 11/16

Table C-10. Double Depth of Screw Threads.

$$D.D. = \frac{1.732}{N} \text{ For V Thread}$$

$$D.D. = \frac{1.299}{N} \text{ For American Nat. Form, U. S. Std.}$$

$$D.D. = \frac{1.28}{N} \text{ For Whitworth Standard}$$

Threads per Inch N	V Threads D.D.	Am. Nat. Form D.D. U.S. Std.	Whitworth Standard D.D.	Threads per Inch N	V Threads D.D.	Am. Nat. Form D.D. U.S. Std.	Whitworth Standard D.D.
2	.86600	.64950	.64000	28	.06185	.04639	.04571
2¼	.76978	.57733	.56888	30	.05773	.04330	.04266
2⅜	.72926	.54694	.53894	32	.05412	.04059	.04000
2½	.69280	.51960	.51200	34	.05094	.03820	.03764
2⅝	.65981	.49485	.48761	36	.04811	.03608	.03555
2¾	.62982	.47236	.46545	38	.04558	.03418	.03368
2⅞	.60243	.45182	.44521	40	.04330	.03247	.03200
3	.57733	.43300	.42666	42	.04124	.03093	.03047
3¼	.53292	.39966	.39384	44	.03936	.02952	.02909
3½	.49485	.37114	.36571	46	.03765	.02823	.02782
4	.43300	.32475	.32000	48	.03608	.02706	.02666
4½	.38488	.28869	.28444	50	.03464	.02598	.02560
5	.34640	.25980	.25600	52	.03331	.02498	.02461
5½	.31490	.23618	.23272	54	.03207	.02405	.02370
6	.28866	.21650	.21333	56	.03093	.02319	.02285
7	.24742	.18557	.18285	58	.02986	.02239	.02206
8	.21650	.16237	.16000	60	.02887	.02165	.02133
9	.19244	.14433	.14222	62	.02794	.02095	.02064
10	.17320	.12990	.12800	64	.02706	.02029	.02000
11	.15745	.11809	.11636	66	.02624	.01968	.01939
11½	.15061	.11295	.11130	68	.02547	.01910	.01882
12	.14433	.10825	.10666	70	.02474	.01855	.01829
13	.13323	.09992	.09846	72	.02406	.01804	.01778
14	.12371	.09278	.09142	74	.02341	.01752	.01729
15	.11547	.08660	.08533	76	.02279	.01714	.01684
16	.10825	.08118	.08000	78	.02221	.01665	.01641
18	.09622	.07216	.07111	80	.02165	.01623	.01600
20	.08660	.06495	.06400	82	.02112	.01584	.01560
22	.07872	.05904	.05818	84	.02062	.01546	.01523
24	.07216	.05412	.05333	86	.02014	.01510	.01488
26	.06661	.04996	.04923	88	.01968	.01476	.01454
27	.06415	.04811	.04740	90	.01924	.01443	.01422

Table C-11. Pitch Diameter Tables For Nos. 575 and 585 Screw Thread Micrometers.

Whitworth Standard

Caliper Reading or Pitch Diameter

for Whitworth Threads $= D - \dfrac{.640}{N}$

Metric Standard

$p = \text{pitch} = \dfrac{1}{\text{No. of threads per inch}}$

$d = \text{depth} = \text{pitch} \times .6495$

$f = \text{flat} = \dfrac{\text{pitch}}{8}$

Diameter Inches	Threads per Inch	Caliper Reading or Pitch Diameter	Single Depth of Thread
D	N	$D - \dfrac{.640}{N}$	$\dfrac{.640}{N}$
. . .	48	. . . . .	.0133
. . .	46	. . . . .	.0139
. . .	44	. . . . .	.0146
. . .	42	. . . . .	.0152
. . .	40	. . . . .	.0160
. . .	38	. . . . .	.0168
. . .	36	. . . . .	.0178
. . .	34	. . . . .	.0188
. . .	32	. . . . .	.0200
. . .	30	. . . . .	.0213
. . .	28	. . . . .	.0229
. . .	26	. . . . .	.0246
. . .	24	. . . . .	.0267
. . .	22	. . . . .	.0291
¼	20	.2180	.0320
⁵⁄₁₆	18	.2769	.0355
⅜	16	.3350	.0400
⁷⁄₁₆	14	.3918	.0457
½	12	.4467	.0533
⁹⁄₁₆	12	.5092	.0533
⅝	11	.5668	.0582
¹¹⁄₁₆	11	.6293	.0582
¾	10	.6860	.0640
¹³⁄₁₆	10	.7485	.0640
⅞	9	.8039	.0711
¹⁵⁄₁₆	9	.8664	.0711
1	8	.9200	.0800
1⅛	7	1.0336	.0914
1¼	7	1.1586	.0914
1⅜	6	1.2684	.1066
1½	6	1.3934	.1066
1⅝	5	1.4970	.1280
1¾	5	1.6220	.1280
1⅞	4½	1.7328	.1422
2	4½	1.8578	.1422
2⅛	4½	1.9828	.1422

Size mm	Pitch	
	Intl. Std.	French Std.
2	.45	.50
3	.55	.50
4	.70	.75
5	.85	.75
6	1.00	1.00
7	1.00	1.00
8	1.25	1.00
9	1.25	1.00
10	1.50	1.50
11	1.50	. . . .
12	1.75	1.50
14	2.00	2.00
16	2.00	2.00
18	2.50	2.50
20	2.50	2.50
22	2.50	2.50
24	3.00	3.00
26	. . . .	3.00
27	3.00	. . . .
28	. . . .	3.00
30	3.50	3.50
32	. . . .	3.50
33	3.50	3.50
34	. . . .	3.50
36	4.00	4.00
38	. . . .	4.00
39	4.00	. . . .
40	. . . .	4.00

Table C-12. Pitch Diameter Table
For Nos. 575 and 585 Screw Thread Micrometers "V" Standard Thread Form.

Caliper Reading or Pitch Diameter for "V" Threads $= D - \dfrac{.866}{N}$

Diameter Inches	Threads per Inch	Caliper Reading or Pitch Diameter	Single Depth of Thread	Diameter Inches*	Threads per Inch	Caliper Reading or Pitch Diameter	Single Depth of Thread
D	N	$D - \dfrac{.866}{N}$	$\dfrac{.866}{N}$	D	N	$D - \dfrac{.866}{N}$	$\dfrac{.866}{N}$
	64	....	.0135	¼	24	.2139	.0361
	62	....	.0140	¼	20	.2067	.0433
	60	....	.0144	5/16	20	.2692	.0433
	58	....	.0149	5/16	18	.2644	.0481
	56	....	.0155	3/8	18	.3269	.0481
	54	....	.0161	3/8	16	.3209	.0541
	52	....	.0167	7/16	16	.3834	.0541
	50	....	.0173	7/16	14	.3756	.0619
	48	....	.0180	½	14	.4381	.0619
	46	....	.0188	½	13	.4334	.0666
	44	....	.0197	½	12	.4278	.0722
	42	....	.0206	9/16	14	.5006	.0619
	40	....	.0217	9/16	12	.4903	.0722
	38	....	.0228	5/8	11	.5463	.0787
	36	....	.0241	5/8	10	.5384	.0866
	34	....	.0255	11/16	10	.6009	.0866
	32	....	.0271	¾	10	.6634	.0866
	30	....	.0289	7/8	9	.7788	.0962
	28	....	.0309	1	8	.8918	.1082
	26	....	.0333	1⅛	8	1.0168	.1082
	..	....	....	1¼	7	1.1263	.1237
	..	....	....	1½	6	1.3557	.1443

Note:—As there is no standard of diameter for the finer pitches this column is left blank.

*These figures give the outside diameter for screws with threads cut theoretically sharp. As it is not practical to make these threads sharp, the outside diameter will measure less than the figures given, the pitch diameter remaining the same.

Table C-13. American Standard Acme Screw Thread Dimensions.

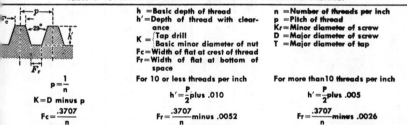

h = Basic depth of thread
h' = Depth of thread with clearance
K = {Tap drill / Basic minor diameter of nut
Fc = Width of flat at crest of thread
Fr = Width of flat at bottom of space

n = Number of threads per inch
p = Pitch of thread
Kr = Minor diameter of screw
D = Major diameter of screw
T = Major diameter of tap

$p = \dfrac{1}{n}$

K = D minus p

$Fc = \dfrac{.3707}{n}$

Kr = D minus 2h'

For 10 or less threads per inch

$h' = \dfrac{P}{2}$ plus .010

$Fr = \dfrac{.3707}{n}$ minus .0052

T = D plus .020

For more than 10 threads per inch

$h' = \dfrac{P}{2}$ plus .005

$Fr = \dfrac{.3707}{n}$ minus .0026

T = D plus .010

Threads per inch (n)	Depth of Thread with Clearance (h')	Flat at Top of Thread (Fc)	Flat at Bottom of Space (Fr)	Space at Top of Thread	Thickness at Root of Thread
1	.5100	.3707	.3655	.6293	.6345
1⅓	.3850	.2780	.2728	.4720	.4772
2	.2600	.1854	.1802	.3146	.3198
3	.1767	.1236	.1184	.2097	.2149
4	.1350	.0927	.0875	.1573	.1625
5	.1100	.0741	.0689	.1259	.1311
6	.0933	.0618	.0566	.1049	.1101
7	.0814	.0530	.0478	.0899	.0951
8	.0725	.0463	.0411	.0787	.0839
9	.0655	.0412	.0360	.0699	.0751
10	.0600	.0371	.0319	.0629	.0681
12	.0467	.0309	.0283	.0524	.0550
14	.0407	.0265	.0239	.0449	.0475
16	.0363	.0232	.0206	.0393	.0419

Table C-14. Different Standards for Wire Gauges
in use in the United States Dimensions of Sizes in Decimal Parts of an Inch.

Dimensions of Sizes in Decimal Parts of an Inch

Starrett Wire Gage Catalog Numbers

Number of Wire Gage	No. 281 No. 282 American or Brown & Sharpe	No. 188 No. 189 Birmingham or Stubs' Iron Wire	No. 287 Washburn & Moen, Worcester, Mass.	W. & M. Steel Music Wire	No. 295 No. 280 American S. & W. Co's. Music Wire Gage	Stubs' Steel Wire	No. 283 U.S. Standard Gage for Sheet and Plate Iron and Steel	Number of Wire Gage
00000000	....	....	....	.0083	....	....	....	00000000
0000000	....	....	....	.0087	....	....	....	0000000
000000	....	....	....	.0095	.004	....	....	000000
00000	....	....	....	.010	.005	....	.46875	00000
0000	.460	.454	.3938	.011	.006	....	.4375	0000
000	.40964	.425	.3625	.012	.007	....	.40625	000
00	.3648	.380	.3310	.0133	.008	....	.375	00
0	.32486	.340	.3065	.0144	.009	....	.34375	0
1	.2893	.300	.2830	.0156	.010	.227	.3125	1
2	.25763	.284	.2625	.0166	.011	.219	.28125	2
3	.22942	.259	.2437	.0178	.012	.212	.265625	3
4	.20431	.238	.2253	.0188	.013	.207	.250	4
5	.18194	.220	.2070	.0202	.014	.204	.234375	5
6	.16202	.203	.1920	.0215	.016	.201	.21875	6
7	.14428	.180	.1770	.023	.018	.199	.203125	7
8	.12849	.165	.1620	.0243	.020	.197	.1875	8
9	.11443	.148	.1483	.0256	.022	.194	.171875	9
10	.10189	.134	.1350	.027	.024	.191	.15625	10
11	.090742	.120	.1205	.0284	.026	.188	.140625	11
12	.080808	.109	.1055	.0296	.029	.185	.125	12
13	.071961	.095	.0915	.0314	.031	.182	.109375	13
14	.064084	.083	.0800	.0326	.033	.180	.09375	14
15	.057068	.072	.0720	.0345	.035	.178	.078125	15
16	.05082	.065	.0625	.036	.037	.175	.0703125	16
17	.045257	.058	.0540	.0377	.039	.172	.0625	17
18	.040303	.049	.0475	.0395	.041	.168	.05625	18
19	.03589	.042	.0410	.0414	.043	.164	.050	19
20	.031961	.035	.0348	.0434	.045	.161	.04375	20
21	.028462	.032	.03175	.046	.047	.157	.0375	21
22	.025347	.028	.0286	.0483	.049	.155	.034375	22
23	.022571	.025	.0258	.051	.051	.153	.03125	23
24	.0201	.022	.0230	.055	.055	.151	.028125	24
25	.0179	.020	.0204	.0586	.059	.148	.025	25
26	.01594	.018	.0181	.0626	.063	.146	.021875	26
27	.014195	.016	.0173	.0658	.067	.143	.01875	27
28	.012641	.014	.0162	.072	.071	.139	.0171875	28
29	.011257	.013	.0150	.076	.075	.134	.015625	29
30	.010025	.012	.0140	.080	.080	.127	.0140625	30
31	.008928	.010	.0132	....	.085	.120	.0125	31
32	.00795	.009	.0128	....	.090	.115	.0109375	32
33	.00708	.008	.0118	....	.095	.112	.01015625	33
34	.006304	.007	.0104	....	....	.110	.009375	34
35	.005614	.005	.0095	....	....	.108	.00859375	35
36	.005	.004	.0090	....	....	.106	.0078125	36
37	.004453	....	....	....	....	.103	.00703125	37
38	.003965	....	....	....	....	.101	.006640625	38
39	.003531	....	....	....	....	.099	.00625	39
40	.003144	....	....	....	....	.097	....	40

Table C-15. Allowances for Fits.

Class	Nominal Diameters	Up to ½ Inch	9/16–1 Inch	1 1/16–2 Inches	2 1/16–3 Inches	3 1/16–4 Inches	4 1/16–5 Inches
Tolerances in Standard Holes							
A	High Limit Low Limit Tolerance	+0.00025 −0.00025 0.0005	+0.0005 −0.00025 0.00075	+0.00075 −0.00025 0.0010	+0.0010 −0.0005 0.0015	+0.0010 −0.0005 0.0015	+0.0010 −0.0005 0.0015
B	High Limit Low Limit Tolerance	+0.0005 −0.0005 0.0010	+0.00075 −0.0005 0.00125	+0.0010 −0.0005 0.0015	+0.00125 −0.00075 0.0020	+0.0015 −0.00075 0.00225	+0.00175 −0.00075 0.0025
Allowances for Forced Fits							
F	High Limit Low Limit Tolerance	+0.0010 +0.0005 0.0005	+0.0020 +0.0015 0.0005	+0.0040 +0.0030 0.0010	+0.0060 +0.0045 0.0015	+0.0080 +0.0060 0.0020	+0.0100 +0.0080 0.0020
Allowances for Driving Fits							
D	High Limit Low Limit Tolerance	+0.0005 +0.00025 0.00025	+0.0010 +0.00075 0.00025	+0.0015 +0.0010 0.0005	+0.0025 +0.0015 0.0010	+0.0030 +0.0020 0.0010	+0.0035 +0.0025 0.0010
Allowances for Push Fits							
P	High Limit Low Limit Tolerance	−0.00025 −0.00075 0.0005	−0.00025 −0.00075 0.0005	−0.00025 −0.00075 0.0005	−0.0005 −0.0010 0.0005	−0.0005 −0.0010 0.0005	−0.0005 −0.0010 0.0005
Allowances for Running Fits ★ ★							
X	High Limit Low Limit Tolerance	−0.0010 −0.0020 0.0010	−0.00125 −0.00275 0.0015	−0.00175 −0.0035 0.00175	−0.0020 −0.00425 0.00225	−0.0025 −0.0050 0.0025	−0.0030 −0.00575 0.00275
Y	High Limit Low Limit Tolerance	−0.00075 −0.00125 0.0005	−0.0010 −0.0020 0.0010	−0.00125 −0.0025 0.00125	−0.0015 −0.0030 0.0015	−0.0020 −0.0035 0.0015	−0.00225 −0.0040 0.00175
Z	High Limit Low Limit Tolerance	−0.0005 −0.00075 0.00025	−0.00075 −0.00125 0.0005	−0.00075 −0.0015 0.00075	−0.0010 −0.0020 0.0010	−0.0010 −0.00225 0.00125	−0.00125 −0.0025 0.00125

Formulas for Determining Allowances

Class	High Limit	Low Limit	Class	High Limit	Low Limit
A	$+\sqrt{D} \times 0.0006$	$-\sqrt{D} \times 0.0003$	X	$-\sqrt{D} \times 0.00125$	$-\sqrt{D} \times 0.0025$
B	$+\sqrt{D} \times 0.0008$	$-\sqrt{D} \times 0.0004$	Y	$-\sqrt{D} \times 0.001$	$-\sqrt{D} \times 0.0018$
P	$-\sqrt{D} \times 0.0002$	$-\sqrt{D} \times 0.0006$	Z	$-\sqrt{D} \times 0.0005$	$-\sqrt{D} \times 0.001$

★Tolerance is provided for holes, which ordinary standard reamers can produce, in two grades, Classes A and B, the selection of which is a question for the user's decision and dependent upon the quality of the work required; some prefer to use Class A as working limits and Class B as inspection limits.

★★Running fits, which are the most commonly required, are divided into three grades: Class X, for engine and other work where easy fits are wanted; Class Y, for high speeds and good average machine work; Class Z, for fine tool work.

Index